Understanding Effective Advocacy to the Government

Michael J. O'Bannon

This publication is the exclusive intellectual property of The EOP Foundation.

Without limiting the rights under copyright reserved below, no part of this publication may be reproduced, stored in or introduced into an electronic retrieval system, or transmitted by any means without the prior written permission of the copyright owner and publisher; The EOP Foundation.

The EOP Foundation has published nine other publications in our Understanding series which explore critical aspects of the manner in which the government functions. Our titles include: *Understanding the Budget Policies and Processes of the United States Government; Understanding Leadership in the United States; Understanding Effective Writing in the Federal Government; Understanding the Interface between Political & Career Executives in the United States Government; Understanding the United States Government's Regulatory Process; Understanding Transition in the United States Government; Understanding the Presidential Transition Process; Understanding the Diversity Policy of the United States Government;* and *Understanding the Ethics Policy of the United States Government.* The EOP Foundation coordinates with EOP Education to train public and private sector officials in our areas of professional expertise. Our new title, *Understanding Effective Advocacy to the Government* provides additional insight.

For more information on the Foundation's training assistance program or to order copies of the publications at a discount for training purposes, contact the Foundation:

Ryan Martin
The EOP Foundation
819 7th Street, N.W.
Washington, D.C. 20001
(202) 833-8940
rmmartin@819eagle.com

To the career and political Government officials as well as professional private sector advocates who tirelessly work to evaluate the most current and accurate data and analysis to shape policy and legislative alternatives to faciliate public sector decision-making at all levels of Government in the United States.

TABLE OF CONTENTS
UNDERSTANDING EFFECTIVE ADVOCACY TO THE GOVERNMENT

PART II: OBJECTIVITY AND ANALYSIS ESSENTIAL TO ADVOCACY

PART III: CHARACTERISTICS OF EFFECTIVE ADVOCACY

Acknowledgements

The EOP Foundation, in partnership with EOP Education, is proud to acknowledge the many contributions from the professional advocacy community critical to the information prescribed in this volume.

This publication relied on public sources inclusive of materials distributed by the Offices' of Government Ethics and Personnel Management for guidance associated with appropriate conduct and professional behavior by external stakeholders as well as government executives involved in the government decision-making process. The House and Senate Ethics Committees also provided valuable lessons learned based on their public reporting on cases in which they were involved. Finally, insights by both active and retired executives from the professional advocacy community into the government decision-making process are featured throughout the book. Particularly, their expertise helped define the information required to facilitate the content of materials associated with efficient, responsible, and meaningful government decision-making.

Our Foundation and Education staff, particularly James Parkhurst and Stephen Arthur, were essential to achieve the exemplary research which led to the quality of this book.

This volume will quickly become a reference for those in the professional advocacy community who work to influence government decision-making with professionalism, strong character, and ethics which are beyond reproach. Their contributions focus on infusing a philosophy that balance advocacy approaches, methods, and delivery mechanisms that are common to stakeholders on all sides of issues the government decides. We extend our thanks to the political and career executives that contributed to critiquing their views.

The government workforce must ascribe to transparency associated with their interface with the professional advocacy community. Interagency deliberations, advisory committees and their reports, management and human resources deliberations, as well as, the contributions from Government contracts and grants, and federal research organizations, are just as important as contributions external to the government.

Government officials' contributions associated with their articulation of what the most efficient and productive input from professional advocates consist of were critical to the publication. Further, they shared their collective experience with the most effective advocacy delivery mechanisms. They explained how the information supported their deliberations on policy, regulatory, and legislative development. Finally, they were clear when explaining how the quality of their deliberations would suffer without the unique perspective and substance of issues presented to them by professional advocates.

Our thanks are extended to each and every one of our contributors. We hope that all will agree that this book advances everyone's desire to eliminate public mistrust while improving government decision-making through the valuable and unique input of the advocacy community.

Michael J. O'Bannon

Preface

This publication presents a principled, positive, and experienced discourse focused on how government officials with federal, state, and local policy formulation and implementation responsibilities to the American Public should work with the nation's professional advocacy community and vice versa. The insights discussed herein provide government decision-makers and other issue stakeholders with effective methods and techniques to evaluate information that are developed and relied on by non-government sponsored advocacy campaigns as well as the government's interagency decision-making processes.

Social media, when used inappropriately, does a disservice to the substantive value of professional advocacy and associated government deliberations. The analysis and presentations advocates rely on when developed in the right way, has been our approach in this publication.

Professional advocacy campaigns have only one objective. The objective is to prepare government decision-makers to make the most informed and cost-efficient decisions on issues before them. The government's decision-making process is improved when the analytical basis for their ultimate decision is facilitated by a balanced evaluation of the alternatives that are relevant to the policy, legislative proposal, regulation and operations within its purview. Our audience is targeted to the public and private sectors as stakeholders to one another.

In government, those entrusted with protecting the taxpayer's dollars are expected to evaluate issues objectively. Our expectation is that career issue managers and career and political executives conduct or review credible cost versus benefit analysis prior to making a decision. Balancing the pros and cons highlight the criteria critical to equitable decision-making. All analysis should focus on the taxpayer best interests. This publication provides guidance to the career and political government workforce associated with appropriate interface between them and issue advocates.

In the private sector, those entrusted with providing America's consumers with quality products or services are similarly challenged. Their metrics include earnings, maximum profits given market dynamics, sensitivity to preserving public health and safety, and obviously consumer satisfaction. This publication provides guidance to professional advocates that provide expert, specialized, and unique information to enhance government decision-making to address shareholder demands.

Both sectors recognize that high quality advocacy information must be relied on to reinforce equity in government decision-making. This means the information must be accurate, timely, and sensitive to the government's statutory mandate. If not, government decisions will negatively impact the American economy.

The evaluation of issues are conducted and influenced by a government workforce that includes career issue managers and senior executives as well as political executives with decision-making responsibilities. The knowledge and expertise that the workforce applies to decide statutory, regulatory, and program requirements which govern implementation in the private and public sectors must be reached based on hiring criteria beyond reproach. Similarly, the private sector advocate is retained based on their knowledge of the issues relevant to the market place and associated experience delivering high quality services to the consuming public. Their mutual advocacy and decision-making is targeted to maintain a vibrant and competitive American economy.

There is a realization in both sectors that government decision-makers are not usually substantive experts on the issues within their purview. Likewise, professional advocates understand that their credibility and unique knowledge of the substantive issues that government decision-makers must be knowledgeable of represents a daunting responsibility to support responsible government decision-making.

The issue evaluated by the American public is the manner in which the public and private sectors coordinate appropriate advocacy, and its role in government decision-making as they discharge their mutual responsibilities. The bottom line is trust!

While the government expert has *no profit* motive, many in industry as well as the American public believe the government's perspectives on issues are biased. On the other hand, many in government and the American public are suspicious that the private sector is only loyal to its investors. The issue is the extent to which competition between companies seeking the highest market share for their products and services influence policy perspectives and quality of products and services without regard for the interests of the American public. Thus, some in the public see the private sector as anti-public interest and only motivated by the return on investment.

There are others that are involved in the American public's trust issue. These are supply chain manufacturers. As stakeholders, they also influence positions taken and decisions made between the private and public sectors.

There are external influences that significantly impact government decision-making processes. Politics is the first! - Elected and Institutional. Republicans and Democrats evaluate advocacy on the basis of partisan principles. Their respective interpretation of technical/factual data drives their actions. Political principles are articulated in party platforms and in individual candidates' statements to voters. The baseline consideration for a politician is their political value proposition.

Advocates and decision-makers must ascribe to the highest ethical/professional principles. This is a political imperative integral to the elective and institutional political calculus. Any unscrupulous taker devoid of these principles is untenable. The heavily biased government official reflecting a personal agenda is a third force to be reckoned with by the elective and institutional political structure. Their agenda is not based on applying the **neutral competence** metric. The rules and principles are ever changing to eliminate the negative forces within the advocacy profession and government decision-makers.

Thankfully, whether unscrupulous professional advocates or biased government decision-makers, it is a small group that has become a common target. Elected politicians work to eliminate government decision-makers, professional advocates, and private sector executives who are unworthy of our respect. Institutional political forces prioritize the same objective.

The rules of engagement for effective advocacy are clear between and among private and public sector advocates who evaluate data and advocate positions based on their analysis. It is critical that they be managed, fact checked, and validated. Their disparate positions must be vetted based on clearly articulated metrics. The metrics are critical. They must be ethical, fact based, and sensitive to the public's expectations. The principle that both the rule of law and common sense be applied is what ensures that the advocacy profession is both honorable and trustworthy. The manner in which advocacy information is received and applied by government decision-makers are equally critical!

Only when the rule of law and common sense are equally applied can the public's trust in the value of advocacy be supported.

INTRODUCTION TO ADVOCACY

This **First Edition**, *Understanding Effective Advocacy to the Government*, is intended to educate the professional advocacy community on effective and appropriate methods to influence government decision-makers. This publication also provides guidance to advocacy executives and staff regarding the appropriate delivery of their materials to government decision-makers. Our advice focuses on quantitative and qualitative methods that support the development of high quality, unique, and expert advocacy materials. However, the career and political government workforce must be trained to receive, evaluate, and apply the information provided to them by representatives from the professional advocacy community.

We emphasize that the justification associated with alternative policy choices related to the specific issues of concern to both the professional advocate and the government decision-maker should be addressed in a manner that exemplifies the integrity the American public demands from this process. Both the internal and external resources expended in the government's decision-making process are subject to intense scrutiny by the monitoring and investigative groups who have developed over time to ensure the American taxpayer's interest is not compromised. This publication articulates guidance on credible, ethical, and transparent interaction approaches proven to be the most effective between professional advocates and government decision-makers.

The **first section** of the book is focused on the basic principles associated with effective advocacy.

Introduction to Advocacy introduces the purpose of the publication. It addresses each topic discussed in the book. This discussion provides critical insight into the knowledge, methods, and approaches required to be a professional advocate, introduces what this publication will communicate throughout the book, and outlines the contents of each chapter.

Chapter 1 defines advocacy and addresses the differences between baseline advocacy, lobbying advocacy, and educating advocacy. It also defines various advocacy approaches associated with establishing the boundaries of appropriate advocacy methods. Further, the most significant Federal Regulations promulgated to govern advocacy activities in the private and public sectors are explained. Common advocacy techniques applied by professional advocates are also discussed. Finally, the chapter provides a chart that identifies the similarities and differences between the advocacy categories.

Chapter 2 discusses the principles of advocacy. The chapter identifies the most effective advocacy approaches and associated delivery systems. The twenty principles of advocacy with detailed explanations are outlined. These principles apply to all aspects of the advocacy community.

Chapter 3 articulates the most significant ethics rules and criteria that apply to the three professional advocacy categories defined in Chapter 1. This chapter further delineates the differences between professional lobbyists, professional educators, and the general category of professional advocates which includes policy, management, or operational analysts. The chapter discusses the application of the law for Lobbying Disclosure and Ethical Rules for Lobbyists.

Chapter 4 articulates appropriate advocacy approaches to improve the probability of receiving federal grant funding. It focuses on what type of funding is available for the private sector to compete for. It examines who in the government is responsible for managing the procurement and bidding process. Further, the chapter examines the role of the procurement manager, and finally, how professional advocates advocate for financial assistance from the government in an ethical manner.

The **second section** of this book focuses on effective advocacy methods.

Chapter 5 discusses specific methods advocates utilize to communicate their message. The methods outlined in this chapter include: issue identification, issue analysis, information quality control, source credibility, and other information delivery techniques.

Chapter 6 includes a discussion of each advocacy technique associated with the methods discussed in Chapter 5. Note that achieving success requires a combination of the advocate's capability to apply their common sense, experience, and special education while applying the principles of professional advocacy through various methods and techniques.

Chapter 7 describes the importance of applying quantitative methods in the analysis of policy and operational alternatives to government decision-makers. The chapter outlines the metrics associated with the quantitative methods used in the government's decision-making process. The first quantitative tool described in the chapter is cost-benefit analysis. The second section focuses on a detailed explanation of different statistical methods applied to data in order to gain a better understanding of the issue objectively. These statistical methods include basic descriptive statistical analysis, exploratory data analysis, and probability distributions.

Chapter 8 identifies qualitative methods utilized by the professional advocacy community. The chapter examines metrics associated with narratives and storytelling, historical research and visual ethnography, feedback from focus groups, feedback from classical ethnographic studies, and qualitative surveys and interviews.

Chapter 9 discusses the utilization of various delivery mechanisms. The chapter gives a description of three types of visual presentation products (PowerPoint, Prezi, and PowToon) used by advocates to educate, establish common ground, and influence stakeholders and decision-makers. The chapter discusses the metrics associated with effective and ineffective verbal presentations and common written instruments.

The **third section** of the book focuses on communicating and maintaining relationships with stakeholders through advocacy.

Chapter 10 lays out how the advocates should communicate with decision-makers and other stakeholders. Whether written or verbal instruments are employed, the quality of the communication is critical to successful advocacy. The chapter explains the keys to communicating with government decision-makers and outlines the important factors and tips for utilizing the various instruments found in the advocacy process. Lastly, the chapter gives insight concerning improper communication and provides tips to avoid it.

Chapter 11 explains how professional advocates build trust among government decision-makers and other stakeholders involved in issues of interest. The chapter outlines and explains the trust equation and its individual variables. Metrics and principles important to developing ethical trust relationships with government decision-makers and stakeholders are outlined.

Chapter 12 clarifies the necessity, role, and benefits that effective advocates provide to the American Public and the paradox associated with the public's perception of advocacy and the reliance government decision-makers and issue stakeholders have on the professional advocacy community. The chapter identifies the specific aim of policy advocacy and discusses the intended audience for specific policy advocacy efforts.

Chapter 13 provides descriptions and contact information of organizations involved in influencing the public policy process through professional advocacy efforts.

Chapter 14 provides the learning results important to effective advocacy. The chapter illustrates the importance of utilizing case studies and simulation exercises to facilitate the type of training and results in tangible learning results for government decision-makers, professional advocates, and methods and techniques that are critical to the advocacy/government decision-making process. The chapter includes a case study focused on the decision-making process of implementing policies to revitalize the decreasing California condor population, a protected endangered species, as well as a simulation exercise. Additionally included is a case study focused on environmental justice related decision-making and simulation exercise.

Chapter 1

DEFINING PROFESSIONAL ADVOCACY

General Advocacy

There are numerous definitions for **Advocacy**. The Merriam-Webster dictionary definition states that advocacy is any action that speaks in favor of, recommends, argues for a cause, supports or defends, or pleads on behalf of others; another is the act or process of supporting a cause or proposal; a third is the act of pleading for, supporting, or recommending e.g. active espousal.

The term **Advocacy** originates from Roman law. A professional advocate pleaded cases in front of Roman courts. Synonyms for advocacy are: champion, upholder, supporter, backer, promoter, proponent, exponent, spokesman, spokeswoman, spokesperson, campaigner, fighter, crusader, propagandist, apostle, apologist, and booster. There are seven, types of advocacy:

- **Self Advocacy** – This is characterized by acting as your own champion or promoter. An individual makes an informed decision associated with their issue, and takes responsibility for supporting and defending their position versus status quo; thus, *creating reality!*

- **Peer Advocacy** – This is characterized by sharing a similar position with other stakeholders seeking change; thus, *creating reality!*
- **Best Interest Advocacy** – This is characterized by changing the status quo to reflect the best interests of issue stakeholders who have the knowledge required to make an informed decision; thus, *creating reality!*
- **Statutory Advocacy** – This is characterized by an advocate with the legal responsibility to represent and appropriately discharge their duty e.g. a welfare guardian; thus, *creating reality!*
- **Crisis Advocacy** – This is characterized by an advocate protecting another who is at risk in the short term of being mistreated or excluded from government benefits due to crisis; thus, *creating reality!*
- **Professional/Specialist Advocacy** – This is the most recognized form of advocacy and is characterized by providing specialized advocacy services e.g. EOP Group; thus, *creating reality!*
- **Political Advocacy** – This is similar to the above, but is characterized by lobbying for the advancement of particular political viewpoints on behalf of a group of people; thus, *creating reality!*

The theme is that all professional advocates seek to create a new reality in a cost effective and beneficial manner for the American public! This is a goal shared by the U.S. Government who is charged with continuously enhancing the American quality of life.

Professional advocates present credible alternatives to issues. Their intent is to influence the government's decision-making process in order to benefit the American public. A professional advocate's responsibility is to ensure that public officials have the most current, credible, and pertinent information associated with issues of concern. The information should enhance the decision-making process. Cost beneficial decision-making which is consistent with policy, statutory, or regulatory responsibilities is what the American public hold the government accountable for. Further, the public expects its' officials to conduct its' government responsibilities in an informed and ethical manner. This expectation is paramount notwithstanding pressures on those officials to decide issues in favor of small but powerful special interests. The three categories of professional advocates that assist government officials in the United States include *baseline, lobbying,* and *education advocates*.

CATEGORIES OF ADVOCACY

The most important element of effective advocacy is building trust through ethical behaviors and demonstrating impeccable character.

This principle and the assurance that professional advocates' practice this principle as prescribed assist decision-makers gain an enhanced command of the facts. They also are exposed to varying perspectives on the issues being debated and decided in the public domain. Since stakeholders advocate for alternative approaches, a decision-maker's ability to trust and rely on the accuracy of the advocacy communities' assertions and facts is key to integrating the government's decision-making process with professional advocacy campaigns.

Detailing the key points of the research that support a position, as well as, points that challenge assertions held by opposing stakeholders often results in recruiting new supporters for an approach. When opposing stakeholders change their position, the new support is associated with the compelling nature of the analysis supporting a differing position. However, it is critical that the data and evidence that supports the position being taken is validated.

Baseline Advocacy

The first category of advocacy is generic and is categorized as **baseline advocacy** (BA). The nomenclature is generic in that professional advocates in the category are objective, analytical, and transparent. All professional advocates do not subscribe to our BA metrics. Our BA metrics are based on a thoughtful assessment of alternative approaches that issue stakeholders and government decision-makers can be certain are credible and reflect the most current data available. Further, baseline advocates are driven by pursuing the public's best interest.

Baseline advocacy relies on an objective evaluation of policy alternatives. Policy alternatives are focused on identifying differences between possible actions or approaches that are credible and can be implemented to address an issue or problem. There should always be three alternatives. Their definitions follow: (1) a controversial but credible political position; (2) a status-quo, no change position based on a current cost-benefit analysis of the existing government program, policy, or statutory interpretation as well as the career bureaucracy's institutional memory; and (3) a credible approach that differs from both status quo and the prevailing political position notwithstanding a consensus associated with a need for change held by some internal and external stakeholders.

The BA criteria are both measurable and realistic. Baseline criteria compare/contrast and validate differing policy alternatives related to goal attainment. This criteria is the basis for analyzing and comparing different policy alternatives.

Alternatives are derived from various sources such as: brainstorming sessions, case studies of real world experiences, defining the problem from others' perspectives, ideal outcomes and results, worst case scenarios, or the modification of existing solutions or policies. Once each alternative solution has been identified, advocates analyze the alternatives using criteria associated with the specific issue. Criteria for evaluating and analyzing policy alternatives include:

- **Cost** – Determines the financial burden of implementing each alternative;

- **Reliability/Validity** – Determines if outcomes are replicable and observable in the real world. The alternative is reliable and valid if the outcomes are consistent across studies. Repeated measurements of the same alternative should produce the same result;
- **Rationality** – Determines if the alternative is logically appropriate to achieve goals and objectives;
- **Invulnerability** – Determines weaknesses through a vulnerability assessment process that identifies, quantifies, and prioritizes (or ranks) the vulnerabilities of each alternative solution;
- **Flexibility** – Determines if the alternative has mechanisms for adapting in changing environments and is generalizable across impacted cultures and communities;
- **Riskiness** – Determines the likelihood that an alternative will be successful in the current political and economic environment. It identifies risk factors and a cost benefit analysis of associated mitigation plans;
- **Communicability** – Determines identifying factors associated with all issue stakeholders for measuring expected results associated with each alternative;
- **Merit** – Determines if the alternative is of good quality and meets its goals within its estimated budget and time line;
- **Simplicity** – Determines if the alternative is logical and succinctly articulates the facts of quantitative and qualitative information analysis in a manner all issue stakeholders comprehend;
- **Compatibility** – Determines if the alternative is sustainable over time and is in the best interest of the impacted communities over generations;
- **Reversibility** – Determines processes for developing plans in the event of emergency or to mitigate the impacts of negative unexpected consequences; and,
- **Robustness** – Determines how the alternative differs and improves on the status quo/current policy and determines a measurement for quantifying that difference.

After analyzing the alternatives utilizing the above criteria, the most effective BAs present three alternatives to government decision-makers and issue stakeholders that articulate:

1. A controversial, but credible political position;
2. Status-quo, no change position based on experience with existing government programs, policies, or statutory interpretation and the career bureaucracy's institutional memory; and
3. A credible approach that oppose both status quo and the prevailing political position notwithstanding a consensus of some internal and external stakeholders.

The baseline advocate is measured pursuant to specific metrics associated with their activities and effectiveness. The metrics include: (1) provision of information based on objective analysis of alternatives available to government decision-makers; (2) research encompassing the most current and peer-reviewed information sources supporting the alternatives; (3) application of quantitative and qualitative methods in the conduct of their analyses; (4) transparency in the description and explanation of the positions of other issue stakeholders' positions; and (5) clear and concise analyses of the information associated with each alternative.

BA is always based on an objective examination of the alternatives from which a decision-maker's conclusion and associated analysis justifies a particular position. The application of defined metrics and criteria is integral to presenting credible arguments for and against a certain alternative.

The following define the action baseline advocates engage in:

- **Testifying before a legislative committee** – provides objective information and analysis regarding the potential positive and negative impacts associated with a change in policy;
- **Presenting non-partisan analysis** – presents results of a non-partisan analysis of issues. The results of research efforts are provided to the decision-makers by baseline advocates. The delivery mechanisms are detailed in chapter 10 and include: Powerpoint presentations, Prezi presentations, PowToon Presentation, grasstop/grassroots advocacy, grant proposal preparations, loan guarantee applications, issue correspondence, whitepapers, emails, press releases and media, speeches, lectures, and testimony;
- **Meet with other stakeholders on an issue** – engages other stakeholders such as members of the local school board, city council members, congressional state representatives, State officials, a chamber of commerce, civic clubs, and relevant trade associations. The objective is to work together to analyze and present alternatives to government decision-makers;
- **Hosting or attending appreciation celebrations** – participates in luncheons, breakfasts, or legislative sessions, but not fundraisers;
- **Sponsoring for candidates' forums** – does not endorse a single candidate or take a position on an issue to be voted on, such as a referendum or constitutional amendment. However, a baseline advocate can sponsor or participate in candidate's forums; and,
- **Providing information by the request of a government official** – responds to a decision-maker request for more information and uses that opportunity to educate them on the specifics associated with policies, and/or legislative or budget issues.

Lobbying Advocacy

The second category of professional advocacy is lobbying advocacy. Lobbying is considered specialized due to the manner in which it is perceived given the American public's expectations of private and public sector interface.

Chapter 1: Defining Professional Advocacy

Lobbying advocates are requires to register with the Senate Office of Public Records in accordance with the Lobbying Disclosure Act of 1995. This registery facilitates transparency in the lobbying sector. The Office of Public Records documents which individual and which organizations lobby specific bills and other government action items. They also document how much time and money was spent lobbying. This type of advocacy is defined by statute. However, lobbying advocacy can be measured by specific metrics. The lobbyist's' specific intent is to successfully convince a decision-maker to decide an issue in the manner presented and on the basis of the lobbyist's subjective position. The specific metrics include those listed under the Baseline Advocate. However, there are additional metrics: (1) registration as required by statute; (2) compliance with restrictions pursuant to applicable law and regulations; and (3) full disclosure and transparency of the companies and bills lobbied.

Lobbying originated in the 19th-century when individuals would gather in the "lobby" outside of a legislative chamber in hopes of meeting legislators or political decision-makers. As efforts to influence legislators grew in popularity, the public grew skeptical of the aspect of lobbying that was associated with gift giving, favors, and campaign contributions as a quid-pro-quo for their vote and continuing support.

The American public views favors to the decision-makers, elected and nonelected, as inappropriate. The result is that lobbyists as a group are maligned. As the media reported on these practices, lobbyists became subject to increased scrutiny and assertions of unethical behavior.

The U.S. began the process of defining appropriate and inappropriate activities in the Federal Regulation of Lobbying Act of 1946. The statute required the lobbyists register with the government. Further, registered lobbyists were required to report contributions and expenditures when lobbying a government decision-maker. Several iterations of the statute were enacted governing the lobbyist's behavior and their activities.

As a result of cumulative attempts to regulate lobbying and reform unfair practices, all lobbying and associated records are available for public inspection at any time. This has resulted in many creative interpretations concerning lobbying vs. advocacy vs. education activities. These factors will never change. As it relates to lobbying, advocacy, and education, clarity will always be regarded as suspicious by the American public. They all have a potential "gray" interpretation as many are incentivized to ensure "gray" is there!

Subjectivity associated with a lobbying campaign should be assumed by the target of the lobbying campaign unless objective analysis is provided. Lobbyists by nature are subjective. They hold a specific stance on an issue and intend to influence the decision-maker towards making a decision that supports that stance.

There are various approaches to lobbying a policy maker that holds a position on a specific and pending legislation, a policy, or a regulation in an attempt to influence a government decision-maker's position. Generally, there are two approaches.

Direct lobbying[1] is any effort to influence legislation through communication with any member or employee of a legislative body, or with a government official or employee who may participate in the formulation of legislation or a regulation/policy that implements statutory intent.

Grassroots lobbying is any effort to influence legislation through an attempt to affect the opinions of the general public or any segment of the general public.

The difference between the two is that direct lobbying is the time spent *persuading a legislator* to act or not to act, and grassroots lobbying involves *persuading other people* to contact legislators to influence the public policy process.

Lobbying Advocacy in the Non-profit Sector

Lobbying advocacy is an effective way for non-profits to create awareness about how a community is either positively or negatively impacted by public policy, and to generate interest in and support for an organization's mission.

The American public does not clearly understand the significance and contribution of the work of lobbying advocates because the lobbying profession has received such an unfavorable reputation due to negative attention the actions of a few highly publicized individuals over time. Just like any other salacious, profitable industry, [e.g., investment banking, hedge funds, venture capital, acting, etc.] throughout our nation's history, non-profit and grassroots advocacy has led to fundamental and constructive public policy reforms in our society. Throughout history, non-profit advocacy played a critical role in ending slavery, securing the right of women and Blacks to vote, technological advancements, energy and environmental improvements, advancements in workforce compensation policy, and creating consumer protection standards.

At all levels of public and private decision-making, non-profit advocacy work has made a positive difference for many causes, communities, and individuals. By examining case studies and success stories, the general consensus is that charitable non-profit advocacy is under-utilized, under-researched, and under-funded. The need for increased advocacy was discussed in a survey report developed by CLPI with Johns Hopkins University's Center for Civil Society. The report states that many charitable non-profits indicated an interest and even a duty to engage in the democratic process, but most devote less than 2% of their annual budget to this activity. The survey participants identified increased funding for dedicated advocacy staff and for general

---

[1] **Direct lobbying** - As a public employee, it is unlawful to use public funds for lobbying. This includes work time, as well as a work phone and other resources needed to respond. So while one can exercise their rights and responsibilities, they will have to utilize their own resources. Then, it is of no consequence to the program

support as the top two changes that would enable them to engage more robustly in the government's decision-making process.

The following define actions of a lobbying advocate:

- Asks a government decision-maker to vote for a bill or policy and take a specific position on the policy change.
- Asks other stakeholders and individuals in the general public to contact decision-makers to support a specific position.
- Sends a letter to a government decision-maker and other issue stakeholders requesting them to take a supporting position on the issue of interest.

Lobbying Reform

The lobbying reform movement is continuously controversial. President Obama was the first President to state on record that his administration would focus their efforts to ban lobbyists and close the revolving door would be a priority. The rationale was to enhance government transparency.

President Obama signed Executive Order (E.O.) 13490, which banned federally registered lobbyists from being appointed to federal advisory boards and commissions. The initial principles of E.O. 13490 were to reform lobbying by adjusting how business was conducted between the private and public sector, while also preventing national agenda issues from being altered disproportionatley in favor of special interests.

However, the Administration's fervor for lobbying reform has eroded over time and the President's views became less intense. His lobbying reform priority has transitioned from once banning registered lobbyists from serving in the federal government to restricting registered lobbyists' roles in the federal positions. Due to loopholes, lobbyists have the option to de-register as a lobbyist, or be issued a waiver categorizing them as "uniquely qualified" lobbyists.

Obama's intent was to lessen the clout of special interest groups' influence on the public policy process. Practically speaking, there were unintended consequences that the Administration recognized. Removing lobbyists that understand the specifics of certain industries' issues, and their realities, limited the quality of information decision-makers had during their deliberations on complex issues. If appointees who have the best command of the breadth of specific issues critical to decision-making in the public interest are banned, the government is ill served.

Education Advocacy

Education advocacy is the third category. It is composed of many of the factors found in the baseline advocacy category. Its distinctions can be generalized as education advocates provide objective and factual information that was developed following academic protocols and data validation techniques. Government decision-makers and other issue stakeholders are usually comfortable with recognized academician's contributions. The information education advocates provide apply the expertise found within institutions of specialized learning, think tanks, and policy divisions within major corporations. Typically the policy development division within private industry is populated by policy analysts and other academic disciplines. All stakeholders expect an academician's contributions to meet a higher quality standard. This reality is the clear distinction between education advocates and advocates populating the other two professional advocacy categories. Thus, if an education advocate's presentation does not reflect well researched, practical, and credible data associated with issues of concern, the representative should not be considered as an education advocate.

Education advocacy is bound by a moral code. The code speaks to objectivity, transparency, and the application of factual data. The metrics applicable to education advocates include: (1) peer-review; (2) recognition through published articles, books, and studies; (3) expertise recognized and demonstrated on the lecture circuit; (4) expert testimony at administrative and congressional hearings, and (5) as an expert witness for either the government or non-government organizations in and concerning litigation surrounding controversial issues.

Education advocacy efforts are all fact-based by definition. However, decision-makers must be cautious that an academician's interpretation of the facts does not include unsubstantiated bias. Education advocacy is an asset in the decision-making process when conducted in accordance with the unique metrics articulated above. Education advocacy targets legislation, policy, or regulations formulated pre-implementation or a study which targets performance.

Factual presentations are the defining tools utilized during an education advocacy campaign. The exception is when an educator's interpretation of specific facts skews the objective articulation of the facts, therefore crossing the line into lobbying advocacy.

COMPARITATIVE ANALYSIS OF APPROACHES UTILIZED BY THE PROFESSIONAL ADVOCACY COMMUNITY

The table below delineate various differences and similarities between baseline, lobbying, and education advocates. Note, some characteristics are particular to one approach while others apply to all approaches. Some of these shared characteristics cause "blurred lines" between private and public sector interactions. Professional advocates have to be mindful to adhere to the metrics specific to their category and not blur the lines between their intentions and their action.

Figure 1.0 Distinctions in Approaches to Influencing Public Policy

	Lobbying Advocacy	Baseline Advocacy	Education Advocacy
Providing a service to a client for a direct purpose for profit.	X		
Arguing in favor of a specific cause, idea, or policy.	X	X	
Providing objective points of view regarding a particular issue so all perspectives are represented.		X	X
Contacting or urging the public to contact policy makers for the purpose of proposing, supporting, or opposing legislation.	X	X	
Specific limits placed on the budget.	X	X	X
Focused mainly on educating people about a specific issue without an attempt to influence legislation.		X	X
Working in/with coalitions.	X	X	X
Coordinating an educational seminar to discuss all perspectives of issues.		X	X
Any effort to influence legislation through communication with any member or employee of a legislative body, or with a government official or employee who may participate in the formulation of legislation.	X	X	
Any effort to influence legislation through an attempt to affect the opinions of the general public or any segment of the general public.	X	X	
Providing general information regarding the importance of policies and/or legislative or budget issues.		X	X
Testifying at a legislative committee, giving balanced information about both the positive and negative potential impact of the legislation.		X	X
Asking others to contact their legislator and ask them to vote for or against legislation.	X	X	

	Lobbying Advocacy	Baseline Advocacy	Education Advocacy
Empowering decision-makers with knowledge and reliable research.	X	X	X
Sponsoring a candidates' forum, as long as they do not endorse a candidate or take a position on an issue to be voted on, such as a referendum or constitutional amendment.	X	X	X

Chapter 2

PRINCIPLES OF EFFECTIVE ADVOCACY

This chapter explains the principles guiding the professional advocacy community. Our 20 principles of effective advocacy reflect the experience of successful advocates in the three categories of advocacy outlined in this publication. Professional advocates present both government decision-makers and issue stakeholders with credible alternatives to current policies, their unique reasoning associated with an issue, or testimony based on expert knowledge associated with an issue. When these principles are applied in practice, the likelihood that an advocacy campaign will be successful is enhanced.

Four Categories of Advocacy Principles

The principles of professional advocacy are categorized into four groups. The first category targets the audience the advocacy campaign seeks to influence. Advocates must be knowledgeable about every stakeholder position and unique quirks associated with each and every issue stakeholder. The evaluation of each stakeholder's priorities and related concerns must be diagnosed to determine the best and most appropriate approach to alter their perspective. The probability that an advocacy campaign will be successful is lessened if an advocate fails to account for and address each stakeholder's position.

The second category focuses on building trust with government decision-makers and other issue stakeholders. Professional advocates must conduct themselves in a manner that ensures long term relationships based on a bond of trust between the parties. Effective interface between government decision-makers, government officials with responsibility for actions bearing on the issue, and other issue stakeholders are defined by the trust between the parties.

The third category requires the professional advocacy community to develop and implement a methodology that characterizes issues accurately. The advocacy campaign must be designed to address all activities and expectations impacting the public policy decision-making process. Each component of the methodology to be employed must be carefully evaluated from the perspective of realism, practicality, and political acceptability.

The fourth and final category focuses on professional advocates' ethics and behavior during advocacy campaigns. In advocacy, practical and political actions matter at all times.

I. Know Your Audience

Identify supporting government decision-makers and other stakeholders – Determine who the issue stakeholders are in the private and public sectors and their respective positions. It is important to understand how deeply invested stakeholders are in matters relevant to the issue.

Identify the opposition stakeholders – Understand the opposition's position and all viewpoints on the issue. Compare the analysis of opposing stakeholder's positions with other credible interpretations. Ensure that this analytical step underscores your commitment to honestly, clearly, and concisely articulate the opposition's positions on the issue.

Conduct due diligence in understanding the government decision-makers' and stakeholders' position – Take time to develop personal relationships and connections between issue stakeholders in order to facilitate open discussion and more serious consideration of perspectives.

Identify the issue stakeholder's questions or concerns about an issue – Anticipate questions and prepare answers to them. Identify areas of concern that are not clearly understood at the beginning of the decision-making process in order to develop and present answers as the campaign moves forward. Amplify and prioritize information that government decision-makers and other stakeholders are unlikely to know so they can be assured that the facts represent the most current and comprehensive information available.

II.   Build Trust

Build trust by being honest – Provide accurate, factual, and objective information to decision-makers and other issue stakeholders. Identify all real or perceived biases associated with informational material being presented. Be transparent with decision-makers and stakeholders as it facilitates a more effective and efficient decision-making process.

Build trust by maintaining constructive relationships with issue stakeholders – Communicate with all stakeholders about progress and new developments associated with the issue. This demonstrates an advocate's respect and commitment to those involved in the advocacy campaign.

Build trust by being direct – Articulate clearly and directly with government decision-makers and other stakeholders to facilitate the highest quality policy alternatives. No value accrues on any stakeholder position by presenting either ambiguous or poorly analyzed data in the analysis of alternatives. A confusing presentation leads to more questions and less actions.

Build trust by staying current – Provide issue stakeholders with the most up-to-date information and analysis. Private and public sector executives direct continuous research and analysis on the issues. The decision-making process is based on the information effectively delivered. Stakeholders' expectations are to receive the most up-to-date data and analysis from the professional advocacy community thus facilitating effective policymaking.

Build trust by being objective – Provide clear, concise, and factual analysis from all perspectives associated with an issue. Apply academia's uniform standards in your methodology to ensure that the analysis others rely upon can be replicated by those trained to conduct similar analyses.

III.   Apply A Strategic Methodology

Approach issues thinking big, but realistically – Advocates must be realistic in their goals and objectives. Complete success attaining advocacy objectives is rare. When every alternative and potential outcome is thoroughly evaluated, it is appropriate to prioritize which of the objectives should not be compromised. Success if often interpretative. Thus, strategic compromise is a critical component of a realistic and practical advocacy campaign. It is often unrealistic for a government decision-maker or issue stakeholder to affirm the entirety of your position.

Approach aspects of the issue in specific terms – Clearly identify and address factors specific to the issues. This approach facilitates a clear understanding of the supporting and opposing stakeholder positions. Decision-makers and other stakeholders armed with clear and objective information enables the most effective decision-making practices.

Approach issues by utilizing credible sources – The integrity of the information relied on enhances credibility with government decision-makers and issue stakeholders. This in turn improves the public policy decision-making process. Government officials and private sector executives require information quality control, thus, validating the sources of information provided in advocacy presentations and campaigns is critical to the success of these efforts.[1]

Approach issues by working with local and national stakeholders – Identify grasstop and grassroots opportunities to build local and national support on the issues. Cooperation between local, state, and federal level stakeholders demonstrate that public leaders who are in agreement about how to address an issue enhances the likelihood the advocacy campaign will be successful.

Approach issues by building coalitions to increase support and attention – Developing coalitions links individuals and organizations striving to achieve similar goals and objectives. It demonstrates flexibility and mutual respect between the general public, professional advocates, issue stakeholders, and government officials seeking timely issue resolution. Consensus within a coalition improves the likelihood of gaining additional support, and provides credible justifications for decisions and ideas initiated within the coalition.

Approach issues thoroughly in follow-up meetings and presentations – Advocates utilize follow-up meetings to respond to comments, clarify details of various stakeholders' positions, and answer questions from issue stakeholders. These meetings and presentations provide another opportunity for professional advocates to influence the government's decision-making process, or impact "next steps" associated with implementing a decision-maker's approach.

IV.   Exemplify Professional Comportment

Advocates must be credible issue experts – Government decision-makers rely on advocates to provide detailed, accurate, and objective information relating to the issue of concern. Professional advocates demonstrate their expertise to a government decision-maker or other issue stakeholder to gain trust and prove they are a valuable resource to the decision-making process.

Advocates must be patient and diligent throughout advocacy campaigns – Advocacy campaigns do not have an easily predictable timeframe. There are competing stakeholders that often influence the timeframe due to strategically and tactically extended deliberations on issues. Therefore, professional advocates must remain flexible and patient to enhance the likelihood their campaign will achieve their goals and objectives. The advantage of being flexible enables professional advocates to re-strategize their advocacy campaign in light of new developments, address all aspects of the issue thoroughly, and re-prioritize their arguments based on tactics employed by their competitors and new developments.

[1] This process is generally known as "fact-checking."

20

Advocates must treat all issue stakeholders as equal participants in the decision-making process – Baseline, lobbying, and educating advocates must demonstrate respect and humility when addressing issue stakeholders, government decision-makers, and their respected staff persons to enhance the likelihood of a successful advocacy campaign.

Advocates must be comprehensive in the presentation of issue positions – Be exhaustive in the presentation of stakeholder perspectives to effectively influence the government's decision-making process. Providing a comprehensive analysis facilitates positive and constructive policy making and implementation.

Advocates must never burn bridges – Regardless of success or failures, advocates must maintain their composure and respect when discussing issues or meeting with government decision-makers and issue stakeholders. Advocates often compromise on less important sub issues. Strategic compromising is an effective approach that allows advocates to get a "foot in the door" on policy alternatives decision-makers oppose; this is an effective approach. This approach is often the basis for trust between stakeholders. Your long term credibility demands that bridges to other stakeholders are always maintained.

The literature associated with professional advocacy validates the aforementioned principles. The Association for Progressive Communications writes extensively on effective advocacy techniques, and their corroborating principles are published in *Advocacy Strategies and Approaches Toolkit.*[2]

Implementing Effective Advocacy Principles

The most common methods advocates utilize throughout advocacy campaigns are applicable to baseline, lobbying, and educator advocates:

Issue Correspondence

Issue correspondence provides a platform to propose changes to a current program or policy. Correspondence is also an appropriate delivery mechanism to provide an on record position, or inform an issue stakeholder about new published information. Correspondence should be written in your own words. This provides the decision-maker a clear and focused understanding of the advocate's passion and biases associated with aspects integral to the issue.

A well organized, short, and concise piece of correspondence is the most effective, and should apply the principles discussed earlier. When using issue correspondence to communicate, the unwritten objective is maintaining the relationship with government decision-makers and other stakeholders. This is achieved by clearly articulating both their position on the issue and yours within the context of the issue. Finally, the benefit

---

[2] Advocacy Stragies and Approaches: Overview. Association for Progessive Communication. hhtp://www.apc.org/en/node/9456.

is ensuring that you do not put yourself in a position to receive an unexpected reaction or response.

Teleconferences

Teleconferences are more personal than written issue correspondence or answering questions during a committee hearing. Whether various stakeholders are involved or a one-on-one conversation, the principles of effective advocacy should be followed throughout the conversation. There are points throughout the advocacy campaign when teleconferences are the most effective medium of communication. If there is a misunderstanding among parties, calls quickly clarify the misunderstanding.

Another arena in which a teleconference is effective occurs when a decision-maker is being informed on an issue that requires immediate action. Though rare, this delivery mechanism is used to prevent unnecessary delays caused by bureaucratic formaility.

Regular teleconferences allow advocates to maintain relationships with decision-makers and stakeholders on a more personal level. Stakeholders can easily judge the commitment of the advocate by the way they conduct themselves during teleconferences. An advocate's credibility is compromised when they fail to provide corroborating evidence to support their position or articulate objective facts about the issue. Sharing information to all stakeholders provides another platform for advocates and decision-makers to build trust with one another.

Personal Meetings

The principles of advocacy must be observed during face-to-face meetings with government decision-makers and issue stakeholders. Because of the legislative pace, it is difficult to predict a legislator's availability for personal meetings. Advocates should call ahead of time and make an appointment with their desired party and provide a brief summary of the purpose of the meeting.

Personal meetings are conducted for professional advocates to clearly articulate the issues to government executives or other stakeholders, present them with policy alternatives, articulate their own position on the issue, or provide new information about an issue. Advocates should only meet face-to-face with an issue stakeholder or government decision-maker after they have completed due diligence associated with the issue. Advocates, lobbyists, and educators that meet with decision-makers should practice out loud verbalizing their message before the meeting so they understand and are comfortable with their talking points. If an advocate has met with the decision-maker previously, they should implement a strategy or approach they know has been successful in delivering information effectively.

A personal meeting should also make effective use of the government decision-maker's and stakeholder's time. This is done by comprehensively preparing for the meeting and articulating the talking points in a concise manner and in plain language. A successful advocate is one that understands their audience, has built trust with that audience, has developed a strategic plan to effectively deliver information to that audience, and conducts him/herself in a manner that facilitates a constructive relationship over time.

It is not appropriate to try and force a decision-maker into changing their position on an issue they are fully committed to. It is fair to ask them their position on the issue and explain how their decision was reached. Advocates need to respect the government executive or stakeholder's position and work on a strategic compromise if your views are in opposition.

At times a senior executive decision-maker may not be available to meet with you at the scheduled time and sends a staff member instead; it is important to respect that staff member's role. Be flexible in who you are willing to meet with, and patient with government executives and the decision-making process. Demonstrate the same respect with their proxy you would show the decision-maker. The staff member's opinion and insight into the meeting will impact future meetings and correspondence as they report back to the government executive or issue stakeholder.

Testifying before Committees

Where appropriate, addressing an advisory or legislative committee is an effective method for advocating for an issue. Public testimony is "on the record" and is a useful reference for government decision-makers and issue stakeholders to rely on in future advocacy campaigns. While providing testimony, it is important to maintain objectivity and support your position using information that has been through a quality control process.[3] Quality-controlled information incorporates the input of various groups that are seeking to provide facts on a particular subject. This results in the development of new coalitions and networks of additional issue stakeholders.

There are risks associated with providing poorly prepared testimony. The advocate can build support for their cause by effectively articulating the issue and the proposed changes. However, if poorly prepared, the advocate increases the risk of losing support they may have already gained and eliminating the credibility they previously had.

Often, the purpose of a committee hearing is to educate decision-makers. Hearings provide an open forum to verify the information being presented by advocates to government decision-makers. Government executives and other issue stakeholders use their staff to research and analyze the validity of the information being presented. Being honest, sincere, and passionate throughout the hearing will positively impact the advocate's credibility with the deciding committee. If the committee finds the advocate is being untruthful or is untrustworthy, the advocacy campaign is unlikely to be successful.

During a committee hearing, it is permissible for committee members to interrupt witnesses to ask them questions. It is important that an advocate has provided factual

---

[3] A description of quality control mechanisms is found in Chapter 4.

and honest answers throughout their testimony so they are prepared to address questions regarding the information they have presented. If unsure of an answer to a question from a government decision-maker or issue stakeholder, either defer to another witness who is more knowledgeable on the subject, or commit to supplying the answer as soon as possible.

Advocates may be asked during their testimony whether they would support a different alternative than the one they have presented. Do not publicly commit yourself to a position you have not previously stated on public record. Advocates must maintain consistency throughout their testimony in order to articulate their intended message. Note, baseline advocates present objective policy alternatives, lobbying advocates demonstrate a specific solution is superior to other alternatives, and education advocates objectively educate and provide facts about the issue to the audience.

In many cases, even if you are sure that your position will not be approved, your testimony will still be useful. For example, it will help to gain respect for your organization and educate government decision-makers and issue stakeholders in ways that may not be immediately apparent. Another example is your testimony and responses to questions become part of the public record associated with the issue, which documents your participation and involvement in the government's decision-making process.

Chapter 3

THE ETHICS OF PROFESSIONAL ADVOCACY

The purpose of this chapter is to demonstrate that our principles for professional advocacy and the associated advocacy categories are consistent with statutory ethics requirements as well as societal and common sense related guidance governing ethical behavior.

Ethical behavior is mandatory in the conduct of professional advocacy, underscored by our definition. Again, our definition is, *ensuring that the consuming public is represented by public officials that have the most current, credible, and pertinent information to rely upon in order to decide the best policy, statutory, or regulatory approach to conduct the government's responsibilities.*

The chapter addresses general ethical considerations, ethical considerations for baseline advocacy, ethics rules for lobbying advocates, and ethics rules for education advocates. The chapter distinguishes the audience to which the rules apply and for which non-statutory guidance is most relevant. Obviously, the federal audience includes the Executive and Congressional Branches of government. However, much that is stated in this chapter is similar in state and local governments' codification of Federal rules and guidance. These factors are relevant because our premise is that professional advocacy is similar whether targeted to federal or state level decision-makers.

Judicial Ethics

Some believe that advocacy to the judicial sector is separate and distinct. The American Bar Association (ABA) employs an entire certification process for those with a legal education to be officers of the court. Theoretically, this results in a higher standard of responsibility for an attorney's performance and compliance versus other professional advocates involved in government decision-making. This publication does not take a position on whether the rules of professional conduct established by the ABA are more significant to the legal profession than the body of ethics law governing professional advocates. However, it is important to note that attorneys, baseline, lobbyists, and education advocates are all professional advocates.

Table 3.0 demonstrates the differences associated with who and how adjudication takes place when lawyer advocates and lobbyist advocates are accused of an ethical violation:

Table 3.0

Advocacy Category	Ethics Rules Author | 1st Rules	Formal Enforcer	Informal Enforcer	Violator	Potential Impacts of Violation
Lawyers—specific ethics rules	ABA | *ABA Canons of Professional Ethics (1908)*	ABA	Clients, competing lawyers	Offending Lawyer	• Loss of credibility • Loss/suspension of ABA license • Loss of business • Fines
Lobbyists –LDA registration/ reporting / disclosure	Congress | *Foreign Agents Registration Act (1938)*	US Attorney's Office	The public, government officials, competing lobbyists	Offending Lobbyist	• Loss of credibility • Imprisonment • Loss of business • Fines
Lobbyists –specific ethics rules	Governmental Institutions— Federal/State | *Constitution Art. II, Sec. 1, Clause 8 & Art. VI (1787)*	Governmental Institutions— Federal/State	The public, competing lobbyists	Offending Government Official	Government Official: • Loss of job • Loss of credibility • Future employment restrictions Lobbyist: • Loss of credibility • Loss of business

The first thing to note is that these differences only concern ethical violations; lawyers, lobbyists, and government employees and officials are treated the same if convicted of a criminal offense.

The second difference to note is that lawyers are self-regulated by the ABA, which is an independent, non-governmental professional organization with a publicized primary goal of serving its members.[1] By comparison, lobbyists must adhere to rules set forth by Congress, the Executive Branch, and the Judiciary through case law. Federal ethical standards were those imposed on the President and Congress in the Constitution. Over 120 years later, ethical rules were developed and applied to lawyers and 30 years later, the first ethics statutes enacted and applied directly to lobbying advocates.

Another difference is that lobbyists did not write the rules which apply to them. The Congress developed and enacted the rules and the Executive Branch enforces those rules whereas the ABA developed and enforces its own rules governing its members. The Federal government has an internal review process which can involve several different agencies when a decision is appealed.

Informal enforcement is carried out by any third party who casts light onto ethical violations which may subsequently be prosecuted within formal enforcement channels. Regardless of profession, there are individuals who seek to utilize ethics rules against others to gain an advantage, whether justified or not. For lawyers, violations arise from the attorney-client relationship. That relationship is protected by statute. There is no requirement for public disclosure. Lobbyists' actions are subject to public review. Public disclosure is the primary purpose behind the Lobbying Disclosure Act (LDA). This act requires lobbyists to register, report, and disclose specific activities associated with their professional advocacy.

Another factor is shown by examining the "Violator" column. Both lawyers and lobbyists can be directly liable for ethics violations but only lobbyists are held accountable for the ethics violations committed by the parties they work with—e.g., government officials. Neither lawyers nor lobbyists are held accountable for the actions of their clients unless they knowingly or negligently participated in the unethical behaviors.

Finally, differences between the penalties facing lawyers and lobbyists are stated. There is a loss of credibility for both when an ethics violation is proven. Further, lobbyists and lawyers are subject to fines and a loss of business. However, only lobbyists face imprisonment given the statutory prescription. Lawyers only face temporary or permanent suspension of their license to practice, as directed by the ABA.

General Ethical Considerations

General ethical considerations apply regardless of profession, specialization, or context. Most ethical standards are taught and learned before we enter the workforce. Family members teach and reinforce moral and ethics-related principles. These principles include respect for others, interpersonal sincerity, and exhibiting character in interactions with others. The societal rules and standards governing one's ethics education is also conducted by other institutions, e.g. the religious and educational. Finally, friends

---

[1] Available at: http://www.americanbar.org/about_the_aba/aba-mission-goals.html

and other interpersonal influences such as the media and the entertainment industry reinforce ethics standards.

Table 3.1

General Ethical Metrics	Family	Executive Branch	Professional Advocate			
			Baseline	*Lobbyist*	*Educator*	*Lawyer*
Honesty	"Your word is your bond."	101(f)	Be truthful	2 U.S.C. 1606(a)	I(A)1	4.1
Loyalty	"Blood is thicker than water."	101(a), (j)	Keep your commitments	e.g. OGE 101(a), (j)	I(B)4	1.9
Fairness	"You & your brother/sister will share."	101(h)	Be transparent, comprehensive, and objective	e.g. OGE 101(h)	II	3.4
Transparency	"We don't keep secrets from each other."	101(k)	Preserve confidentiality, otherwise keep an open record	2 U.S.C. 1604	I(A)5	7.1
Appearance of Impropriety	"Don't embarrass the family."	101(n)	Ensure your conduct is above reproach and your client's objectives are not unclean	e.g. OGE 101(n)	III	8.3
Respect for Others' Property	"Take care of it as if it was your own."	101(c), (i)	Do not disrespect other stakeholders or their work product	e.g. OGE 101(c), (i)	I(A)6	1.15
Equality	"Walk a mile in their shoes"	101(m)	Do not discriminate	e.g. OGE 101(m)	I(A)4	6.2
Integrity	"You are what you do, not what you say you'll do."	101(b), (d), (g)	Be objective and transparent	e.g. OGE 101(b), (d), (g)	I(B)2	8.4
Responsibility	"Do your chores."	101(l)	Be accountable when discharging commitments	e.g. OGE 101(l)	I(A)9	1.1
Diligence	"If it's worth doing, it's worth doing right."	101(e)	Be consistent and quality control presentations	e.g. OGE 101(e)	I(A)2	1.3

The above Table 3.1 illustrates that general ethical considerations exist regardless of profession. The chart's references are from the Executive Branch; parallel rules are in place for all Congressional Members and their staffs.

There are punishments and rewards to reinforce the ethical metrics. The government and private sectors, inclusive of educational and legal professionals, use similar methods to reinforce ethical behavior for those that did not learn during their upbringing. Depending on the gravity of the violations, the penalties for violations are subject to:

- OGE rules are subject to Office of Personnel Management jurisdiction and the imposition of reprimand, suspension, demotion, and removal.
- LDA rules may result in fines up to $200,000 or 5 years imprisonment.
- ABA standards include punishments such as disbarment, suspension, interim suspension, reprimand, admonition—e.g., private reprimand, probation—and other penalties such as restitution, practice limitations, continuing education.

The Ethics of Baseline Advocacy

The differences between the specific rules applied to each profession are numerous. The following table 3.2 illustrates the relationship between our general ethical metrics and baseline advocacy compared with nuances in other advocacy scenarios:

Table 3.2

General Ethical Metrics	Advocacy Scenarios		
	Baseline	*Lobbyist*	*Educator*
Honesty	Be truthful emphasizing alternatives	Be truthful emphasizing your client's position	Be truthful emphasizing conclusions of the research
Loyalty	Keep your commitments	Keep your commitments	Keep your commitments
Fairness	Be transparent, comprehensive, and objective	Be transparent and comprehensive when explaining your position	Be transparent and comprehensive when explaining issues in your specific area of expertise
Transparency	Preserve confidentiality, otherwise keep an open record	Comply with confidentiality agreements, otherwise maintain an open record	Maintain an open record
Appearance of Impropriety	Ensure your conduct is above reproach and client's organization's position is clear in context with other stakeholders	Do not undermine the credibility of your client's position	Do not undermine the credibility of the research
Respect for Others' Property	Do not unfairly characterize a competitor's position or work product	Emphasize your client's position and work product	Only discuss research, and studies within your area of expertise
Equality	Do not discriminate based on different positions	Emphasize your position without discrediting other stakeholders	Do not discriminate against other experts' research or standing

29

General Ethical Metrics	Advocacy Scenarios		
	Baseline	**Lobbyist**	**Educator**
Integrity	Be objective, transparent, and comprehensive concerning alternative approaches	Be comprehensive in presenting options and analysis to your client and governmental decision makers	Be comprehensive, peer-review, and accurately source the analysis within your area of expertise
Responsibility	Fulfill commitments	Fulfill commitments	Fulfill commitments
Diligence	Quality control presentations	Quality control presentations	Quality control presentations

The Ethics of Lobbying Advocacy[2]

Lobbyists must comply with specific requirements associated with our metrics. A simple guide to these requirements organized by metric follows:[3]

- **Honesty** – No bribery and campaign contributions are limited.
- **Loyalty** – Restrictions associated with lobbying for former employees and officers of the Federal government.
- **Fairness** – Restrictions on gift-giving associated with limitations based on value, relationship, and circumstances, such as symbolically between individuals inclusive of awards or food at a "widely attended" event.[4]
- **Transparency** – Register as a lobbyist within 45 days of the requisite lobbying contacts or within being employed to make such contacts.[5] Provision of reports that identify the lobbyist; clients; specific issues being lobbied; bill numbers, earmarks, any specific executive branch actions; who was lobbied; the covered interests of foreign entities; estimated revenues and expenditures; political, campaign, and other similar contributions; and a certification associated with following gift rules.[6]
- **Appearance of Impropriety** – Undisclosed contingency fees. Congressional contingency fees are defined as additional compensation paid out based upon the success of the lobbying efforts to influence a specific outcome. Outlay of Federal funds as contingent compensation is prohibited under Subpart 3.4 of the Federal Acquisitions Regulations (FAR) which apply to all government contracting.
- **Integrity** – Do not use federal funds to finance lobbying activities.[7] Senators are prohibited lobbying Congress for two years after leaving the Senate.

---

[2] For more in depth coverage of this topic, please refer to the EOP Foundation's *Understanding the Ethics Policy of the United States Government* publication.
[3] CRS Reports: Lobbying Congress: An Overview of Legal Provisions and Congressional Ethics Rules
[4] Please see the EOP Foundation's *Understanding the Ethics Policy of the United States Government* publication, pages 70-78 for details.
[5] LDA
[6] LDA and Foreign Agents Registration Act (FARA)
[7] LDA, FAR

The Honest Leadership and Open Government Act of 2007 (HLOGA) prescribes circumstances under which a lobbyist may be held accountable for bringing a Congressional Member or staffer into conflict with internal ethical rules. For example, violations of gift rules where the lobbyist manipulates or otherwise induces a Congressional staffer to accept an impermissible gift can result in direct penalties to the lobbyist.

The following table 3.3 provides additional detail on current ethics rules as updated by the HLOGA, which are also discussed in our publication, *Understanding the Ethics Policy of the United States Government*:

Table 3.3

Name	Regulation
Lobbying Registration (LD-1 & LD-2 Reporting)	• Income threshold for lobbyist registration is $2,500 during a quarter.[4] • Expense threshold for lobbyist registration is $10,000 during a quarter.[5] • Disclosure—a 20-year look-back on government service for LD-1 and LD-2. • Disclosure—by coalitions and associations of members who "actively participate" in the registrant's lobbying activities and pay at least $5,000 per quarter. • Every lobbyist/entity must file semi-annual certifications of ethics compliance and disclosure of contributions and payments.

Executive Order Governing Political Appointees	• Political Appointees are required to adhere to certain gift and employment restrictions:
	  o Political Appointees may not accept gifts from lobbyists.
	  o Political Appointees may not contact anyone in the executive branch if they become lobbyists upon leaving the Obama Administration.
	• Communications between lobbyists and agency officials on "stimulus bill" funding are required to be disclosed by the agency within three days of contact.
	  o Oral communications regarding specific projects are prohibited by all parties between the submission of a grant application and the awarding stage.

Name	Regulation
LDA Guidance	• Lobbying Registration-clarification that initial registration of a potential registrant must be filed at the earliest time a potential registrant employs a person meeting the definition of lobbyist. • Quarterly Reporting-emphasizes registrants that make an LDA Section 15 election, they may not subtract lobbying expenses for state, local, and grassroots lobbying activities from their total reported on Line 13 of LD-2. • Semiannual Reporting of Certain Contributions- o Each lobbyist who is listed or required to be listed on an LD-1 or LD-2 must file an LD-203 for the period listed on those forms. Filers are expected to know requirements and exercise reasonable care completing and submitting forms. o Contributions to state and local candidates and to party committees not required to be registered with the FEC do not have to be disclosed on an LD-203. o A charitable organization established by a person before that person became a covered official is not considered to be established by a covered official as long as no relationship to the organization exists after the individual becomes a covered official. o A covered official's *de minimis* contribution to a charity is not an indication of the covered official's financing the charity. o Costs relating to sponsorship of a non-preferential multi-candidate primary/general election debate for a particular office do not have to be disclosed on an LD-203. • Termination of a Lobbyist/Registrant—This section provides additional information regarding the circumstances under which a registrant may remove a lobbyist from its active lobbyist list and emphasizes a lobbyist is only relieved from having to file an LD-203 by proper removal, on Line 23 of LD-203, for all clients for whom the lobbyist was listed.

The Ethics of Education Advocacy

In order for educators to be credible, they must adhere to requirements established within the scientific and academic communities. These requirements are not legislated or part of a licensure, such as with lobbyists and the ABA for attorneys, respectively. Rather, they are established and enforced by their peers. The purpose of these standards is producing accurate and replicable research results educating the public across communities and cultures, and providing credit to the experts who ensure our competitiveness in the world.

The principles beyond the baseline which apply to our metrics follow:

- **Attribution** - Work product conducted by others is properly cited. 'Respect for Others' Property' is the applicable metric.
- **Accuracy** - Work product is conducted and complied with methodologies relevant to the field of study. 'Diligence' is the applicable metric.

- **Accumulation** - Work product and associated information is accessible and transparent so that it can be tested, verified, and built upon by others within the academic / scientific community. 'Transparency' is the applicable metric.

There are more institutions and standards than this chapter can cover. The following table 3.4 provides examples in a variety of disciplines:

Table 3.4

Ethical Metric	High School	College	Graduate School	Scientific Research	Pharmaceutical Research
	National Scholastic Model Code[6]	*American Association of University Professor[7]*	*Harvard Medical School Guidelines[8]*	*National Academy of Sciences[9]*	*International Federation of Pharmaceutical Manufacturers & Associations[1]*
Attribution	Be Honest	They practice intellectual honesty.	Everyone who has made substantial intellectual contributions to the work should be an author.	The principle of fairness and the role of personal recognition within the reward system of science account for the emphasis given to the proper allocation of credit.	Quotations should not change or distort the intended meaning of the author or the significance of the underlying work or study.
Accuracy	Be Accurate	They respect & defend the free inquiry of associates, even when it leads to findings & conclusions that differ from their own.	Everyone who is listed as an author should have made a substantial, direct, intellectual contribution to the work.	Organized and searching skepticism as well as an openness to new ideas are essential to guard against the intrusion of dogma or collective bias into scientific results.	The industry has an obligation and responsibility to provide accurate information about its products to healthcare providers in order to appropriately use prescription medicines.
Accumulation	Be Accountable	Professors encourage the free pursuit of learning in their students	Investigators should review each proposed manuscript.	Scientists have to decide the best ways to work with others and exchange information.	Information provided must be objective, truthful and in good taste.

Chapter 3: The Ethics of Professional Advocacy

The following provides samples of actual ethics standards and rules—a set of standards for educators set by a national organization, a students' code set by an institution of higher learning, and a code of ethics for the scientific community set by professionals within a scientific field:

The following table provides quotes from ethics standards and matches them to each of the metrics discussed above:

Rule Set	Responsible Party	Attribution	Accuracy	Accumulation
The National Education Association (NEA) provides a two-part ethical standard[1] 1	Educator	Shall not use professional relationships with students for private advantage.	Shall not deliberately suppress or distort subject matter relevant to the student's progress.	Shall not unreasonably deny the student's access to varying points of view.
Dartmouth's "The Academic Honor Principle"	Students	Any form of plagiarism violates the Academic Honor Principle.	Note: Students are held to a reduced standard of accuracy versus professionals because they are supposed to be learning the appropriate methods and diligence to perform professional-quality research.	Use of the same work in more than one course. Submission of the same work in more than one course without the prior approval of all professors responsible for the courses violates the Academic Honor Principle.
The American Psychological Association (APA) Ethical Principles of Psychologists and Code of Conduct	Professional Psychology Educators	Psychologists do not steal, cheat or engage in fraud, subterfuge or intentional misrepresentation of fact.	When engaged in teaching or training, psychologists present psychological information accurately.	In academic and supervisory relationships, psychologists establish a timely and specific process for providing feedback to students and supervisees. Information regarding the process is provided to the student at the beginning of supervision.

Chapter 4

Government Policy, Budget, Financial Assistance, and Advocacy

Professional advocates interface with government decision-makers in the conduct of authorized government operations and budgeted government extramural programs. Professional advocates seek to influence or change current policies or programs funded by the local, state, and federal government. Professional advocates also assist their private sector clients respond to governmental requests for private sector goods and services. It is important to note that there are professional advocates that specialize in assisting non-government organizations successfully compete for federal financial assistance. The EOP Group is an example of a firm that includes grant writers and other members of its workforce assisting in the drafting of applications for other forms of federal financial assistance.

The first focus is the broadest. This is the area in which government executives and the professional advocacy community combine their efforts to improve the manner in which the government manages its responsibilities. Improving internal controls, maintaining accounting standards, and aggressively pursuing excellence in the conduct of government programs are the emphasis in this category. This focus encompasses the government's decision-making and implementation associated with changes in policy, regulation, guidance, and program operations.

The second focus is associated with changes to the United States budget. This includes annual changes to the budget and new initiatives resulting in increases or decreases to existing programs. Congressional deliberations on the budget are a part of the process resulting in changes to existing priorities.

The third focus is associated with the government's extramural activities. The emphasis is on government solicitation to the private sector; followed by competitive award of financial assistance following the government's evaluation of private sector responses.

Approximately $500 billion in annual procurement and additional federal financial assistance to the private sector encompasses the most significant interface between the nation's private sector professional advocates and the government's program and procurement bureaucracy. Through this interface, the government determines what solicitations are necessary to retain assistance from the private sector in order to achieve mission critical objectives. This federal financial assistance is targeted to the non-governmental organization (NGO) community, industry, research organizations, higher education institutions, and innovative energy, homeland security, environmental, transportation, agricultural, and health priority areas within the federal government. Specifically, the federal financial assistance awarded to private sector organizations include grants, loans, tax credits, contracting and purchases of goods and services from the government, investment in efforts such as research demonstration and development projects, and financial assistance to facilitate innovation in other areas of government responsibilities.

Professional advocates mount campaigns targeting government decision-makers to influence their priorities. Success for the advocate is a request for proposal (RFP) that mirror priorities successfully resulting from the advocacy campaign.

The primary objective of the professional advocacy community is to change the status quo and facilitate new and improved approaches to government operations. The intent is to demonstrate that the proposed alternative approaches are more cost-effective than status-quo for government operations.

In order to ensure that the government and private sectors' ethics are beyond reproach, the rules, methods, and techniques discussed in sections two and three of this publication are critical to understand and apply. The mechanism to address the American public's suspicion of bias within the methods and techniques employed by both the government and private sectors is the continuing evaluation of procurement best-practices and undertaking leadership changes when warranted. The result is that programs under government stewardship are conducted in a manner beyond reproach and the government enhances its effectiveness through use of private sector capabilities.

This is the principle justification for the government to provide the private sector with financial incentives to conduct research, demonstrate, and develop new technologies and approaches in the issue areas for which the federal government is responsible. Similarly, it is the justification for the private sector to partner with government organizations that conduct continuing analysis of scientific, technical, and experience related data developed with government financial assistance.

The rules governing government solicitations and the response from the private sector underscore the sophisticated, complex, and politically-sensitive competition leading to award financial assistance. The decision-making process results in changing established policies or approving changes to program budget allocation.

The government's written and peer reviewed solicitations and the private sector's response to those solicitations must specifically address the government's requirements. These imperatives apply in the full range of solicitations that the government prepares. Examples of the diversity associated with the advocacy campaigns include everything from regulations governing dietary restrictions in schools, funding research in order to find cures for infectious diseases, developing appropriate disposal protocols for nuclear waste, demonstrating techniques to strengthen cement used in road construction, and establishing refuges and sanctuaries inclusive of financing alternatives to save populations of birds.

Changes in Government Policy

Congress, departments, and agencies in the Executive Branch are charged with enacting and interpreting statutes which authorize the government's operations. Government operations are implemented pursuant to policies inherent in legislation and later interpreted via regulation and other written guidance. The nation's industries routinely propose and advocate changes to both the Congress and the Executive Branch when a determination is made that the government's performance can be improved. The public has an expectation that the government will act whenever an opportunity to reduce costs to consumers and improve one's daily lifestyle exists. The private sector pursues policies whose objectives are opening new markets, enhancing net profits, and building consumer loyalty to their product line and services. Success in achieving these objectives requires cooperation between the government and the private sector. Thus, the interface between private sector advocates and a decision-maker's consideration of issue-specific information developed in conjunction with an advocacy campaign becomes an invaluable resource to government decision-making.

Changes in the Government's Budget

Formulating the President's budget has become a yearlong process. The first phase is examining the performance and utility of the government's existing programs. This involves evaluating the cost-benefit of the government's program related expenditures; it is important to evaluate the government's success attaining Congressional intent for the program being implemented.

Each year departments and agencies complete the aforementioned process which concludes in a presidential budget message, legislative agenda, and budget proposal transmitted to Congress for action. Stakeholders for the government's programs advocate their interests in the different phases of the annual budget process.[1] Political initiatives undertaken by elected officials comprise the most controversial component of budgetary decision making and therefore are most subject to advocates seeking to influence the outcome. The politics of budgetary decision-making is divisive. The government–(Executive, Legislative, and Judicial branches—and the private sector are generally partners in determining priorities for federal financial assistance as well as allocations and reallocations impacting policy. Further, the politics between the Republican and Democratic parties have become more ideological warfare. Again, the budget requires cooperation between the public sector and private sector.

Case Study Illustration 4.3: CA Condor and the DOI Budget

In the development of policy alternatives related to the declining condor population the baseline advocate includes a cost-benefit analysis. This analysis clearly indicates how the costs associated with each alternative differ, and by how much. No recommendation is made by the baseline advocate but their presentation informs the Department of the Interior, the agency responsible for implementing programs associated with protecting endangered species, evaluates these alternatives and proposes to Congress the amount needed to implement a new policy.

The lobbying advocate uses their cost-benefit analysis to demonstrate why the captive breeding program is the most cost effective for the Congress to implement. The lobbyist uses their trust and understanding of the current political environment to gain support for the captive breeding program. By gaining the support of government decision-makers the lobbying advocate can influence and impact the allocation of funds from the federal budget to assist in the implementation of the program.

The education advocate simply presents objective data regarding the costs of specific actions. Using academic studies and the analysis of similar policies the education advocate can arm decision-makers with the knowledge they need to understand how these policies will impact the department's budget.

---

[1] A detailed explanation of the federal budgeting process can be found in EOP Education's *Understanding the Budget Policies and Processes of the United States Government*

The Role of Federal Financing Instruments

The federal government's responsibility is to the American public. The federal government discharges its responsibilities whether operational or seeking new and innovative approaches by partnering with the private sector. When program managers select contractors to conduct research or provide goods and services the selection criteria is efficiency, quality, and timely and efficient implementation of government mandates. The process includes competitive proposals from organizations seeking to advance government priorities. The types and definitions of federal financial assistance are listed and described below.

Contracts

Federal contracts are developed between the service providing contractor and the federal government for a specific good or services requested by an agency, department, or program. The federal government procures all its goods and services through contracts. These contracts range from procuring desks and chairs to equip an office to jet bombers to meet national security specifications. RFPs are similar for any government procurement. The government employs contracting officers to coordinate with program executives who ultimately select a private sector vendor to provide goods or services.

Many companies that seek financial renumeration in furtherance of their business model apply to be part of the General Service Administration's (GSA) schedule. The GSA schedule exists to expedite federal department and agency procurement capabilities. The companies that are listed meet the requirements and specifications that governmental departments and agencies rely on. The companies also benefit in that they can be selected based on similar previous contracts without having to start the bidding process over again when a new RFP is released.

The federal procurement process is designed to facilitate competition between highly selective pools of applicants. Applicants must first conform to the criteria outlined in FAR .[2] The regulations contained within FAR help eliminate unacceptable vendors and con-men.[3] The Federal Acquisition Act (FARA) requires that the FAR "shall ensure that the requirement to obtain full and open competition is implemented in a manner that is consistent with the need to efficiently fulfill the Government's requirements.

The procedures governing the contracting process include:

- **Sealed bids** – These are offers submitted in response to invitations for bids (IFBs); opened publicly at a specified time and place; and evaluated without discussions with the bidders, with the contract being awarded to the lowest-priced responsible bidder.[4] The Competition in Contracting Act (CICA)

---

[2] 48 CFR Chapter 1
[3] Such as "shell" corporations or de facto "shell" corporations.
[4] See 48 C.F.R. § 14.101(a)-(e).

requires that agencies solicit sealed bids if (1) time permits their solicitation, submission, and evaluation; (2) the award will be made on the basis of price or price-related factors; (3) conducting discussions with bidders about their bids is not necessary; and (4) there is a reasonable expectation that more than one sealed bid will be received.

- **Competitive Proposals** – This is when agencies use competitive proposals whenever "sealed bids are not appropriate" in light of the previous four factors.[5] Competitive proposals are offers received in response to RFPs. RFPs generally provide for negotiation between the government and at least those offerors within the "competitive range," with the contract being awarded to the responsible offeror whose proposal represents the "best value" for the government.

- **Combinations of competitive procedures** – This is a two-step sealed bidding process in which the government receives the submission, evaluates it, and discusses the technical proposals from each bidder without pricing information. Then, sealed bids are based on a proposal's initial acceptability to the government.

- **Procurement of architectural or engineering services** – This is conducted in accordance with the requirements of the Brooks Act (40 U.S.C. §§541-559). The Brooks Act allows the selection of architects and engineers based upon their qualifications without consideration of the proposed price for the work. Awards must be made to the highest-ranked offeror unless a reasonable price cannot be agreed upon.

- **Competitive selection of basic research proposals** – This is a result from a general solicitation and peer or scientific review of proposals, or from a solicitation conducted pursuant to 15 U.S.C. §638 (research and development contracts for small businesses).

- **Procedures established by the GSA for its multiple awards schedule program** – These are procedures that are recognized as competitive so long as participation in the GSA program is open to all responsible sources, and orders and contracts under GSA's procedures result in the lowest overall cost alternative to meet the government's needs.[6]

- **Procurements conducted in pursuant to 15 U.S.C. §644** – This addresses "set-asides" for small businesses, among other things. Such set-asides are competitive so long as all responsible businesses entitled to submit offers under Section 644 are permitted to compete for the contract.

Procedures established by the GSA for its multiple awards schedule program is particularly significant because it allows agencies to use the so-called "Federal Supply Schedules" (FSS) or "GSA schedules." These schedules enable agencies to take advantage of a "simplified process" for obtaining commercial supplies and services by issuing task or delivery orders directly to contractors listed on the schedules without issuing IFBs or RFPs.

---

[5] See 10 U.S.C. § 2304(a)(2)(B) & 41 U.S.C. § 253(a)(2)(B).
[6] See 41 U.S.C. § 259(b)(1)-(5).

Loans

Loan guarantees eliminate the default risk to the lender by shifting it entirely to the government, enabling the borrower to obtain much more favorable loan rates. Often, without the guarantee, the company seeking the loan would not have been approved at all. In other cases, the corresponding interest rate would have been higher than the federally backed loan.

For loan guarantees, the interest rates and other fees charged to borrowers rarely included enough of a premium to cover the large defaults on which the government is responsible. These high default rates are due to government lending that targets higher risk ventures than do private lenders, and conduct less stringent risk assessments prior to approving loans. For example, defaults on direct and guaranteed loans from both the US Export-Import Bank and the US Rural Electrification Administration (the predecessor of the Rural Utilities Service) have historically been a large percentage of outstanding obligations. Lenders normally charge higher interest rates for riskier loans, and the differences in rates between borrowers of different grades can be larger. Rates to smaller exploration firms would be even higher. For many industries, the larger the portion of capital that can be met through access to federal loans, the better.

An example and discussion of the step by step process of the loan guarantee cycle utilized in the Department of Interior can be found in chapter 10.

Small business loans are loans managed by the Small Business Administration (SBA) and focus primarily on federal financial assistance in encouraging entrepreneurship and the creation of jobs. There are different types of SBA loans:

- **General Small Business Loans** – The 7(a) program is the SBA's most common loan program. It includes financial help for businesses with special requirements.
- **Microloan Program** – This provides small, short-term loans to resolve small business concerns and certain types of not-for-profit child-care centers.
- **Real Estate & Equipment Loans** – The CDC/503 program provides financing for major fixed assets such as equipment or real estate.
- **Disaster Loans** – These low-interest loans are issued to businesses of all sizes, private non-profit organizations, homeowners, and renters following a natural disaster.

Tax-Credits

Tax credits are authorized incentives provided by the Internal Revenue Service (IRS) to implement public policies and initiatives. Congress, in an effort to encourage the private sector to provide a public benefit, allows a participating taxpayer a dollar for dollar reduction of their tax liability for investments in projects that are unlikely to occur or cost prohibitive without an additional incentive. Examples of various tax credits are outlined below.

- **The Research & Experimentation Tax Credit or R&D Tax Credit** – This is a general business tax credit for companies that incur research and development (R&D) costs within the United States.
- **Federal Historic Rehabilitation Tax Credit** – This is a legislative incentive program to encourage the preservation of "historical buildings". Congress instituted a two-tier tax credit incentive under the 1986 Tax Reform Act which includes a 20% credit for the rehabilitation of historical buildings and a 10% credit for non-historic buildings, first placed in service before 1936.
- **Renewable Energy/Investment Tax Credit (ITC)** – This investment tax credit incentivizes organizations to make investments into renewable energy projects by providing the following types of credits; solar fuel cells ($1500/0.5 kW) and small wind (< 100 kW) are eligible for credit of 30% of the cost of development, with no maximum credit limit; a 10% credit for geothermal, microturbines (< 2 MW) and combined heat and power plants (< 50 MW). The credit is generated at the time the qualifying facility is placed in service.
- **Renewable Energy/Production Tax Credit (PTC)** – This credit provides an income tax credit of 2.3 cents/kilowatt-hour (as adjusted for inflation for 2013) for the production of electricity from utility-scale wind turbines, geothermal, solar, hydropower, biomass and marine and hydrokinetic renewable energy plants.
- **Low Income (Affordable) Housing Tax Credit (LIHTC)** – This program allocates tax credits to each state based on that state's population. These credits are then awarded to developers who, together with an equity partner, develop and maintain apartments as affordable units. Benefits are derived primarily from the tax credits over a 10-year period.
- **Work Opportunity Tax Credit (WOTC)** – This is a federal tax credit providing incentives to employers for hiring groups facing high rates of unemployment, such as veterans, women, and minorities. WOTC helps these targeted groups obtain employment so they are able to gain the skills and experience necessary to obtain better future job opportunities.
- **American Opportunity Tax Credit (AOTC)** – This credit replaced the Hope Scholarship credit for Tax Years 2009 and 2010, and increased the benefits for nearly all Hope credit recipients and many other students by providing a maximum benefit of up to $2,500 per student, 100 percent of their first $2,000 in tuition and 25 percent of the next $2,000. It also expanded the income range over which taxpayers can claim a credit, and made the credit partially refundable.
- **State tax credits** – These credits are provided in approximately forty three states. These include Brownfield credits, Film Production credits, Renewable energy credits, Historic Preservation credits and others. The amount of credit, the term of credit and the cost of the credit differs from state to state. These credits can be either in the form of a certificate, which can be purchased as an

asset, or in a more traditional pass through entity. The tax credits can generally be used against insurance company premium tax, bank tax, and income tax.

Grants

Federal grants are financial assistance awards from a federal agency to a private sector recipient to carry out a public purpose of support authorized by statute. Grants provide financial assistance to individuals, for-profit and non-profit organizations, educational institutions, states, and US territories. Federal grant opportunities are very competitive and specific. The granting agency uses a grant offering as a way to promote a R&D project, educate a certain population on an initiative promoted by the administration, demonstrate a new technology, or study an environmental or other type of phenomenon. Grants are packaged in many different instruments and can be 100% funded by the government. Grants can be packaged as a cost-sharing, matching, or requiring cost participation indicating the federal government splits or shares the cost of the project with the grantor. In other words, the government provides funding for a pre-described percentage of the costs.

The grant process is very competitive and highly scrutinized. The review process varies by agency, but every private sector grant proposal is evaluated by two and often three reviewers. If the grant application is not rejected, the reviewers read and independently score sections of the proposal following the evaluation criteria. Evaluation scoring includes the statement of need, statement of objectives, program description, agency and staff experience and qualifications, and other elements including strength of community partners, recommendations, etc. Proposals scoring lower than a predefined cutoff are rejected. Proposals scoring higher than the predefined cutoff are recommended for funding. Recommendation for funding does not mean funding will be granted, but that the proposal has been determined to meet the baseline qualifications. The ultimate decision for funding is determined by the number of qualifying proposals, the amount of funding available, and each proposal's ranking. A full length step by step example of the grant proposal and award cycle can be found in chapter 10.

Subsidies

Federal subsidies are benefits given by the government to groups, businesses, or individuals usually in the form of cash or tax reduction. The federal government provides subsidies to remove a specific type of burden or to prop up an industry or business that is facing unfair competition from foreign entities. Additionally, subsidies are given to promote a social good or an economic policy. Federal subsidies provided to individuals are done in the form of social welfare programs such as food stamps, welfare payments, and unemployment benefits. Examples of subsidies provided to industry are found within the farming industry.

Roles of Advocates within Government Financial Opportunities

NGOs, private sector for profits, non-profits, educational institutions, and state and local governments all jockey for federal financing opportunities. In 2015, the federal government spent over $2 trillion on grants, contracts, loans, and other financing assistance. To ensure fair treatment and efficient spending of the US tax payer's money, the methods used to spread federal dollars across all non-federal entities are closely monitored.

Navigating the GSA and the FAR is a challenging task for any organization interested in providing goods and services to the government. Often many organizations look for assistance in this navigation. To assist an organization in navigating the FAR process, many organizations retain firms with contracting and procurement experience within the federal government. Former procurement and contracting officers become valuable assets and are highly sought after following their retirement from government service.

The second option used by organizations looking to break into the federal sales marketplace is to hire a professional advocacy organization. The professional advocacy organization's role is to use their relationships within procurement and contracting offices along with expertise in the federal procurement process to provide guidance and assistance to companies looking to gain a foothold within federal procurement circles. Additionally, professional advocates educate the private sector company's leadership on how to navigate the processes governing federal procurement. Furthermore, they educate government decision-makers on the value and warrants associated with the organization's goods or services.

The professional advocacy community consists of non-profit special interest organizations, business oriented organizations, trade associations, individuals (former Congressional members, Governors, Ex-Government employees), grassroots organizations, law firms with lobbying and advocacy units, lobbying firms, consulting firms, boutique consulting firms, think tanks, and environmental groups. These types of organizations represent directly, or in-directly, the values and interests of an organization, the collection of organizations, or an industry.

Chapter 5

EFFECTIVE ADVOCACY METHODS

This chapter discusses specific methods which should be employed by professional advocates in their dealings with government decision-makers. These methods require a combination of an advocate's knowledge, skills, and abilities (KSAs), common sense, experience, and special education as the basis for effectiveness.

The following definitions will enhance your understanding of our methodologies and descriptions. The government's KSAs are defined as the attributes required to perform in a federal job that are generally demonstrated through experience, education, or training. Common sense is defined as the application of logic and social awareness to a routine task. Experience is defined as having worked in a position which required regular and routine interface with decision-makers in the government on issues of concern for a minimum of three years. Special education is defined as completing a legal, a public policy, business administration, or a leadership/policy analysis curriculum. Other graduate level curricula may also qualify as special education under our definition.[1]

While redundant, we re-emphasize that the most important scenario to apply as a professional advocate is to be straight forward, honest, transparent, and trustworthy with whomever you seek to influence.

The methodology and process for effectively advocating to government decision-makers includes five steps:

Issue identification – The statement of the issue must be clear, succinct, and neutral.

Analysis of the issue – The analysis should be quantitative/qualitative and practical. Both quantitative and qualitative analyses must meet uniform academic standards of excellence and include an evaluation of alternatives.

Information quality control – It is critical that any application of data or qualitative information be evaluated against uniform quality standards.

Legitimate sources – Evaluate sources of data and other reference material, e.g. studies, expert statements etc., to be certain of their credibility.

Effective delivery – Strategize and determine the most appropriate presentation alternative, e.g. PowerPoint, letter, etc. The choice should be made based on the audience, timeframe, and effective utility with the decision-maker you seek to influence.

Issue Identification

The single most important written articulation for professional advocates is the statement of the issue. Decision-makers require a clear, concise, and accurate understanding of the issue being addressed in the government decision-making process. They are unable to address concerns raised by stakeholders that are:

- Too broad;
- Too narrow;
- Too subjective;
- Too superfluous;
- Too unclear;
- Too technical; and of course,
- Too political.

Professional advocates have found that framing the issue as a question is the most effective method to identify the issue. A well structured question can narrow the issue to the simplest factors requiring resolution.

---

[1] Additional information relevant to qualifying curricula and training is found in EOP Foundation's Understanding Leadership in the United States Chapter 9 Page 105.

Issues are decided within the government's dynamic decision-making process. The government's process is predictable. Advocates must understand the dynamics of the government's decision-making process when commencing their efforts to work within it. Therefore, a clear and direct question articulates the specific issue and what needs to be resolved in a neutral fashion and facilitates the government's deliberations.

Once the issue has been narrowed by developing a direct and pointed question, the professional advocate is ready to prepare an issue analysis inclusive of the preferred alternative.

Example 5.0

Statement of the issue: Should the endangered California condor continue to breed in the wild?

Analysis of the Issue

The analysis of the issue must be comprehensive, transparent and accurate. Transparency requires that specific policy or program alternatives be articulated for government officials and decision-makers. The issue analysis must be accurate in that it communicates the facts associated with the issues. Additionally, the analysis must identify sources of information, employ replicable analytical methods, and identify arguments that are subjective, or reflect only certain perspectives.

Transparency is defined as the openness in communications with decision-makers and accountability for the outcome; successful or not.

Subjectivity or bias is associated with advocating for a single outcome from a singular perspective. Presentation to government officials and other stakeholders is amplified by relying on data and information that reinforces the decision being sought. Therefore, bias is defined as being prejudiced in favor of one position on an issue versus another. Prejudice is defined as having a strong inclination as well as a preconceived perspective about the issue of concern.

When the basis for presenting an evaluation of alternatives represents factual, comprehensive, and objective statements distinguishing the differences between the alternatives, the optimal environment for decision-makers has been achieved. Straightforward articulation of different perspectives is useful, but is not as beneficial to government officials as an objective comprehensive analysis of alternatives. The reason is that different perspectives can be evaluated against criteria that are not comprehensive and balanced. The following example is beneficial to illustrate the point:

Example 5.1

Each of the alternatives is credible and could be implemented. The following example reflects an effective articulation of the alternatives.

- Alternative 1: The political decision-makers articulated position is presented objectively in the following alternative.

  Example: Continue condor breeding in the wild without intervention.

- Alternative 2: The status-quo alternative reflects the change that public/ private sectors support based on scientific studies and analysis believed to be in the public interest.

  Example: Initiate condor captive breeding programs.

- Alternative 3: The most credible opposition alternative is articulated and forms the bases for conducting an objective issue analysis provided to all issue stakeholders.

  Example: Continue condor breeding in the wild, but remove environmental hazards by acquiring condor habitat and promulgating command and control regulations governing the habitat.

If these considerations are the basis of the methodology applied by professional advocates in developing alternatives, government executives can be expected to accept the information as realistic and useful. The decision being influenced through this methodology represents the range of alternatives that are most prominent in the public debates. Thus, government executives have to evaluate and address the issues associated with each alternative. There are credible and expert perspectives associated with each of the three alternatives presented. This is the backdrop during the decision-making process. The key to its effectiveness is judged on the basis of clarity and transparency.

Completing an issue analysis as a professional advocate is critical prior to interfacing with government decision-makers. Effective interface between the parties relies on researching the facts bearing on the issue inclusive of expert testimony, studies, reports, and other analyses of the issue. A professional advocate's credibility is dependent on the answers to the following six questions:

1. What are the sources of data and information relied on in your analyses and presentation?
2. Where are the studies', reports' and experts' biased in their manipulation of data and emphasis in their presentation?

3. Did you address each of the stakeholder's positions and associated analyses objectively in your representation of their perspectives in your presentation?
4. Were any of the facts you relied on interpreted differently by other experts or stakeholders?
5. Did you address the government decision-makers' political considerations in your analysis and presentation?
6. Did you balance your comprehensive analysis by presenting competing data and information associated with the issue of concern?

Once again, the key is transparency and accuracy. The sources cited and used to generate the alternatives and how the facts are applied in an advocacy campaign defines whether baseline advocacy, lobbying advocacy, or education advocacy is the appropriate classification.

Information Quality Control

Professional advocates must ensure that their sources are current and reputable to the government. Quality control measures are important. The level of detail and energy associated with quality control must be beyond reproach. The methods employed to validate information, sources, and finally the interpretation of information presented to government decision-makers must similarly be beyond reproach.

Editing a document and associated quality control which results in zero changes is rare. Whereas, presenting arguments in a document with only minor revisions is more likely among advocates.

It is important to distinguish between internal quality control and external quality control methods. Internal quality control involves proofreading or editing your own work, whereas external quality control involves peer-reviewed fact checking.

All professional advocacy campaigns require quality controlled information. With the widespread availability of information from internet sources, social media generated rumors, and the presentation of biased information, additional diligence is required. Controlling the quality of information is of the utmost importance because people have a tendency to perform quick Google searches and believe the results.

Conversely, scientific journals and other professional reports institute safeguards to ensure that information relied on is credible and reputable. The review process subjects scientific research papers to higher levels of scrutiny. Newspapers, magazines, and websites are not put through the same rigorous reviews before they are published. Thus, the probability that some percentage of the information is biased or incorrect is likely.

Quality Control Methods

The following quality control methods should be used as appropriate to ensure the highest level of quality controlled information can be relied upon and is presented by the advocacy community:

Traditional Proofreading – A proofreader examines a portion/section of text and provides substantive, grammatical, or textual remarks. Proofreaders are expected to be accurate given their role in external quality control before publication. The term proofreading is also referred to as copy editing. Proofreaders, or the act of copy editing, mark queries for typesetters, editors, or authors. From an organizational standpoint, advocates should ensure all issue papers or reports submitted to government decision-makers and other issue stakeholders are proofread prior to delivery. Management should implement a proofreading/quality control process that ensures multiple layers of review that result in the highest level of quality.

Copy holding or copy reading – Employs two readers editing an electronic or paper copy of a publication's text. The first reads the text aloud literally as it appears; usually at a comparatively fast but uniform rate. The listener/second reader follows along and marks any pertinent differences between what is read and what was typeset. This method is appropriate for large quantities of boilerplate text where it is assumed that the number of errors will be comparatively small. Attorneys use this method often when drafting contracts or legal memorandums.

Double reading – A method that utilizes a single proofreader checking a proof in the traditional manner then passes it on to a second reader who repeats the process. Both proofreaders initial the proof. Note that with both copy holding and double reading, responsibility for a given proof is necessarily shared by two individuals.

Editing (Supervisory Control) – The professional advocate considers the feedback provided by the peer reviewers prior to making a decision about whether the suggested changes should be made. The following are the most common editorial decisions include:

- **Acceptance** – Accept document without any changes. The advocate uses a staffer's document in its original form;
- **Acceptance with minor revisions** – The advocate uses a staffer's document but requires small corrections;
- **Conditional acceptance** – The advocate does not use the staffer's document without requiring substantial changes suggested by other reviewers;
- **Conditional rejection** – The advocate rejects the staffer's document. The advocate indicates the willingness to reconsider the paper in another round of decision-making after major changes have been made; and,
- **Outright rejection** – The advocate will not even reconsider a staffer's document because it is not fixable and will not publish the paper or reconsider it even if the authors make major revisions.

Post-publication review – Reviews that are submitted after publication depend on public accessibility. Post-publication reviews can add valuable information to published papers. For example, a highly controversial paper regarding California wind farms negatively impacting the endangered condor population appearing in a journal may motivate a number of supportive or critical post-publication reviews. The overall evaluation from these public reviews impacts the attention given to the paper by potential readers. The actual text of the reviews may help readers understand and judge the details of the paper. Advocates can use these comments as the basis for how the public views the issue.

Peer Review

There are four specific peer review methods that the professional advocacy community relies on. In generic terms, peer review is the evaluation of work product by one or more individuals of similar expertise to ensure the quality of the work product that will be used in an advocacy campaign.

In academia, peer review is often used to determine whether an academic paper is of sufficient quality to be published. Quoting peer-reviewed reports is a commonly used method in baseline advocacy, lobbying advocacy, and education advocacy to get the most unbiased, accurate, and credible information to the appropriate decision-maker.

The following peer review methods are also employed to improve an advocate's performance and credibility with issue stakeholders and government decision-makers.

Open peer review – Open peer commentary is an extension of peer review and occurs after the date of publication, whereby, experts comment on the published article. Advocates can use the comment period to assess public opinion regarding the publication. This review can be used to quiet dissenting voices, revise the publication, and promote the publication to new audiences.

Peer-review of government policy – The technique of peer review is also used to improve government policy. OMB's peer review bulletin requires that U.S. federal regulatory agencies submit all "influential scientific information" to peer review before the information is publicly disseminated. This process provides validity to government-issued reports; however it does not ensure their accuracy. Government review processes can be requested by the government. Advocates should be cognizant of potential bias in government reports and should evaluate data utilizing data integrity as the driving evaluation principle.

Single-blind peer-review – A single-blind peer review keeps the identity of the reviewer anonymous, but reveals the author's name and their affiliation. The advantage to this approach is that the reviewer is free to provide edits and comments without fear of repercussion or pressure from the author or others in their organization. The disadvantage is that the reviewer may have a preconceived bias, whether implicit or not, against the author, the author's institution, or their political affiliation.

Double-blind peer-review – This method is similar to the single blind peer review. The difference is that the reviewers and author's identities are concealed throughout the review process. The double blind peer review process eliminates potential bias by a reviewer. This allows the reviewer to critique the paper in the most honest and transparent manner. This method addresses the issue of credibility and trustworthiness. Double blind peer reviews produce higher quality work and more trustworthy data because the bias and potential prejudices held by the reviewer are mitigated. The intent is to ensure that only the facts and methodologies used are evaluated for validity and accuracy.

Legitimate Sources

It follows that evaluating the legitimacy of sources is critical to the advocacy community, government decision-makers, and issue stakeholders alike.

When presenting advocacy materials, advocates must determine that without a doubt the information being presented is legitimate. It is imperative to identify differences between industry funded and inspired studies, scientific reports, and specific point-of-view pieces published by other organizations.

Advocates must understand that the sources they select and cite are integral to the validity of their analysis and presentation.

The information advocates present is evaluated by government decision-makers for its level of credibility based on the sources the advocate's provide. Government decision-makers view certain sources as more credible than others. Further, government decision-makers are sensitive to sources that are accepted or rejected by other issue stakeholders. In some cases, the media's spin on an advocate's list of sources has influence on the way government executives and the public perceive the information.

This publication takes the position that the sources of information listed below fall into three categories relevant to a government decision-makers perspective: factual, objective, and subjective.

Factual	Objective	Subjective
Database Presentations	Subject Matter Articles	Newspaper Editorials
Encyclopedia	Academic Journal Articles	Association Websites
Almanacs	Reference Books	Biographical Works
Congressional Committee Publications	Guidebooks	Monographs
Congressional Hearings	Indexes and Abstracts	Magazine Articles
Chronologies	Manuals	Books
Directories	Task Force Reports	Patents
Survey Research	Theses	Letters
Official Records of Organizations/Gov Agencies	CBO Reports	Interviews
Proceedings of Meetings, Conferences, and Symposia		Email Communications
Investigating Articles		Diaries
Laboratory Experiment Findings		Debates by Congress Persons
GAO Audits		Advisory Committee Member Testimony
Congressional Investigation Reports		Trade Associations Reports
Legislative Oversight Testimony		

Identifying Credible Sources

Credible Websites

The following outlines characteristics associated with different aspects of evaluating whether information found on a website is credible. Often times, well designed websites can be scattered with bias or inaccurate information. When determining if a website is providing credible information, first look at the home page or main page of the site. The home page will identify the last time the page was updated, who to contact with questions regarding the information provided, and the sources relied on for their research purposes. If a website does not provide the aforementioned information, the website is not providing credible information.

Authorship

In some cases, authors become "discredited" for publishing information they manipulated to appear as if it were accurate and true. Authors should be well researched and their body of work evaluated. If there is no author or organization claiming responsibility for the information, use different material.

Sponsorship

Often times, specific organizations sponsor material printed on web pages. The sponsoring entity can provide insight into the level of objectivity or subjectivity to be expected. Determine who sponsors and operates the page and if that organization is reputable. If determined that it is, the source may be appropriate to use, even if no individual author is credited. If you cannot determine what group or individual developed the site or provided the material, think twice before using the source.

Date

For many disciplines, how current the information is becomes the key factor associated with credibility and utility. Advocates should provide the most accurate and up-to-date information available to issue stakeholders and government executives.

Site type

When using a search engine like "Google.com" do not assume that the top results are programmed to identify most credible results. Search engines have different methods for organizing and ordering results and many times the top option is a paid advertisement. Using filters such as Google.com/scholar provide results acceptable to academia criteria.

Advocates should avoid using blogs or websites owned by an individual unless you can verify the owner's credentials. A popular site type for quick answers to questions is a "wiki page." A wiki page is a Web site where any user can modify and edit the information. Thus, there is no way to verify authorship or credibility of the information provided.

Online periodicals or online versions of print publications are often credible sources of information but are sometimes spun or prejudiced towards one particular position on an issue. Examples of online periodicals include Slate.com; Salon.com; and Wired.com. Examples of print publications on the Web include Nytimes.com and Newsweek.com.

Editorial Board Meetings

An editorial meeting, whether with an editorial board, or a single editorial writer, is a unique opportunity for the professional advocacy community to present their viewpoints on issues to the press and broadcast media. Editorials present opinions, thus advocates utilize editorial meetings to explain policy alternatives, attempt to gain support for one particular policy approach, or educate their target audience and the media about a specific issue, policy, or program.

When preparing for an editorial board meeting, it is important for advocates to follow these steps:

- **Access the appropriate time to schedule the meeting** – It is appropriate to schedule a meeting when you are launching a new campaign or program, releasing a report which provides newsworthy information, or to refute a recent news story opposing an action be taken on your issue of concern;
- **Build a team** – Determine which individual(s) are the most knowledgeable and useful in conveying the essential aspects of the advocacy campaign. If more than one person addresses the board, assemble a team that can articulate the same message providing expert analysis in all essential areas. For example, include a baseline advocate to explain the policy alternatives, an industry expert to provide technical expertise on the issue, and a policy expert that can articulate the processes and regulations bearing on the issue;
- **Prepare advocacy materials for dissemination** – Once the meeting is secured, send the board a packet of information that includes an agenda for the meeting. Materials should include proposed/enacted legislation, press releases, graphs/charts and white papers related to the issue, and common questions/answers that are asked. Determine the subject areas that are especially pertinent to government executives and issue stakeholders. Be sure to include that information in the packet;
- **Moderate the meeting** – The individual who scheduled the meeting should act as the moderator. The moderator outlines the purpose and objectives for the meeting and introduces participants. In addition, the moderator should address the coverage, whether positive, negative, or non-existent, as it relates to the issue being discussed. This serves to provide new or additional information to government decision-makers and issue stakeholders;
- **Engage knowledgeable participants** – Each participant should be knowledgeable, succinct, and comprehensive within their expertise. They should speak no more than three to five minutes. The moderator should ask for questions and direct them to the appropriate member of the team;
- **Communicate the impact** – Include issues that deserve attention and discuss those who will benefit and those who will be affected. Discuss, objectively, how recent proposals will be a win-win solution for decision-makers and other issue stakeholders;
- **Closing the meeting** – Conclude the meeting by requesting an action from the editorial board. The "ask" depends on the issue and phase in the decision-making process. If the newspaper or an industry related publication has not published an editorial on the issue, then ask them to publish an editorial focused on educating readers. Lastly, provide the editorial board with handouts and contact information for further review and additional resource materials.

Verbal Communication

Effective verbal communication is essential for advocates. Advocates build and connect relationships, discover solutions, educate the public, and advise decision-makers. Verbal communication with stakeholders and face-to-face interaction is an essential component of any professional advocacy campaign. Verbal communication skills impact how effectively one communicates their intended message; thus, usefulness to decision-makers and those being educated. Additionally, advocates must adapt the skills in their repertoire to account for all settings and environments ranging from the office, a restaurant, a bar, a conference, an event, or an encounter with an issue stakeholder at a widely attended event.

Effective Verbal Communication Skills

Clarity of speech, remaining calm and focused, being polite, and following some basic rules of etiquette will aid the process of communicating effectively with all issue stakeholders and government decision-makers. Advocates who master these skills are positioned to effectively deliver new knowledge and influence the public policy process. They are better equipped at bridging relationships, keeping communication lines open and fluid, and are successful in influencing the decision-making process. This following discussion addresses metrics associated with effective verbal presentations.

Opening remarks are vital to making the right first impression. First impressions are the most significant factor governing the likelihood of further communication between the parties in the future. Meeting and exceeding first impression expectations create a baseline standard for how future meetings or correspondences proceed. Failing to meet or exceed those expectations decrease the probability of further communication.

The following performance metrics serve as a standard to ensure positive first impressions with issue stakeholders:

- Introduce yourself, shake hands, making eye contact, and then initiate small talk on a neutral topic;
- Demonstrate a friendly disposition to encourage open communication, avoid sitting or standing with your arms crossed; and,
- Demonstrate you are well informed about the government's perspectives on the issue as well as other key issue stakeholders. This builds confidence required to meet and exceed their expectations.

Reinforcing behaviors such as combining encouraging words with non-verbal gestures such as supporting head nods, warm facial expressions, and maintaining eye contact are ways to encourage openness in others. Encouragement and positive reinforcement signify interest in other stakeholder's comments, establishes a pathway for development and/or maintenance of relationships, allay fears, and provides reassurance to the audience.

Active listening is vital to effective verbal communication as well. Generally, most people spend more energy deciphering their next words, in lieu of listening to the person speaking; therefore, limiting the potential constructiveness of the discussion.

The following precepts serve as guidance to active listening:

- Be deliberate in listening to government decision-makers and other stakeholders;
- Keep an open and objective mind while concentrating on the main points of the speaker's message;
- Avoid distractions, especially cell phone usage;
- Allow the speaker to finish speaking before articulating your opinion or asking questions; and,
- Avoid prejudices. A perception that you have personal issues with one's gender, ethnicity, social class, appearance, or dress will negatively impact your advocacy efforts.

Effective questioning is an essential skill advocates must utilize while conducting verbal presentations. Your ability to: (1) obtain information; (2) start a conversation; (3) test the audience's comprehension of your message; (4) show interest in other stakeholders and their message; and, (5) seek support or agreement based on your questions and comments. The following two methods are useful to categorize effective questions:

1. Closed questions seek a one or two word response (often 'yes' or 'no') and, in doing so, limits the scope of the response. An example of a closed question is "Has the California condor population been in decline?" When this type of question is asked, the questioner maintains control of the answer. However, this is an ineffective method to start a conversation. Closed questions can be useful for focusing discussions and obtaining clear, concise answers when needed.

2. Open questions broaden the scope for responses in that they facilitate further discussion and elaboration. For example, "What do you believe would be necessary to restore the condor population to healthy levels?" Answers to open questions are unpredictable, but they provide the respondent more scope for self-expression and encourage fluid and open communication.

Professional advocates must reflect on the key points of the conversation. Their reflection assures that the message communicated by speakers can be articulated in your own words. In doing so, the significance of the facts and feelings expressed, communicate your comprehension of the speaker's message. This is useful because it validates your understanding of the message. You can demonstrate that you have interest in, and respect for, what the other stakeholders have to say, and acknowledge the fact that you are considering the other viewpoints. During this reflecting process you also clarify what was communicated by the speaker. If there has been a misunderstanding of a key point the speaker can take this opportunity to correct you.

Summarizing can also serve a similar purpose as reflecting; however, summarizing allows both parties to review and agree about what the key points of the discussion were. It helps to remind the participants of what they just talked about. When used effectively, summaries may also serve as a "next steps" discussion that outlines what each participant will do moving forward.

The conclusion of the verbal interaction will impact the way a conversation is remembered by the participants. For example, some people may avoid eye contact or use behaviors such as looking at a watch or cell phone too frequently. These non-verbal actions indicate to the other person that the initiator wishes to end the communication.

An appropriate time to make future arrangement comes at the conclusion of the interaction. This time will also be accompanied by a number of socially acceptable parting gestures such as a hand-shake or a hug depending on the nature of the relationship.

Verbal presentations and face to face interface is necessary for operating in a professional environment. Advocates who demonstrate a history of success influencing stakeholders prepare well in advance and effectively organize their thoughts and approaches to government decision-makers and issue stakeholders.

Chapter 6

PRACTICAL ADVOCACY TECHNIQUES

This chapter discusses the techniques professional advocates utilize along with the application of our principles when drafting effective written instruments and associated patterns of interaction with government decision-makers. It provides guidance for advocates who seek to influence the public policy development process through written instruments, face-to-face meetings, hearings, and other forums involving government decision-makers and issue stakeholders.

Government decision-makers allocate their time based on the conduct of their highest priority issues. Their performance criteria require that meetings and associated internal and external communications are focused and purposeful. The most successful professional advocate articulates their position with sensitivity to meeting the government decision-maker's needs while minimizing their time considering the advocate's information.

Issue Correspondence

The government is encouraged to view taxpayer or constituent correspondence as a priority. In fact, most presidential appointees and senior executives have correspondence control units and associated staff to manage the flow of correspondence.

Issue correspondences employ the following metrics:

- **Proper format** – Should be a maximum of two pages. Must be dated and include the complete address of both the government executive to receive the correspondence and the advocate transmitting it. All correspondence should be printed on letterhead when it's transmitted;
- **Identifies critical information in a clear and concise manner** – Should articulate the advocate's position in the first paragraph. Paragraphs that follow should justify and reinforce the advocate's position. The final paragraph should recommend proposed next steps for the decision-maker and other issue stakeholders;
- **Includes cogent analysis** – Summarize the quantitative and qualitative data sets relevant to the issue. Lay out conclusionary analysis for the audience;
- **Articulates the preferred actions to implement the proposal** – Should present strongest arguments and impacts of the advocate's position. Should not cut and paste or copy information associated with proposal other information, rather; discuss the proposal in your own words referencing all sources that were relied on;
- **Addresses only one issue** – Should carefully focus arguments so that the stakeholder is not confused about the preferred outcome;
- **Utilizes vocabulary familiar to all issue stakeholders** – Do not introduce any terminology or rhetoric unknown to government decision-makers or issue stakeholders;
- **Avoids redundencies** – Should provide current and unique information that is neither threatening nor pro-forma; and,
- **Develops clear follow-up plan** – Should state that the correspondence follows-up on previous message delivery and either thanks the decision-maker or restates impacts of no action. Sending a brief follow-up request if you don't receive a reply in a reasonable amount of time is appropriate. The follow-up plan must be transparent whether the issue was decided in your favor or not as the advocate seeks feedback.

Teleconferences

Many government decision-makers and private sector executives delegate advocate's calls to members of their staff. This is particularly true if the perception is that the call is to further reinforce positions and restate arguments that are already on-the-record. Teleconference that decision-makers participate in must provide new or additional information or to position the information so its relevance to the decision-making process is clear. Remember time is invaluable to government executives; therefore, requesting a call should add significant value to the process.

Baseline advocates use teleconferences to inform issue stakeholders, government decision-makers, and their staff about policy alternatives bearing on issues of interest. They seek to provide objectivity and balance to the government's decision-making process. When scheduling a teleconference, baseline advocates explain why their agenda for the call is important and adds value to those that will participate.

Lobbying advocates rely more on their personal relationships with government executives to induce them to participate in teleconferences. They demonstrate their clout when they make unscheduled calls to obtain a status report from executives "in the know" about the process. A short call can also be extremely fruitful to government executives in that they can quickly learn the most up-to-date information about their issue. Education advocates provide new technical information to decision-makers or provide further explanation of an issue. These advocates participate in teleconferences when they have received requests for further information, or to provide an expert perspective relevant to the issues of interest. The information they provide is simply to educate and not influence the decision-makers to adopt changes to the status quo. When conducting teleconferences with government decision-makers, a professional advocate should employ the following techniques:

- **Schedule the call in advance** – Scheduling a call time allows all parties to properly prepare for the call. It focuses participants on a specific subject and helps them to organize their materials, prepare any questions they plan to pose, or gather/request more information;
- **Keep the call as brief as possible** – Start by identifying the participants on the call. The issue should be articulated immediately following introductions, and the objective of the call articulated. Disseminating an agenda for the call is always effective to coordinate participants and improve efficiency;
- **Use the call to obtain information about the government's position on an issue** – Provide the decision-maker the opportunity to articulate their position as well as their rationale. Remember the decision-maker's perspective and rationale is important to strategize and focus advocacy around;
- **Provide the government executive with the information they request during the call or as quickly as possible** – The decision-making process can move more rapidly than anticipated. Thus, provision of both unique or the most up-to-date information is important to decision-makers as soon as it is available; and,
- **Follow the call with a note thanking them for their time** – Use the note as an opportunity to briefly restate the issue, any alternative approaches that were discussed and your position.

Face to Face Interface

Face to face interaction is one of the most effective techniques professional advocates utilize to communicate with government decision-makers and issue stakeholders. Like teleconferences, decision-makers are selective in how and with whom they spend their time. This means that the time used for the meeting must add value to the decision-making process. The results of personal meetings must be tangible and reportable. Moving the process towards issue resolution requires focused discussions and sensitivity to the decision-maker's needs.

Chapter 6: Practical Advocacy Techniques

Many advocates make *cold calls* or contacts to government officials they do not know, perseverance is the critical factor when an appointment is not scheduled in a timely fashion. The following is guidance for the professional advocacy community desirous of meeting with government decision-makers and other issue stakeholders:

- **Schedule a meeting with appropriate government executives** – It is unprofessional and inappropriate to show up unannounced. Further, many government officials would be offended by such an action;
- **Before the meeting, be clear about the purpose** – Identify all meeting participants and affiliations. Providing each meeting participant with a short issue brief as well as being transparent about the purpose of the meeting yield a positive environment and constructive dialogue. Inform the decision-maker and/or their staff who is expected to attend in advance of the meeting;
- **Before the meeting, practice a three-minute statement of the information you plan to present** – This forces advocates to think about their intended message and why the meeting is justified given the decision-makers limited time to consider alternative positions;
- **Before the meeting, prepare materials that explain your principle arguments** – Prepare handouts or a packet of information for attendees to review during and post meeting. This becomes a permanent record as well as reference material for government officials. Be sure to include your current contact information on each page of the materials provided at the meeting. This facilitates government officials with questions a simple means to quickly and effectively contact advocates;
- **Before the meeting, research the attendees** – Thoroughly research government officials and other stakeholders who are expected to participate in the meeting. The smart advocate uses commonalities and similar points of view held by other stakeholders to drive the decision-making process;
- **Identify the meeting affiliations** – Transparency is essential to building relationships with government decision-makers. Insure that meeting attendees have the baseline knowledge required to intelligently participate in the discussion. Articulating affiliated organizations with the same background information increases transparency and opens the door to a larger network supporting a change to status quo;
- **Identify your respective roles** – Let the decision-maker know what your goals and objectives are and who you represent in the advocacy campaign;
- **Be on time for your scheduled meeting** – Be on time and patient with the other attendees. Decision-makers are often late or fail to attend because they have hearings or other meeting requests that could not be anticipated or go overtime. You must be patient;
- **Keep meeting participants to a minimum** – Do not bring more than three people. All participants must have an acknowledged role and add value. Keep your visits brief; plan for a 30 minute meeting as your time horizon for the meeting;
- **Explain the issue and the alternative solutions during the meeting** – If the government decision-maker is not up to speed on the issue, use the meeting

to educate them. This approach goes a long way to insure that they feel comfortable with the issue and to demonstrate your expertise. This is helpful as many government executives deal with a large number of issues. Make sure you are clear and concise about all policy alternatives to assist in their decision-making;

- **Avoid "burning bridges," be courteous** – Never let any disagreements lead to harsh or personal attacks. If you lose your temper or prevent other stakeholders from being heard, you will compromise your ability to get their support. Further, it is likely that your information would be disregarded. Finally, keep a constructive attitude and never forget you may need their support on other issues in the future;
- **Maintain a clear position** – Remain consistent in your position throughout the meeting. Do not try to force the decision-maker into changing their minds or to commit themselves to a particular approach when they don't want to or before they are comfortable doing so;
- **At the end of the meeting, recap the main points** – Meetings should conclude with a quick summary of what was discussed and next steps; and,
- **At the conclusion of the meeting, thank the attendees for participating and discuss the next meeting** – Generally, issues are not solved in one face-to-face meeting. Plan to follow up and schedule a follow-up meeting. If you can tentatively schedule the follow-up meeting, the path forward is clear and the goal attainment become easier.

Committee Testimony

Where appropriate, addressing an advisory or legislative committee provides a great opportunity for advocates to present their issue to government decision-makers. Public testimony is always on the record and is an effective reference in any advocacy campaign portfolio. Metrics for presenting effective testimony are discussed below.

- **Prior to the hearing, research the audience** – Review the committee roster to familiarize yourself with committee members, the top issues within their individual portfolios, and their positions on the issues;
- **Prior to the hearing, submit written testimony to the committee** – In addition to the testimony, an executive summary summarizing the main points should be prepared to disseminate to whomever participates in the hearing. The summary should be no more than two pages long;
- **Begin your testimony by identifying yourself and who you represent** – Be brief in your opening statement and speak for no more than 5 minutes. Summarize the main points of your written testimony at the beginning. Practice your statement numerous times before the hearing to become an expert on the material you plan to present;
- **Dress appropriately** – Appearance is as important to some decision-makers as what you say and how you say it;
- **Throughout the testimony, use language familiar to those who follow the issue** – Use a vocabulary in your testimony familiar to all issue stakeholders.

Refrain from using jargon, acronyms, and abbreviations so there is not confusion about what has been stated;

- **Conclude your testimony by thanking the committee members and offering to answer any questions that the decision-makers have** – This is the time to restate the key points of your testimony and provide answers to questions. It is advisable for advocates to inform the committee members what next steps on the issue are planned; and,

- **Even if you are certain that your proposal will not be supported, your testimony should present your best case with the objective being to improve your stature among stakeholders** – Your testimony becomes a part of the record on the issue. Thus, opportunities to enhance trust among fellow colleagues and improve your organization's stature and respect for the delivery of credible information are worthwhile. Testimony also reinforces your position and documents your participation in the decision-making process.

Answering Questions

Committee members often have questions during a hearing or following sworn testimony. Further, government decision-makers often have questions following presentations or meetings where new information is provided. There are metrics governing interface with government officials as well as other issue stakeholders. The inherent principles that guide professional advocates should remain at the forefront when implementing these techniques; the metrics follow: Answer questions honestly – If you do not know the answer, say so and offer to provide the answer at a later date. If necessary, defer to another witness or colleague who is more knowledgeable on the subject;

- **If asked whether you would support an alternative other than one you have committed to, indicate where there is flexibility in your position** – There is a chance that a compromise position will emerge during the process. An appropriate response is that your organization will re-analyze the issue and the alternatives and report back to the decision-maker as soon as possible;

- **If asked an irrelevant or rhetorical question, use the opportunity to restate your position** – If the question is out of context, do not bring attention to it. Restate your position on the issue; and,

- **Remain calm if you are asked a hostile or personal question** – Avoid confrontation at all costs. Diffuse hostility with humor. Government-decision makers expect to hear the most accurate and credible information in order to make appropriate decisions. Inappropriate questions are applied to distract advocates and observe their reaction.

Widely Attended Events

Widely attended events and informal settings are places that advocates have chance interactions with issue stakeholders and government officials. At widely attended events there are opportunities for discussion about specific issues of interest "off the record." These conversations occur frequently and are not deemed unethical if the event meets specific criteria. A *widely attended event* is defined as one that at least 100 people are expected to attend. The value of free admission is not valued at more than $250, the views and interests of the attendees are diverse, and free attendance is not controlled by the event sponsor. A government official may attend an event classified as "widely attended" as a speaker or attendee on behalf of their agency if the officials' participation is considered necessary for them to perform official duties.

The Senate Select Committee on Ethics and the House committee on Standards of Official Conduct have published specific rules that define acceptable gifts government officials are allowed to receive so as not to create a conflict of interest and to promote fairness among the private and public sectors. Within their rule set they list exemptions such as the gift provision in the Ethics House Rule XXV, clause 5(a) (3). The widely attended events provision permits free attendance at events such as: conventions, conferences, dinners, and other similar events where (1) the event is open to individuals from throughout an industry or profession, or those in attendance represent a range of persons interested in similar issues, and there is reasonable expectation that at least 25 persons will attend, other than Members, officers, or employees of Congress; (2) the invitation is provided by the sponsor of the event; and, (3) the Member or employee reasonably determines that attendance at the event is related to his or her official duties.

Chapter 7

APPLY QUANTITATIVE METHODS TO SUPPORT ADVOCACY ANALYSIS

Defining Quantitative Methods

Quantitative methods emphasize objective measurements and the statistical, mathematical, or numerical analysis of data collected through polls, questionnaires, and surveys, or by manipulating pre-existing statistical data using computational techniques. They focus on gathering numerical data and generalizing it across groups of people or to explain a particular phenomenon.[1]

General Advocacy of Quantitative Research Approaches

Professional advocates apply quantitative methods to present information in a factual, objective, and concise manner. This chapter identifies the most effective quantitative methods. It also explains quantitative techniques and metrics used by baseline, lobbying, and education advocates. Government officials and other stakeholders rely

[1] Babbie, Earl R. *The Practice of Social Research*. 12th ed. Belmont, CA: Wadsworth Cengage, 2010; Muijs, Daniel. *Doing Quantitative Research in Education with SPSS*. 2nd edition. London: SAGE Publications, 2010.

on credible, accurate, and current information provided by the advocacy community. Most argue that quantitative analyses and methods are the most credible approach for advocates to utilize when presenting new information. Quantitative methods use hard data as the basis for conducting analysis on issues of concern. Further, government decision-makers prefer a numbers-driven approach to support policy changes. Quantitative approaches are neither perceived as interpretive or political.

Advocates vary methods and types of analyses based on the audience. By using quantitative methods, advocates build and maintain professional relationships, trust, and credibility with all issue stakeholders. Delivery mechanisms vary but the basis for delivering the message remains consistent. Further, utilizing quantitative methods enhances advocates' capability to control, select, analyze, and highlight various aspects of an issue.

There are many methods that are equally effective associated with presenting quantitative information. Baseline advocates are more direct and objective when applying data. Lobbying advocates add spin to the data and associated results to make their subjective argument. Educator advocates are similar to baseline advocates in their interpretation of data and associated analyses; however, some cross the line from educating to advocating for a specific outcome.

Professional advocates employ quantitative methods as a systematic approach to defining and justifying their arguments to government decision-makers. By applying different quantitative methods to facilitate issue analysis and presentation of alternatives, advocates provide decision-makers an improved platform to form their conclusions based on hard data and evidence rather than intrinsic emotions or opinions.

Baseline advocates have distinct metrics when applying quantitative tools. These metrics assist baseline advocates to develop the issue-related alternatives. The metrics focus on describing the facts associated with each alternative objectively. These metrics are:

- Present the most accurate and up-to-date data available;
- Present objective data that issue experts accept; and,
- Present reliable, valid, and statistically significant data.

Lobbying advocates operate under a similar but slightly different set of metrics associated with the use of quantitative tools. The metrics associated with their advocacy approach is closely aligned with the how their client wants to proceed through the decision-making process. A lobbyist intends to fulfill the needs of the client therefore should implement the following metrics:

- Present data which supports their client's position;
- Present reliable, valid, and statistically significant data supporting a specific position; and,

- Present data supported by experts with a similar issue positions.

An education advocate utilizes similar metrics as baseline advocates, but is held to a higher level of quality control to ensure accurate data. The metrics associated with an education advocate are:

- Present data accepted by academia as the most recent, objective, and accurate to the issue;
- Present data that is held to the highest level of quality control and has been subject to industry peer review processes; and,
- Present data that highlights credible sources to corroborate results and conclusions.

Advocates that perform their own research, studies, or analysis are best served when they adhere to the common structure and formatting associated with quantitative research designs. Those are to:

- Introduce the topic and problem being researched or analyzed;
- Describe the research methodology;
- Present the results; and,
- Discuss the analysis and significance of findings.

Quantitative research designs are associated with the following characteristics:

- Data is gathered using structured research instruments, e.g. questionnaires, computer software, or other data collection methodologies;
- Sample sizes are representative of the population being studied e.g. analysis of internal systems, processes, or public opinion;
- Experiments can be replicated or repeated to ensure credibility, reliability, and validity;
- All methodologies are clearly articulated and written down before data is collected; and,
- Results are generalizable to various groups to help to predict future results or investigate causal relationships.

Advocates using quantitative analysis seek to ensure credibility. For a quantitative analysis to be credible advocates follow these rules:

- The quantitative methodology is replicable;
- The researcher is qualified to perform the analysis;
- The analysis is performed within an appropriate timeframe producing useful and timely results;
- The advocate has access to the appropriate means for quality data selection; and,
- The analysis and data are objective.

General Advocacy

Effective advocates apply quantitative methods to analyze information for presentation to public officials. This is particularly true when issues of concern lend themselves to quantitative analytical methodologies followed by appropriate delivery mechanisms for presentations. To the extent the most current, credible and pertinent data has been analyzed and indicates that a change in policy, statutory or regulatory approach could improve the government's operations, a government decision-maker will likely be constructively influenced. In order to provide credible and factual information, advocates can either rely on research performed by another organization, such as academia or a trade association. Other sources such as credible for-profit organizations, applications of clinical results, or even self-perform studies, research, or analyses can be credible sources of data.

Baseline Advocacy

Quantitative analysis is an effective tool for baseline advocates because it provides government officials with the necessary data they need to make educated and effective policy evaluations.

As outlined in Chapter 2, baseline advocates rely on the evaluation of policy alternatives available to government decision-makers. These policy alternatives are derived from various sources or actions such as: brainstorming sessions, case studies, redefining of the problem, considering ideal solutions, determination of the worst case scenario, or the modification of existing policies. Alternatives presented to government decision-makers do not carry any weight unless there has been credible and thorough quantitative analysis performed on each potential outcome. Professional advocates presenting an alternative position to government officials must corroborate their claims using metrics and quantifiable outcomes as well as justify why those alternatives should be considered.

Lobbying Advocates

It is the lobbying advocate's objective to convince a government decision-maker to decide on an issue in a manner that benefits the lobbyist's subjective position. Lobbying advocates will, of course, use the same techniques as other advocates, but they add subjective spin to the analysis section. Lobbying advocates can be selective in their research designs to ensure results that lean in their position's favor. This is done through sponsored studies or through specific selection bias.[2] Selection bias is not unethical or illegal but does reduce the credibility of a conclusion.

Quantitative analysis is very important in the lobbying advocates' profession. Government decision-makers understand that lobbying advocates have a subjective

---

[2] Selection bias is the selection of individuals, groups or data for analysis in such a way that proper randomization is not achieved, thereby ensuring that the sample obtained is not representative of the population intended to be analyzed. It is sometimes referred to as the selection effect.

position; therefore, the lobbying advocate overcomes the perceived decision-makers bias by using credible quantitative metrics that tell the same story the lobbying advocate is telling.

Educator Advocates

Educator advocates seek to educate government decisions-makers about an issue in a clear, concise, and objective manner. Educator advocates do not support any specific policy alternative or provide any spin on the issue. They simply present the decision-maker with findings and conclusions and discuss the objective impacts of the status quo, or the projected impacts of alternative approaches to the issue.

Education advocates use quantitative analysis to present the facts and figures associated with their studies of an issue. They'll present the data graphically, in tabular format, or statistically as basic data providing the decision-maker no interpretation, spin, or policy alternatives.

Educator advocates will use non-biased research studies or institutions to provide the research or analysis to maintain credibility and respect within their industry. Often universities are funded through federal grants to perform the studies of interest and are considered credible, objective, and peer reviewed.

Examples of Quantitative Methodologies

This publication highlights eight of the most common quantitative methods used within the professional advocacy community.

Cost-Benefit Analysis:

Cost-benefit analysis is a procedure which estimates the net economic value of a policy or regulation. It converts all costs and benefits into a monetary metric. The analysis then measures whether the benefits outweigh the costs.

This methodology is used to analyze and compare the costs associated with a policy alternative or project, including opportunity costs. The analysis also computes the benefits of the project including revenues or savings that would result. This tool is employed to quantify long term projects or policies that have substantial upfront costs with benefits to be experienced over time. This tool is common to government officials as it is also part of the regulatory and statutory processes for policy development.

Generally this tool is rather complex because an advocate or policy analyst must have a clear understanding of all the potential costs and benefits associated with the policy to effectively model the impact.

Example 7.0

Statement of the Issue: Should the endangered California condor continue to breed in the wild?

New Program: Implement a California condor captive breeding program.

Alternative Option: Continue breeding California condors in the wild, but remove environmental hazards through regulation.

Estimating Cost

A determination of the costs of a program/policy and the costs of the alternative option should be evaluated on the following elements: (1) primary costs including capital investment, operational costs, and maintenance costs; and, (2) secondary costs including post implementation monitoring costs, and opportunity costs.

Estimating Benefits

A determination of the benefits of a California condor captive breeding program and the benefits of the alternative option should be evaluated on the following elements: (1) the value of the species and the benefit to be derived from continued preservation of an endangered species; (2) the extent to which to which protection of particular habitat areas will actually benefit the species; and (3) ancillary benefits that may result from the protection of habitat areas and ecosystems on which the species depends.

California Condor Captive Breeding Program Cost Benefit Analysis	
Cost	Benefit
Primary Costs • Capital Investment - $500,000 • Operational Costs - $750,000 • Maintenance Cost - $150,000 Secondary Costs • Monitoring and Research - $250,000 • Opportunity Cost - $1,000,000 Total Cost = $2,650,000	• Value of species - $1,500,000 • Population increase - $1,250,000 • Ancillary benefits - $2,125,000 Total Benefit = $3,750,000
Net Present Value	$1,100,000

Removal of Environmental Hazards Through Regulation Cost Benefit Analysis	
Cost	Benefit
 • Regulatory costs - $1,250,000 • Compliance costs - $1,500,000 • Opportunity Cost - $1,100,000 	 • Value of species - $1,500,000 • Population increase - $1,250,000 • Ancillary benefits - $2,125,000
Total Cost = $3,850,000	Total Benefit = $3,750,000
Net Present Value	- $100,000

Cost-Benefit Decision

Program	Cost	Benefit	Net Benefit	Favorable/ Unfavorable
Captive Breeding	$2.65M	$3.75M	$1.1M	Favorable
Wild Breeding	$3.85M	$3.75M	-$100K	Unfavorable

Based on the above example, a cost-benefit argument can be used to support or strengthen advocacy efforts or simply report data.

Baseline Approach – This approach uses the above data to support a captive breeding program.

"The cost-benefit analysis indicates that a captive breeding program investment is a better investment than the alternative because there is a net benefit of $1.1M compared to a net cost of $100K."

Lobbying Approach – A lobbying firm representing an energy company specializing in wind projects may use the information to argue against the alternative wild breeding program because increased regulations negatively impact the company's bottom line as new regulations would increase compliance cost and limit wind power development in the regulated area.

"The Federal Government should not continue breeding condors in the wild through new regulations because the costs associated with the program outweigh the benefits."

Educator Approach – An educator uses the above analysis to present data on both the new program and alternative program.

> *"The cost-benefit analysis indicates that a captive breeding program investment of $2.65M would result in a benefit of $3.75M and that an alternative wild breeding program investment of $3.85M would have costs that outweigh the net benefit by $100K."*

The Cost-Benefit Analysis methodology can be used in a more complex and detailed manner. Advocates that need to perform a more detailed analysis of an issue or policy alternative can perform the following detailed methods:

- **Net-Present Value** – The present value of an capital investment or a project taking into account all cash inflows and outflows. The NPV provides whether the project or investment is worth the investment made by providing what the current value of the project would be.
- **Internal Rate of Return** – A metric used to determine the profitability of a project or capital investment.
- **Socio-Economic Impact Assessment** – This methodology examines how a proposed policy change or policy will affect the lives of current and future constituents. Quantitative measures within the assessment are demographic, market analyses, demand, employment/income levels, and aesthetic qualities.
- **Economic Impact Study** – Develops and quantifies the direct impacts (jobs created), indirect impacts (indirect jobs created), and induced impacts. This is used often when determining whether a new policy will be a job creator and meets standard baselines for job creation.

Descriptive Statistical Analysis

This methodology is used to analyze and summarize large amounts of data and facilitating descriptive data points reflecting the population or sample being evaluated. This approach is used throughout the regulatory and statutory process when evaluating how policies will affect the American public.

Descriptive statistical analysis summarizes data and presents it in various ways e.g. tabular, graphical, or numerical.

Examples of this methodology are used throughout the government, but are used predominantly by the US Census as they rely on these data to articulate information about household income, household pricing, or population shifts.

Example 7:1

Statement of the Issue: Should the endangered California condor continue to breed in the wild?

The population mean for the amount of California condors capable of breeding in the wild in 1990 was 210 condors. In 2000, the population mean for condors capable of breeding in the wild was 150. This shows that the number of condors breeding in the wild from 1990 to 2000 has declined, in this example they have declined by 28.6%.

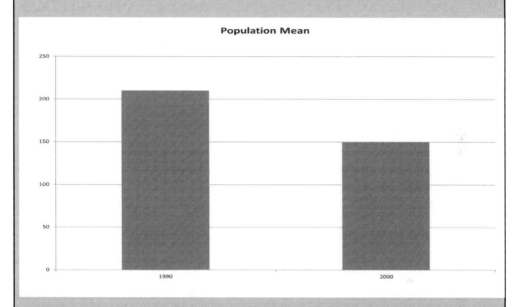

Baseline Advocate's Approach – Baseline advocates use the above data to support the position that the California condor population will continue to decline without intervention.

"Without intervention, the condor population of 150 is likely to continue to decline. The intervention approaches involve:

- *Continue condor breeding in the wild without intervention hoping the birds breed on their own;*
- *Initiate condor captive breeding programs; or*
- *Continue condor breeding in the wild, but remove environmental hazards by acquiring condor habitat and promulgating command and control regulations governing the habitat."*

Lobbying Advocate's Approach – A lobbyist representing a client's interest uses the data to support their preferred alternative.

> *"The data clearly shows that a captive program is a better solution than the current policy because the number of condors breeding in the wild from 1990 to 2000 has declined by 28.6%. This decline cannot be reversed by simply eliminating environmental hazards or letting nature run its course. A captive breeding program is a far more effective option because it focuses on ensuring that the condors are given opportunity to reproduce, and environment in which their offspring can survive."*
>
> **Educator Advocate's Approach** – An educator presents the data objectively.
>
> *"The number of condors breeding in the wild from 1990 to 2000 has declined 28.6%, from 210 to 150 total condors capable of breeding in the wild."*

Descriptive statistical analysis consists of four distinct measurements.

Measures of Location

- **Mean** – A measure of central location computed by summing the data values and dividing by the number of observations;
- **Median** – A measure of central location provided by the value in the middle when the data are arranged in ascending order;
- **Mode** – A measure of location, defined as the value that occurs with greatest frequency;
- **Percentiles** – A value such that a least x percent of the observations are less than or equal to this value and least (100 –x) percent of the observations are greater than or equal to this value; and,
- **Quartiles** – The 25th, 50th, and 75th percentiles are referred to as the first, second and third quartile respectively. Quartiles are used to divide the data into four parts.

Measures of Variability

- **Range** – A measure of variability, defined to be the largest value minus the smallest;
- **Interquartile Range (IQR)** – A measure of variability, defined to be the difference between the third and first quartiles;
- **Variance** – A measure of variability based on the squared deviations of the data values about the mean;
- **Standard Deviation** – A measure of variability computed by taking the positive square root of the variance; and,
- **Coefficient of Variation** – A measure of relative variability computed by dividing the standard deviation by the mean and multiplying by 100.

Measures of Distribution Shape, Relative Location, and Outliers

- **Skewness** – Is the measure of the shape of a data distribution. Data skewed to the left result in negative skewness; a symmetric data distribution results in zero skewness; and data skewed to the right result in positive skewness;
- **Chebyshev's Theorem** – A theorem that can be used to make statements about the proportion of data values that must be within a specified number of standard deviations from the mean. Not all data sets are normally distributed and, because of this, the Empirical Rule cannot be used for all data sets. Chebyshev's Theorem outlines that ¾ of the data lie within two standard deviations of the mean. Also that 8/9 of the data lie within three standard deviations of the mean;
- **Empirical Rule** – A rule that can be used to compute the percentage of data values that must be within one, two, or three standard deviations of the mean for data that exhibit a bell-shaped distribution. The Empirical Rule outlines that roughly 68% of the data will lie within plus or minus one standard deviation, 95% of the data will lie within plus or minus two standard deviations, and 99.7% of the data will lie within plus or minus three standard deviations of the mean; and,
- **Outliers** – An unusually small or unusually large data value outside of plus or minus three standard deviations from the mean. Outliers are a rare occurrence and should be treated as such. Outliers should occur less than .3% of the time, however if they begin to occur more frequently the experiment should be examined for human error or unusual circumstances.

Measures of Association between Two Variables

- **Covariance** – A measure of linear association between two variables. Positive values indicate a positive relationship; negative values indicate a negative relationship; and,
- **Correlation Coefficient** – A measure of linear association between two variables that takes on values between -1 and +1. Values near +1 indicate a strong positive relationship; values near -1 indicate a strong negative linear relationship; values near zero indicate a lack of a linear relationship.

Inferential Statistical Analysis

Inferential statistical analysis is the process of making inferences based sample data (confidence intervals, margin of error, and hypothesis testing). Inferential statistics use random samples of data taken from a population to describe and make inferences relating to the population as a whole. Inferential statistics are valuable when it is not convenient or possible to examine each member of an entire population.[3]

---

[3]   http://support.minitab.com/en-us/minitab/17/topic-library/basic-statistics-and-graphs/introductory-concepts/basic-concepts/descriptive-inferential-stats/

Example 7.2

Statement of the Issue: should the endangered California condor continue to breed in the wild?

Suppose you want to know the average age of all the condors in a state of California. Because it isn't very practical to try and get the age of each condor in the state, a sample of the total population can be used to make an inference about the entire population.

Population	150
Sample Size	10
Age of Sample Size	15,31,8,57,43,60,22,4,19,37 = 296
Sample Average Age	296/10 = 29.6
Inference	**Average life span of a California condor is 45 years. The average age of the current population demonstrates an aging condor community.**

Baseline Advocate's Approach – This approach uses the above data to support the position that the California condor low population provides further evidence for intervention.

"Intervention is necessary in order to make an impact on the declining population of the California condor. The average age of the condor population demonstrates the current population is entering the final years of their life cycles are not reproducing at a rate that will sustain their existence."

Lobbying Advocate's Approach – A lobbyist representing a client's interest uses the data to support their preferred alternative.

"In California there are 150 condors in the wild with an average age of 29.6 years. The condors exhibit an aging community, the sample demonstrates that no condor has been born in the last 8 years."

Educator Advocate's Approach – An educator uses the above analysis to present the data objectively.

"The current condor population in California has an average age of 29.6 years. Assuming the population continues to decline at this rate of 28.6% over the next ten years, there will be 107 wild condors in California."

Advocates performing their own research will likely need to be able to implement complex sampling methodology. Below is a list of more complex and accepted sampling methods.

- **Stratified Random Sampling** – The probability sampling method in which the population is first divided into strata and a simple random sample taken from each stratum;
- **Cluster Sampling** – The probability sampling method in which the population is first divided into clusters and then a simple random sample of the clusters;
- **Systematic Sampling** – This equal probability method is a progression through the sampling list is treated circularly; returning to the top once the end of the list has passed;
- **Convenience Sampling** – The nonprobability method of sampling whereby elements are selected on the basis of convenience; and,
- **Judgment Sampling** – The nonprobability method of sampling whereby elements are selected for the sample based on the judgment of the person doing the study.

Time Series analysis

Time series analysis assists the advocacy community in their efforts to explain phenomenon observed in the real world over time. This type of analysis helps illustrate what variables influence issues over time and can be used to project how an issue will be impacted by those variables in the future. This is useful for identifying trends as well as developing adjustments over time to mitigate problems and identify solutions to problems before they actually occur.

Time Series Analysis is the examination of past events and the development of a prediction of future events using quantitative metrics.

Time Series Analysis is used by scientific organizations like the Geological Survey, NOAA, and NASA.

Example 7.3

Each year a researcher is measuring the number of California Condors in captivity that are capable of breeding.

Statement of Issue: Should there be a federal captive breeding program for the California condor?

Alternative: California condors should continue to breed in the wild.

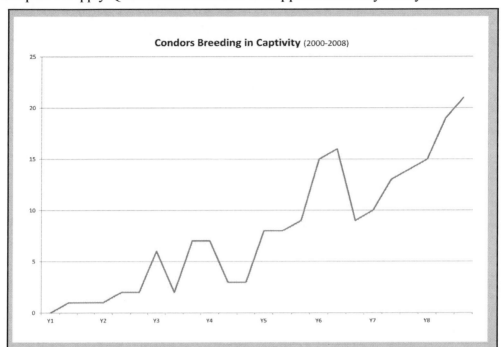

Condors Breeding in Captivity (2000-2008)

Baseline Advocate's Approach – The baseline approach utilizes the above time series data to demonstrate an increase in the number of condors breeding in captivity over time.

"This time series analysis demonstrates that the condor population in captivity increases over an eight year period. Having the condors in captivity improves their opportunity to breed successfully."

Lobbying Advocate's Approach – This approach uses the information to present to government decision-makers that the captive breeding program can be an effective public program for saving the California condor from extinction.

"After eight years the number of captive condors capable of breeding successfully suggests that the Federal Government should implement the captive breeding program to ensure that condors have the chance to survive. The Federal Government should not waste tax-payer money by implementing costly and unproven regulations to remove environmental hazards that do not ensure the condors can successfully breed."

Educator Advocate's Approach – An educator uses the above analysis to the present data objectively that has been collected over the two year period.

"The time series analysis indicates that a captive breeding program increases the number of condors in captivity from 0 to 21 condors over the two year period."

There are detailed and more complex time series methods which an advocate may need to employ. More complex times series patterns are outlined below:

- **Horizontal Pattern** – A horizontal pattern exists when the data fluctuate around a constant mean;
- **Trend Pattern** – A trend pattern exists if the time series plot shows gradual shifts or movements to relatively higher or lower values over a longer period of time;
- **Seasonal Pattern** – A seasonal pattern exists if the time series plot exhibits a repeating pattern over successive periods. The successive periods are often one-year intervals, hence seasons;
- **Cyclical Pattern** – A cyclical pattern exists if the time series plot shows an alternating sequence of points below and above the trend line lasting more than one year;
- **Time Series Decomposition** – The time series method designed to separate or "decompose" a time series into seasonal and trend components;
- **Additive Model** – The additive model applies actual time series values within the time period t is obtained by adding the values of a trend component, a seasonal component, and an irregular component; and,
- **Multiplicative Model** – The multiplicative model is when the actual time series value at time period t is obtained by multiplying the values of a trend component, a seasonal component, and an irregular component.

Forecasting

This methodology is employed most often within the financial areas of advocacy. The advocacy community uses forecasting because it provides evidence as to what the flow of resources will be from projected policy changes.

Forecasting takes historic data and uses quantitative methods to make predictions to meet future needs. Quantitative forecasting can only be employed if 1) historical data related to an issue s available, 2) historical data establishes a pattern, and 3) it is credible to consistently assume in the future.

Forecasting is used in budgetary decision making, debt projections, and financing decisions by every agency specifically OMB, CBO and the Department of Defense.

Example 7.4

Statement of the Issue: Should the federal government implement regulations focused on removing environmental hazard regulations in order to protect the California condor population.

Alternative: Implement a federally funded captive breeding program to revitalize the condor population.

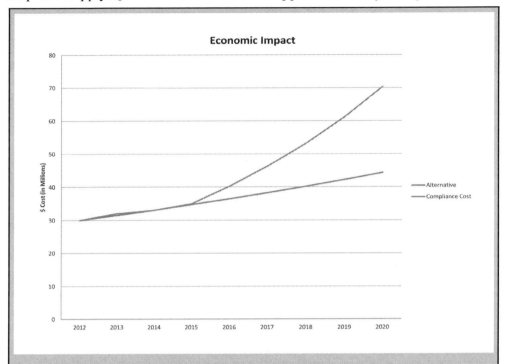

Baseline Advocate's Approach – The baseline approach uses the forecasting analysis to show the impact of policy/program implementation over time.

"An expert study projects current compliance costs associated with the removal of environmental hazards through regulatory measures is likely to be more expensive than implementing the alternative captive breeding program."

Lobbying Advocate's Approach – This approach uses the forecasting model to highlight the increasing cost of the status-quo.

"Expert forecasting analysis demonstrates that environmental regulatory rules are damaging to the economy. Any new rules associated with removing environmental hazards would increase the tax burden of the people of California. In order to protect the condor's population and the people of California the alternative option of implementing a captive breeding program should be implemented."

Educator Advocate's Approach – An educator uses the above analysis to show what the future economic implications are of a policy and any alternatives.

"The forecasting analysis indicates that removing environmental hazards through regulations would increase cost by more than 100% in 2020 while the alternative option would increase costs by 28% 2020."

Advocates use forecasting in order to project future financial events will be impacted by certain changes in cash flows or supply and demand affected by a change in policy. Advocates may need to implement more complex forecasting methods some of which are outlined below.

- **Linear Trend Regression** – The forecasting method building off of the linear regression principles. By analyzing previous data, in a time series, one can calculate the relationship between a scalar dependent variable and one or more explanatory variables (independent variables). The formula derived from this calculation can be used to project future outcomes;
- **Holt's Linear Exponential Smoothing** – Designed by Charles Holt, this extension of single exponential smoothing uses two smoothing constants to enable forecasts to be developed for a time series with a linear trend;
- **Nonlinear Trend Regression** – The most common regression trend analysis is linear, however, not all time series data are linear, and some may be curvilinear or nonlinear. Projecting nonlinear trends make use of the quadratic trend equation;
- **Seasonality** – Examines the effects of seasons on time series data and works, through regression modeling, to smooth out the seasonal effects of the time series. Seasonality works to quantify the effects of seasons throughout a year, or over years depending on the product or data being evaluated;
- **Moving averages** – The forecasting method that uses the average of the most recent data values in the time series as the forecast for the next period;
- **Weighted Moving Averages** – The forecasting method that involves selecting different weight for the most recent data values in the time series and then computing a weighted average of the values. The sum of the weights must equal one; and,
- **Exponential Smoothing** – The forecasting method that uses a weighted average of past time series values as the forecast; it is a special case of the weighted moving averages method in which only one weight is selected, the weight for the most recent observation in the sample.

Hypothesis Testing

This methodology is used by advocates when creating surveys and research instruments to examine a population samples to predict population impacts. Sample data must be replicable from other sources to test hypothesis.

Assumptions associated with population impacts against a hypothesis tests the validity of the impacts. A hypothesis is not ever determined to be true. The hypothesis is simply rejected or not rejected.

Hypothesis testing is used by the regulatory agencies when evaluating whether the population, state, or company is complying with a regulation.

Example 7.5

A California condor expert hypothesizes that the average life span of a California condor living in the in the wild is 45 years. Using hypothesis testing, an advocacy group can determine if this hypothesis is supported by evidence. Using a random sample of 24 birds, the mean life span for condors was found to be 43.05 years. The lives of all such birds have a normal distribution with the population standard deviation of 4.5 years.

- Sample size = 24,
- Sample mean = 43.05
- Population Standard Deviation = 4.5
- Degree of Significance = 0.025

1. State the Null and Alternative Hypothesis
   - Null hypothesis: The average life span of the condor is equal to 45 years. Ho: m=45
   - Alternative hypothesis: The average life span of the condor is less than 45 years. H1: m < 45

2. Using statistical computer software the results indicate that their findings are not statistically significant.

3. Based on the result of not having statistically significant outputs researchers would reject the null hypothesis and determine that the average life span of the condor is less than 45 years.

Baseline Advocate's Approach – The baseline approach utilizes hypothesis testing to support the claim that the average life span is not 45 years.

"Studies have shown there is no statistical significance associated with the life span of the condor equaling 45 years. The government should examine alternative methods and sources to determine the average life span of the birds"

Lobbying Advocate's Approach – A lobbying firm uses hypothesis testing to validate a claim.

The expert's claim that the average life span is 45 years has not been supported by statistical testing. Our analysis determined that the average life span is less than 45 years indicating that the increasing number of aged birds drives our rationale for a captive breeding program."

> ***Educator Advocate's Approach*** – An educator reports on the results of a hypothesis test.
>
> *"The expert's hypothesis was not supported by statistical tests and this organization concludes the mean (average) lifespan is less 45 years."*

When advocates and quantitative researchers perform hypothesis testing there are two types of test they perform. The details of those types of tests are outlined below:

- **One-tailed Test** – A hypothesis test in which rejection of the null hypothesis occurs for values of the test statistic in one tail of its sampling distribution; and,
- **Two-tailed Test** – A hypothesis test in which rejection of the null hypothesis occurs for values of the test statistic in either tail of its sampling distribution.

Probability Analysis

Providing probability analysis to issue analysis allows professional advocates to communicate how likely their policy or program will impact the status-quo and to what magnitude. There are various ways in which quantitative analysts can measure probability. The details of each and every method goes beyond the scope and purpose of this chapter, but the utilization of these methods by professional advocates is essential to developing the most accurate and influential data they can provide.

Probability Analysis is the practice of quantifying how likely something or a specific outcome is to happen.

Probability Analysis is used by federal agencies in order to determine the probability of individuals or areas being affected by a policy change. Also, probability analysis is used by the DOD in order to determine effectiveness of weaponry and impacts of wartime strategy on geographic areas and civilians by continually calculating the how likely the strategy will produce an outcome.

Example 7.6

From actual breeding tests with the California condor, it is estimated that the mean condor lifespan is 36.5 years and that the standard deviation from the mean is q = 5 years. In addition, the data collected indicated that normal probability distribution curve is a reasonable assumption. What is the probability that a condor's lifespan will exceed 40 years?

- Estimated life span = 40 years
- Z-score = (40-36.5) / 5
- Z-score =.70

Using the standard normal probability table, we know that the area under the normal distribution curve extending to the left of a .70 Z-score is equal to .7580. To find the probability that a condor will live to be 40 years old we subtract the value associated with the area to the left of the Z-score. 1.000-.7580= .2420

Conclusion: 24.2% of the birds bred in captivity will reach 40 years of age.

Baseline Advocate's Approach – The baseline approach would use the above data to demonstrate that the captive breeding program will allow about 25% of the condors bred to live to be 40 years old.

"Evidence suggests that 24.2% of birds breed through a captive breeding program will live past the age of 40."

Lobbying Advocate's Approach – This approach would use the data to a captive breeding program.

"The Federal Government should implement a captive breeding program because on average 1 of 4 condors will exceed their expected lifespan of 36.5 years and live to be at least 40. This would result in an increase of condors living longer and providing them more opportunities to reproduce."

Educator Advocate's Approach – An educator would use the above analysis to present data on both the new program and alternative program.

"The analysis indicates that a captive breeding program would result in 24.2% of birds living up to the age of 40."

The implementation of statistical analysis can be a very complex endeavor and one that can provide an advocate an advantage if performed well. More complex statistical analysis methodologies are outlined below:

- **Discrete Probability** – The description of how the probabilities are distributed over the values of the random variable;
- **Discrete uniform probability distribution n** – The probability distribution for which each possible value of the random variable has the same probability;
- **Binomial Probability Distribution** – The probability distribution showing the probability of x successes in n trials of a binomial experiment;
- **Poisson Probability Distribution** – The probability distribution showing the probability of x occurrences of an event over a specified interval of time or space;
- **Hypergeometric Probability Distribution** – The probability distribution showing the probably of x successes in n trials from a population with r successes and N-r failures;
- **Uniform Probability Distribution** – The continuous probability distribution for which the probability that the random variable will assume a value in any interval is the same for each interval of equal length;
- **Normal Probability Distribution** – The continuous probability distribution which is displayed in a bell-shaped and determined by its mean and standard deviation;
- **Standard Normal Probability Distribution** – The normal distribution with a mean of zero and standard deviation of one; and,
- **Exponential Probability Distribution** – The continuous probability distribution that is useful in computing probabilities for the time it takes to complete a task.

Testing and Modeling

Testing and modeling methods are used by the professional advocacy community when they want to test the impact of one or multiple variables, (independent variables) onto one dependent variable. Models are helpful in demonstrating support or opposition to an issue of interest. It helps to isolate and identify influential factors while highlighting less influential ones. Advocates use this models to effectively communicate exactly what variables they believe government decision-makers need to pay the closest attention to and which ones are considered "noise". Regression analysis is one of the popular forms of statistical modeling utilized by policy analyst and the advocacy community.

Testing and Modeling is predominantly performed by two types of regression analysis, simple linear regression and multiple regression modeling. Simple linear regression involves one variable and one dependent variable and quantifies the relationship between the two. Multiple regression models involve two or more independent variables and their impact on a dependent variable.

Example 7.7

Statement of Issue: Should the Federal Government implement a captive breeding program for the California condor?

Alternative: Allow the California condor to continue to breed in the wild without intervention.

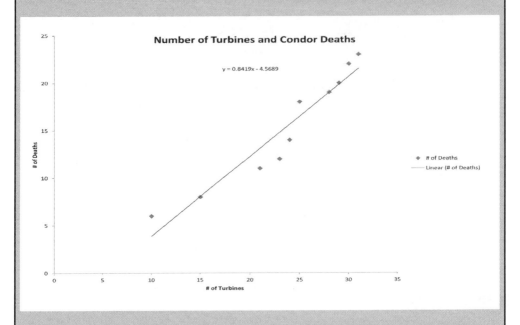

If there are 45 wind turbines built within the California condor habitat the regression model estimates that roughly 33 condors will die using the equation $y = 0.8419x - 4.5689$ y= number of condor deaths and x= number of turbines built. The regression equation is: $33.3166=0.0419(45)-4.5689$.

Baseline Advocate's Approach – The baseline approach would use the above data to suggest that there is a linear correlation between the number of turbines and the number of condor deaths.

"Research indicates that there is a positive linear correlation between turbines and condor deaths."

Lobbying Advocate's Approach – This approach would use the data to support its position supporting a captive breeding program.

"The above estimation shows a direct connection between wind turbine development and the number of condors killed. A captive breeding program will allow the condors a better opportunity to reproduce and allow new energy technologies to be implemented."

Educator Advocate's Approach – An educator would use the above analysis to present data on both the new program and alternative program.

"The regression analysis projects the 33 condors will be killed if California builds 45 additional wind turbines."

- **Simple Linear Regression Model** – Regression analysis involving one independent variable and one dependent variable in which the relationship between the variables is approximated by a straight light. The regression model is denoted as an equation that describes how a change in the *x-variable (independent variable)* is related to changes in value of the *y-variable (dependent variable)* while holding all other possible independent variables as a constant value; and,
- **Multiple Regression Model** – The regression analysis involves two or more independent variables impacting one dependent variable. The model produces a mathematical equation that describes how the dependent variable y is altered by additive effect of each independent variable taken together.

Cost-Effective Analysis

This methodology is used to analyze the effectiveness based on the different costs associated with multiple viable options. This tool is commonly employed within the EPA, DOI, HHS, and other agencies that are developing regulation for healthcare, environment, or other macro challenges with significant amounts of variables.

The cost effectiveness method compares the relative costs to the outcomes of two or more courses of action. This method is used when there are constraints which prevent an advocate from conducting a cost-benefit analysis. For example, a cost effectiveness analysis is used when all the costs and benefits cannot be converted into a monetary metric.

An example of this is the cost of a research project using specific lab equipment versus using another type of lab equipment. The data would be analyzed to determine the effectiveness of expenditures associated with one piece of equipment to address a regulatory requirement with the projected expenditure utilizing another type of equipment and the effectiveness of each. This method is used often in healthcare when a decision whether to use a treatment that consistently produces a certain outcome is a more effective approach than a different treatment modality that is less consistent but incrementally more effective.

Example 7.8

Statement of Issue: Should there be a captive breeding program for the California condor?

Alternative: California condors should continue to breed in the wild, but remove environmental hazards through regulations.

Policy	Benefits (Increase Condor Population, Annually)	Net Cost	Average CE
Captive Breeding	25	$2,500	$100/QALY
Regulation — Alterative	15	$2,800	$187/QALY

Baseline Advocate's Approach – The baseline approach would use the above data to recommend the captive breeding program over the alternative because it is the most cost effective policy option.

"The cost effectiveness analysis indicates that a captive breeding program investment is a more efficient way of spending tax dollars to save the California condor compared to the alternative."

Lobbying Advocate's Approach – This approach would use the data to support its position against removing environmental hazards through regulation.

"The Federal Government should not regulate environmental hazards to save the declining condor population because it is not the most cost effective option."

Educator Advocate's Approach – An educator would use the above analysis to present data on both the new program and alternative program.

"The analysis indicates that a captive breeding program's average cost effectiveness is $100/QALY and the alternative program's average cost effectiveness is $187/ QALY."

Strengths and Weaknesses of Quantitative Methods

Strengths

Quantitative researchers try to recognize and isolate specific variables contained within the study framework. They seek correlations, relationships and attempt to determine causality while attempting to control the environment that the data is collected in to avoid the risk of interference from other variables that may influence outcomes.

Below are strengths the advocacy community can expect to observe by utilizing quality controlled quantitative tools.

- Allows for a broader study, involving a greater number of subjects, and enhancing the generalization of the results;
- Allows for greater objectivity and accuracy of results. Generally, quantitative methods are designed to provide summaries of data that support generalizations about the phenomenon under study. In order to accomplish this, quantitative research usually involves few variables and many cases, and employs prescribed procedures to ensure validity and reliability;
- Applying well-established standards facilitates research that can be replicated, and then analyzed and compared with similar studies; and,
- Personal bias can be avoided by keeping a 'distance' from participating subjects and using accepted computational techniques that control for selection bias and multicollinearity.

Weaknesses

Quantitative methods presume to have an objective approach to studying issue of interest. Where data is controlled and measured to address the accumulation of facts and to determine the causes of behaviors the results may be statistically significant but are often humanly insignificant. It is important to identify the significant findings to issue and continue to explore those. Remember not to get bogged down and buried in unnecessary and inconsequential data points.

Some specific limitations associated with using quantitative methods include:

- Context must be provided and results must be interpreted, this leads to selection bias and can lead researchers to come to different conclusions about the same results;
- Uses a static and rigid approach and so employs an inflexible process of discovery;
- The development of standard questions by researchers can lead to "structural bias" and false representation, where the data actually reflects the view of the researcher instead of the participating subject;
- Results provide less detail on behavior, attitudes, and motivation;
- Researcher may collect a much narrower and sometimes superficial dataset that is not representative of the population they are making inferences about;
- Results are limited as they provide numerical descriptions rather than detailed narrative and generally provide less elaborate accounts of human perception;
- The research is often carried out in an unnatural, artificial environment so that a level of control can be applied to the exercise. This level of control might not normally be in place in the real world thus yielding "laboratory results" as opposed to "real world results"; and,

- Preset answers will not necessarily reflect how people really feel about a subject resulting in data that is not representative.

Chapter 8

APPLY QUALITATIVE METHODS TO SUPPORT ADVOCACY ANALYSIS

General Qualitative Method Applications

The purpose of this chapter is to discuss the role that qualitative analysis plays in professional advocacy. Qualitative analysis is a common method used by both government decision-makers and advocates. Government officials know that qualitative information is perceived to be more subjective than its quantitative counterpart. Conversely, government decision-makers understand that qualitative analysis and associated presentations are more descriptive and reflect institutional positions associated with intra-agency and inter-departmental deliberations on issues. Qualitative analysis is more contextual and comparative than its quantitative counterparts. The optimal scenario is for government decision-makers to receive a combination of quantitative and qualitative analysis in advocacy presentations.

Chapter 8: Apply Qualitative Methods to Support Advocacy Analysis

Professional advocates value to government decision-makers is anchored in their provision of timely, accurate, and contextual information that is pertinent to the issues. Realistically, government executive do not have the time or resources required to conduct and prepare comprehensive analysis on every issue within their scope of authority. Further, government analysts often miss nuances that industry experts, academicians, and other stakeholders believe are critical to the government's deliberations.

Thus, professional advocate's contribution of the information available to government officials is valuable. Government executives face pressure to cut project and program costs and improve services or programs that do not perform in a cost beneficial manner. It is important to maintain institutional political support with stakeholders associated with projects, programs, and operations. Further, government officials are generally not privy to new developments that are competitively sensitive to stakeholders competing in the private sector. Finally, professional advocates provide comprehensive examinations of issues that differ given their perspectives and contexts. These differing analyses provide benefits to government officials working to develop more effective public policy.

The institutional or partisan dimension associated with government decision-making is not quantitative. Whether partisan, bi-partisan, or non-partisan the rhetoric is qualitative. Thus, the political impact of a decision is generally analyzed with an emphasis on conceptual or philosophical rhetoric reinforced by data.

Qualitative methods focus on human elements that underlie issues of concern. The human element has both tangible and intangible variables. Tangible variables are associated with longstanding societal mores.[1] Intangible variables relate to the differences in human behavior, beliefs, opinions, emotions, and the complexities of relationships. Additional intangible variables are socio-economic status, gender, ethnicity, or how religious perspectives are applied or relevant to the issue. A tangible variable is society's consensus that the California condor should be protected and cared for by whatever means necessary to prevent its extinction. Legislation would be easily accepted by communities across America if conservation stakeholders prioritize condor management in lieu of some other bird like a robin.

An example of an intangible variable is the underlying belief system of the individual or community being examined. What groups or subgroups have a vested interest in protecting the condor? Do specific religious groups hold or share a belief that the condor is an important symbol of their beliefs, and if so, what is their perspective?

Credible qualitative research applies the following metrics:

- Clearly articulated variations within stakeholder and government perspectives;
- Clearly defined relationships and descriptions of both tangible and intangible factors;

---

[1] Mores are the essential or characteristic customs and conventions of a community.

- Clear associations between the individual or institution experience associated with an issue; and,
- Clear understanding of the applicability of tangible individual or institutional norms.

Obviously, qualitative methodologies emphasize subjective characteristics in the examination and arguments between alternatives. These include the evaluation of management expertise, experience gained from examining industry's production and service delivery cycles, commitments to continuous research and development, relationship associated with labor impacts, and the public's opinion. These all become critical factors for government decision-makers when evaluating the credibility of an advocate's presentation of facts and the thoroughness associated with their analysis of alternative policy approaches. There must be a logical and systematic methodology that is replicable and transparent to the government's institutions and industry when decision-making relies on qualitative analysis of issues. The following methods are common elements employed in qualitative methodology:

- Narrative or Storytelling;
- Historical Research and Visual Ethnography;
- Focus Groups Feedback;
- Classic Ethnographic Feedback; and,
- Qualitative Survey/Interview.

The objective of each method is to create information and categorize data into a functional format that is used in the development of policy, support of political decisions, and to justify change or maintain status quo.

There are a number of questions generally posed for analysts utilizing systematic application of qualitative tools. The common questions include: Why is a change necessary or warranted and why is now the time to proceed? Who supports this, and why? Does the public support it or is there a fringe group pushing for change? What is the basis for maintaining or changing? Are political environments and the associated government officials in favor of change, or is the political climate unsupportive?

The objective of each qualitative research method is to categorize data into identifiable patterns identifying how and why decisions were made, who and what is involved in the issue of interest, and finally when are these factors most relevant to the decisions the government needs to make.

Qualitative methods must employ the following metrics:

- **Introduction of the issue** – State the issue as well as expected conclusions bearing on the issues resulting from research and the development of policy alternatives;

- **Describing the research method** – Describe the process in which data was collected and the limitations associated with data collection;
- **Presentation of the results** – Describe the results of the research in the context of the method and how it relates to the issue; and,
- **Analyzation of the results** – Describe how results influence the American public and how it is associated with the issue. Discuss how societal trends and the impact of the results has on the affected community. Explain how the methods and the results impact the decision-makers as well as other issue stakeholders.

Applying Qualitative Methods in Baseline Advocacy

Baseline advocates employ unique metrics to qualitative tools:

1. The impact of each alternative policy approach addresses why the alternative is viable and justifies its relevance to the issue and how it relates to issue stakeholders;
2. The analysis is comprehensive, balanced, and comparable by objective facts known about the sample population as they relate to the issue of concern; and,
3. The tangible and intangible variables are highlighted and put into context.

These metrics provide government decision-makers with the compatibility to weigh the impacts from each of the policy alternatives. The most up-to-date and thorough information associated with those impacted by the policy or program is provided by comparison with the other. Finally, baseline advocates always address similar data points and arguments with an emphasis on objectivity.

Applying Qualitative Methods in Lobbying Advocacy

Lobbying advocates present subjective arguments and data based on their unique position utilizing the following metrics:

1. The information highlighted emphasizes the desired outcome;
2. The information is accurate to the issue and is interpreted to support the desired outcome;
3. The information and arguments draw attention to the reasons why decision-makers should support the lobbyist's desired outcome; and,
4. The information presented is selected based on its usefulness to influence government decision-makers and the public to support the desired alternative. No data should be presented that is in opposition to the desired outcome.

Lobbying advocates, as opposed to baseline advocates, produce results that substantiate their position on an issue and guide the decision-maker toward that desired outcome. Lobbying advocates are selective and subjective, yet still present factual and credible arguments and rationale to government decision-makers. Qualitative data presented by lobbying advocates clearly articulate the positive or negative effects, depending on position, that will occur as a result of the supported position. Lastly, lobbying advocates use qualitative methods to provide context to the negative impacts of alternatives in an effort to garner support for their desired outcome.

Applying Qualitative Methods in Education Advocacy

Education advocates utilize similar metrics as baseline advocates because they both present their data objectively. The education advocate's presentation of data are held to a higher standard of scrutiny than baseline and lobbying advocates because the expectation is that they are experts in their field of study and are not presenting materials intended to influence the government's decision-making process. The following metrics apply to education advocates:

1. The data collection methodology is replicable;
2. The data is reliable and determined to be valid; and,
3. The data has been peer reviewed and accepted by leading experts in the related field.

Qualitative tools employed by the education advocacy community are subject to the same level of scrutiny as scholarly reports and articles published in academic journals. Education advocates use qualitative methods to document how and why a government policy has impacted the American public.

Qualitative Tools

There are many different qualitative research approaches and designs that are commonly implemented in advocacy campaigns. The most frequently used qualitative research approaches are discussed individually below.

Narratives or Storytelling

Narratives are obtained from individuals being impacted by a current government policy, and they focus on expressing the individual's opinion about how they are being impacted or how a change in policy will impact them. Advocates use individuals willing to share their experiences and thoughts about an issue to present the human element associated with the issue. Narratives from different individuals experiencing the effects from a policy or event produce different perspectives for decision-makers to consider. The unique perspectives illustrate the impact of the policy and add context for decision-maker to draw conclusions from.

Storytelling is a methodology to document an individual's personal experience surrounding the issue. Video or tape recording individuals are the most effective methods of capturing the exact words and phrases used by the storyteller. Advocates or researchers should not attempt to hand write notes while listening to a story, or try to recall later what the storyteller said. The information received through this method must reflect exactly what the storyteller said, and not what the advocate thought the person said or their interpretation of the story they heard. Advocates utilize stories when communicating with government decision-makers. These anecdotes drum up interest or urgency from government decision-makers and are effective in illustrating a need for intervention.

The advocacy community implements these methods to humanize an issue for government officials. Decision-makers are provided with direct examples from actual people being impacted in their community. It is not uncommon for an individual, with a powerful story, to become the "poster child" of an issue and their story used throughout the advocacy campaign. Grassroots campaigns generate support from the public or directly from government decision-makers through the use of a celebrated case. Individual experiences provide advocates a strong and credible view into the positive or negative impacts associated with the public policy process.

Government officials analyze the stories they learn about to compare the experiences of individuals and groups being impacted by a policy or regulation in their community. The President often uses storytelling during the State of the Union Address as a way to humanize the successes of the administration's implemented policies. Narratives and storytelling are not complex analytical approaches, however, they are persuasive.

Example 8.0

Statement of the Issue: Should the federal government continue to allow the California condor, an endangered species, to continue to breed in the wild without intervention?

A newspaper journalist recently interviewed employees of the conservation team associated with tracking the California condor population. One of the team members told a story that described the feelings they experienced after discovering five dead condors in the last six months located directly beneath newly constructed energy efficient wind turbines. The conservationist mentioned that they have not found this many condors dead in a six month period in the 20 years they have been tracking them.

Baseline Advocate's Approach: This narrative is used by a baseline advocate to provide context and to demonstrate that the issue exists and that alternatives are to be examined. Using effective delivery mechanisms, baseline advocate include a discussion of the conservationist's description of what it is like to be on the "ground floor" of the issue

---

Lobbying Advocate's Approach: This narrative is spun by a lobbying advocate in order to gain support of a captive breeding program. The lobbying advocate presents the conservationist's experience to illustrate the seriousness of the issue, and to point out that their preferred alternative will address the issue.

Education Advocate's Approach: An education lobbyist utilizes this narrative to expresses a cause for action. The education advocate spends time investigating the conservation group and the individual to ensure the information is credible and presents the overall number of condors killed in recent years by other means than nature causes. This allows government decision-makers to determine if the number killed in the area is irregular.

Historical Research and Visual Ethnography

Historical research is a method that examines past and present events in order to develop a historical context of the present condition. Historical research provides advocates with the ability to present answers to questions government decision-makers may have, such as: Where have we come from? Where are we now? Who are we now? How did we get here? Where are we going from here?

Visual ethnography is the data collection and analysis of photographic records, voice records, collages, drawings, and maps. These techniques are used as a participatory qualitative technique and provide contextual and visual evidence for the advocacy community and government decision-makers. Visual methods assist advocates in demonstrating to decision-makers the changes that have occurred over time that otherwise are challenging or difficult to imagine. When the impacts of policies on communities are presented visually through photographs or videos the results are effectively influential on the decision-making process. Photos, videos, and historical context make issues real for decision-makers, and allow them to truly observe results of implemented policies. Government officials interpret pictures differently and so advocates need to draw their attention to specific details in the image; this ensures the intended message is communicated and encourages thought about a particular part of an issue without having to explicitly state it.

Example 8.1

Statement of the Issue: Should the federal government allow the California condor, an endangered species, to continue to breed in the wild without intervention?

Satellite pictures of the condor's migration route are released in a report published by Nature, an academic journal. The pictures, showing the same geographical area over a span of ten years, are used to illustrate the fact that condors have had to avoid new obstacles constructed in their migratory path, such as energy efficient wind turbines and the spread of urbanization into condor breeding zones.

Baseline Advocate's Approach: A baseline advocate presents these photos in their description of the issue to government decision-makers. They objectively illustrate the fact that the landscape occupied by condors is changing. The development of alternatives is derived by ideas as to how to adjust to the changing environment apparent in the provided satellite images.

Lobbying Advocate's Approach: A lobbying advocate uses the photographs to blame wind farm companies for the recent decline in the condor population. They use the photographs to help illustrate to government officials that these wind turbines are detrimental to the wildlife in the area. The lobbyist insists that in order to rebuild the condor population, a captive breeding program is essential.

Education Advocate's Approach: The education advocate uses the photographs to show government decision-makers the path condors use during their migration months, and they inform the decision-makers about how many new wind farm developments have been proposed, permitted and are in construction phases, and projects that have been completed in the bird's migratory path.

Focus Group Feedback

The advocacy community uses focus groups to gather perceptions, opinions, beliefs, and attitudes associated with a concept or potential policy change. Advocates develop numerous focus groups comprised of individuals from different demographics and ideological positions to draw conclusions from, and understand how a sample population reacts or opines about policy alternatives.

The information gathered and compiled from focus groups provides valuable insights into how the affected community would react to a change in a policy or program. Feedback from focus groups helps advocates identify trends, themes, and commonalities among the participant's responses. These commonalities, or lack thereof, creates either a general consensus about an issue or demonstrates disagreement among the public regarding the issue of interest.

Example 8.2

Statement of the Issue: Should the federal government allow the California condor, an endangered species, to continue to breed in the wild without intervention?

The State of California Governor's Office provided a grant for a private sector company to conduct focus group seminars three days a week for six months. The grant instructed the grantee to ask participants questions about the California condor. Following the completion of the seminars, the company compiled and analyzed the findings. The company's conclusions were three fold: 1) On average, 20% of each group knew what a California condor was, 2) When asked if the participants would support the development of a wind farm development in their community, knowing that condors lived in the area, 70% said they would, and 3) 80% of participants agreed that the federal government should use tax payer dollars to protect endangered species.

Baseline Advocate's Approach: The baseline advocate uses the results from this study to shape the development of their alternatives. The results provide insight into what people in the impacted communities know about the condor issue and what their opinions are. Baseline advocates use this feedback as evidence to support of the need for alternative policies that the American public can understand and support.

Lobbying Advocate's Approach: The lobbying advocate uses the same results as support for their desired outcome, a captive breeding program. They highlight that the community supports both wind farms development and increase in tax dollars used to pay for wildlife protection. The lobbyist presents conclusions from the focus groups that lead decision-makers to agree that a captive breeding program would protect the condors from being injured or killed in their early years. The idea has support of the community and it is politically acceptable to spend the money necessary to do so.

Education Advocate's Approach: The education advocate does not make any interpretation of the findings or suggest a particular course of action to the government decision-maker. They report the results from the focus groups to government decision-makers. They present the methodology used and questions asked to participants of the focus group to ensure the outcomes are credible and reliable.

Classic Ethnography Feedback

This method is also called "ethno methodology" or "methodology of the people". Ethnographic research studies a particular culture and their understanding of a particular issue within their cultural perspective. This research is generally documented through observational studies conducted by professional ethnographers or anthropologists who immerse themselves into the culture as if they were a member of that culture.

Advocates use the information gathered from this experience to humanize issues and experience what others from outside the culture may not be able to understand. The testimony and reports documented through the ethnography can give a decision-maker a better perspective as to how a specific culture, geographic area of the US, or in various areas throughout the world would react to a policy decision. Advocates use this methodology in the development of evidence for or against domestic and foreign policy. Additionally, the advocate community employs this methodology to articulate potential cultural barriers that help guide the development of policy alternatives. Instead of individual experiences and narratives, this tool offers insight to how an entire culture is impacted. This is useful to advocates because they add to their arsenal a commentary that speaks for a large group of people. Decision-makers rely on advocates to provide this level of insight because government-decision-makers are not intimately knowledgeable about every group or community of persons.

Example 8.3

Statement of the Issue: Should the federal government allow the California condor, an endangered species, to continue to breed in the wild without intervention?

A professor of Native American studies at the University of California Berkeley completed a study regarding the cultural significance of the California condor within the local Native American tribes. The study concluded that the condor plays a significant role in the local Native American's spirituality especially within an annual religious ritual. The condor migration patterns and times play a major role in how the tribes mark their seasons and religious holidays.

Baseline Advocate's Approach: Baseline advocates use the results from this study to present a government decision-maker with valuable information about how a community may be affected and react to a policy change. This information helps shape the course of potential policy alternatives by informing the decision-maker of certain communities that must be considered during policy alternative development.

Lobbying Advocate's Approach: The lobbying advocate uses the cultural impact study to support their desired outcome, a captive breeding program. They highlight that capturing and breeding the condor ensures the tribe a long lasting population of a spiritually significant icon. The lobbyist presents the information in a subjective manner showing the cultural significance of the condor to the Native American community and the federal government's responsibility to support spiritual freedom and rituals.

Education Advocate's Approach: The education advocate's role is to present the results from the study to the government decision-maker. They would not make any interpretation of the findings or suggest any course of action. Education advocates examine the report to ensure credibility and accuracy, including whether it's been peer reviewed and has been accepted by cultural experts prior to presenting it to government officials.

Qualitative Survey/Interviewing

This methodology employs the collection of detailed information about how individuals experience, understand, and explain the events and affects of policies in their lives. Qualitative surveys or interviewing provides greater detail and depth of responses than standard storytelling or narratives. The professional advocacy community employs this methodology to understand what the public thinks about a policy or policy alternative. Additionally, advocates use interviews to gain new insights from topical experts. This often occurs during a congressional hearing. An advocate may introduce an expert witness to testify about their understanding of the issue and their understanding of the causes and effects of specific policies.

Advocates can use surveys and interviews to develop qualitative context and by developing humanizing sound bites from the population. This methodology captures emotions, beliefs, political expectations, and comprehension. Advocates capture these data points and present them to government decision-makers to ensure the decision-maker has a full understanding of what the public, specific community, or topical expert perceives an issue, and whether they understand it.

Example 8.4

Statement of the Issue: Should the federal government allow the California condor, an endangered species, to continue to breed in the wild without intervention?

The State of California's Governor's Office has been under pressure by environmental groups demanding a policy change that will save the endangered California condor. The State of California wants to know what the general public thinks about the issue so they send out canvasser to ask people on the street a series of questions to gather data and sound bites about the condor issue, what they understand about the issue, and how they react to different potential policy changes. The results were tabulated and made public. The results were that the majority of the affected areas "didn't know the condor lived in their area", that they "felt that the government should step in and help ensure the survival of the condor but only if it doesn't raise taxes" and that they "believed that wild animals should be left in the wild and that humans should get out of the way".

> ***Baseline Advocate's Approach:*** Baseline advocates use survey results to present a government decision-maker with policy alternatives that would be politically acceptable based on how the community feels about the issue. The decision-maker gains insight into potentially politically challenging areas, specifically areas that their constituency would likely be against.
>
> ***Lobbying Advocate's Approach:*** The lobbying advocate uses the sound bites and survey results as evidence that the communities would expect the government to step in and provide protection for endangered animals. Additionally, they present that the public supports government intervention that supports their captive breeding program proposal.
>
> ***Education Advocate's Approach:*** The education advocate presents the results from the survey to government decision-makers to educate them about the perspectives of their constituents. They would not make any interpretation of the findings or suggest any course of action. Education advocates would examine the survey methodology to ensure credibility and validity of the people being interviewed and specifically if they were coaxed into a preferred response or to ensure their responses are authentic.

Strengths of Qualitative Data Analysis

The strength of qualitative data analysis revolves around history, experience, and description of impacts. History, experience, and factual discussion of impacts associated with an issue reinforce realism to an analysis. When interviews, surveys, and testimonials reinforce a policy or operational position, the issue analysis is more credible. This approach also humanizes proposals and recommended actions that government decision-makers and issue stakeholders evaluate. Reinforcing the potential impact of a policy decision by telling the story of those who benefitted from a specific approach to an issue is particularly influential. Baseline advocates often use this approach in their policy development process. Lobbying advocates use these narratives to highlight benefits or risks to justify change. Lobbyists also trigger emotional responses to add perspective to the decision-making process. Education advocates apply this approach to develop case studies and simulations.

Qualitative data analysis creates transparency around an issue. Opportunities to expand on their responses to questions are inherent in this process. The impetus to explain one's rational and justify their perspective is another benefit of the qualitative approach. It facilitates open discussions to offer new perspectives or new solutions being addressed.

When combined with quantitative data, qualitative information can enhance a specific proposal for change. The combination strengthens the justification associated with why the data and narratives support a specific outcome. The narrative provides context to the statistical analysis. It also provides decision-makers with a more holistic perspective to assist in the decision-making process.

Weaknesses of Qualitative Data Analysis

Qualitative data analysis presented without quantitative analysis has predictable weaknesses. First, qualitative analysis is not as compelling as a quantitative presentation. It is easier to generalize. The testimonials, surveys, and interview responses are often less convincing than positions associated with other issue stakeholders.

Another limitation to qualitative research is the reliance on the researcher. Most data that is collected utilizing quantitative methodology is standardized and rarely relies on the interaction between the researcher and the subject. Qualitative data relies on the researcher using their emotional intelligence to analyze and ask the most effective questions associated with the issue. This subjective manner of obtaining information can lead to credibility and validity issues. Researchers are at risk of injecting bias and asking suggestive or leading questions that may influence how individuals respond.

Chapter 9

UTILIZE EFFECTIVE MESSAGE DELIVERY MECHANISMS

Baseline, lobbyists, and educator advocates' use visual aid presentations, and written instruments to communicate their messages to government decision-makers and other issue stakeholders. This chapter provides guidance associated with utilizing appropriate delivery mechanisms to facilitate the most effective advocacy messaging metrics.[1] This chapter also integrates these mechanisms with the application of the metrics associated with incorporating quantitative and qualitative data in the delivery instruments.[2] In this chapter you will find examples of the current delivery mechanisms of choice:

- PowerPoint Presentations;
- Prezi Presentations;
- PowToon Presentations;
- Grasstops;
- Grassroots;
- Grant Proposals/Grant Preparation;
- Loan Guarantee Applications;

[1] Introduced in chapter six.
[2] Discussion of quantitative and qualitative techniques introduced in chapters in 8 and 9.

- Issue correspondence;
- Whitepapers;
- Emails;
- News Outlets and Editorial Commentary Shows;
- Speeches/lectures;
- Testimony; and,
- Questions & Answers.

Government decision-makers have limited time to consider various stakeholder positions on issues. This increases the importance of presentations that provide clear and concise policy alternatives while adding the stakeholder's unique information to the decision-making process. Any presentation should be fine tuned to anticipate questions from the decision-makers point of view.

The stakeholders' choice of mechanism is critical when advocating for a specific issue outcome. Background research is required to determine decision-makers' preferred delivery preferences. Note that more than one instrument may be required to deliver the most effective message.

The professional advocacy community applies fundamental metrics required to develop high quality written instruments and delivery mechanisms. Those metrics are to:

1. Provide clear, concise, timely, and accurate information;
2. Provide comprehensive and balanced analysis inclusive of quantitative and qualitative evidence; and,
3. Provide citations for all sources relied on in the presentation.

Application of these metrics provides decision-makers with credible information to justify the decision they reach. The following sections provide examples of how to use data and enhance delivery effectiveness.

Components of Effective PowerPoint Presentations

The most common digital presentation instrument utilized in educational environments, seminar style lectures, speeches, and issue summary presentations is PowerPoint; Microsoft's visual presentation program. It is used to present arguments, positions, or educational material through the use of computer generated slides to accompany oral delivery of the material. Apple computers come equipped with their visual presentation program, Keynote, and should adhere to the same metrics.

An effective PowerPoint presentation follows the following metrics:

- Establishes a consistent and simple design template using the same font styles, colors, and background themes throughout;

- Facilitates easy reading for the audience by using contrasting colors for text and background color;
- Limits the number of words on each slide and emphasizes key phrases and words especially important to decision-makers focusing on the policy issue;
- Avoids the excessive use of special effects such as animated and lengthy transitions that might distract from the intended message;
- Uses high quality imaging to reinforce and complement pertinent information. Diagrams, graphs, tables, and other quantitative data presented visually allow the audience to view the policy impacts through various media. These instruments are an effective means of communicating messages. It is important to test image resolution before giving a presentation to ensure the images are clearly visible on larger screens;
- Limits slide content to an average of one minute per slide; and,
- Ensures the number of slides for an hour meeting does not exceed 12 slides. This has proven to be the optimal number so that questions can be addressed and time for topical discussion is facilitated. The following example employs the metrics for an effective PowerPoint instrument.

Figure 9.0

Condor Breeding Alternatives

1. Continue condor breeding in the wild.
2. Initiate a condor captive breeding program.
3. Continue condor breeding in the wild but elimate environmental hazards.

Figure 9.0 applies PowerPoint metrics. It is clear, concise, and does not distract the audience with elaborate pictures or designs. It is simple, easy to read, and communicates the alternative policy approaches associated with the condor issue. Finally, the context of the slide is logically associated with the title.

Components of Ineffective PowerPoint Presentations

An ineffective PowerPoint presentation leaves the audience confused, detached, and uninvolved. The metrics to identify ineffective PowerPoint presentations are as follows:

- Too much information on a slide diffuses the message and fails to facilitate productive deliberations;
- Too much illustration exemplified by poorly sized or spaced quantitative and graphic material, such as complex data presented in diagrams, tables, and other graphics, can distract the audience; and,
- Too many words, colors, or information when providing qualitative material on individual slides results in audiences focusing on the slide versus listening to the oral presentation with the slide as a visual supplement. The audience is lost in this circumstance.

Figure 9.1

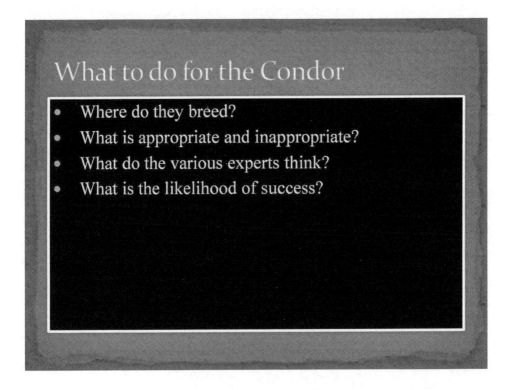

Figure 9.1 is poorly developed PowerPoint instrument. The information does not facilitate decision-making. The title does not correspond with the content of the slide. The slide's content doesn't educate the audience about the policy issue. Specifically, the content doesn't provide information required to support a recommendation, or the impacts of differing approaches.

Components of Effective Prezi Presentations

Prezi presentations facilitate a storytelling approach on a digitally constructed canvass. They convey both quantitative and qualitative material. This method pans and zooms to individual sections of the canvass to emphasize the most significant topics and data points. The zoom component concisely explains the pertinent information.

Effective Prezi presentations utilize the following metrics:

- The template is logical and highlights important information;
- The titles and subtitles are captivating and emphasize significant information;
- The graphics communicate critical information; and,
- The transitions are seamless from one topic to the next summarizing key points.

Figure 9.2 is an effective Prezi presentation. The titles of each circle articulate important topics. The design template simplifies following the presentation from start to finish. The visual "road" articulates the presentation's direction. The example is illustrative of the road to recovering the condor population.

Figure 9.2

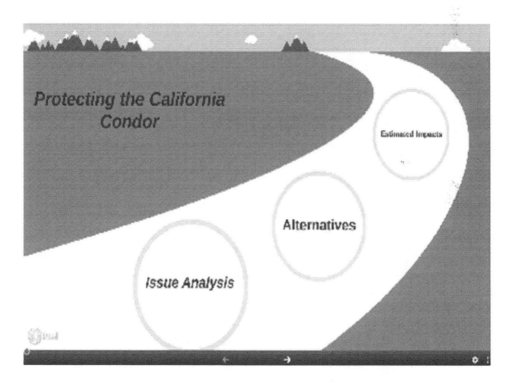

Components of Ineffective Prezi Presentations

Demonstrated below is an ineffective Prezi presentation. It is representative of deficiencies inherent in ineffective PowerPoint presentations, such as:

- Poorly designed templates that are illogical with unarticulated messages;

- Poorly titled headings that do not provide insight into the discussions that lie ahead; and
- Poorly chosen font, text size, color, and design that make it impossible to follow the presentation and understand the presentation as a whole.

Figure 9.3

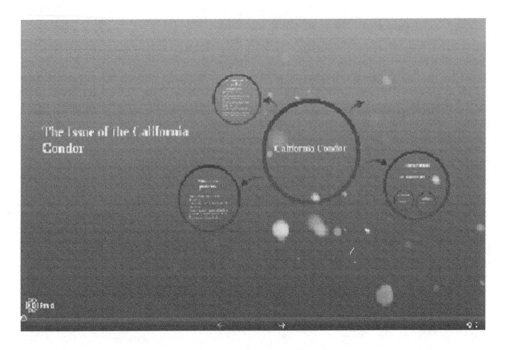

Components of an Effective PowToon Presentation

PowToon presentations are animations which convey specific messages versus written slides. PowToon presentations are creative. Stakeholders and government decision-makers focus on issues in a different manner. The metrics of effective PowToon presentations follow:

- Design animations are objective, influential, and entertaining while both professional and of high quality;
- Use images to communicate issues to government decision-makers and stakeholders;
- Limit the use of quantitative equations or numbers versus graphs, tables, and charts to articulate key points;
- Use similar fonts and placement of titles to ensure the audience focuses on the main point; and,
- Use a logo or an associated graphic to "brand" presentations associated with the message and provide an analysis of the issue to the presenter.

Figure 9.4 is an effective PowToon opening slide. The animation outlining each of the subject topics is not demonstrated in this "still" frame. Nonetheless, the animation is hand writing for each section on the screen. As the audience watches, they see what each topic of the presentation is, the order, and an approximate time of the presentation. The purpose of the presentation is stated in the title, and has an illustration of a large bird soaring in the clouds. The advocacy group's name is written on the bottom of the presentation so the audience can clearly associate the presentation with the presenter.

Figure 9.4

Components of an Ineffective PowToon Presentation

Ineffective PowToon presentations do not create an animated presentation that focuses the audience's attention on the key points associated with the issue of concern. The metrics of poorly developed presentations include:

- Failure to connect the organization to the presentation using words, logos, or graphics;
- Failure to balance purpose with professionalism by appropriately communicating the intended message through animations associated with objective analysis;
- Overwhelming decision-makers with wordy and disjointed paragraphs as well as lengthy bullet point lists; and,
- Confusing decision-makers and diminishing the strength of the intended message by utilizing inconsistent and illogical methods that do not coordinate the information with the animations.

Figure 9.5 illustrates an ineffective opening slide for the PowToon presentation. The animations are not visible in the "still frame" but illustrate that the headings and titles do not convey the information necessary to effectively communicate the topics and the overall issue. Audience members do not know what the issue is beyond the California condor pictured.

Figure 9.5

Visual presentations are not the only mechanisms used by the professional advocacy community to communicate their messages. They will often interact directly with the general public and community leaders in their effort to positively influence the government's decision-making process. Two types of community interaction are Grasstop and Grassroots Advocacy.

Grasstop Advocacy

Baseline, lobbyists, and educator advocates utilize the grasstop approach to influence the public policy process. They are activists or members of an organization that have recognized professional and public profiles. They have demonstrated over time that their ties and influence are credible with appointed and elected officials. Their place in a *power cluster* is associated with established relationships inclusive of businesses, donors, civic leaders, media outlets, and community groups. Grasstop advocates gain support for their position by relying on their vast network of relationships to deliver messages that reinforce the proposed change in policies or programs.

This network of relationships with issue stakeholders defines a *power cluster*. This influential group of issue advocates are some-times referred to as a decision-maker's *political family*.

Government decision-makers often learn about policy impacts from representatives of the high profile organizations delineated earlier. Decision-makers trust these organizations and their representatives to provide current and objective information. Professional advocates raise public awareness and influence government decision-makers by applying this grasstop approach. The delivery mechanisms are one of the written instruments accompanied with direct communication by these groups with the decision-makers.

Metrics associated with successful grasstop advocacy campaigns include:

- Targeting local organizations that influence decision-makers. The advocate knows and respects members of the ***power cluster*** or ***political family***;
- Choosing the appropriate grasstop advocates requires a due diligence scenario to ensure the right issue stakeholder is identified. Their current and former jobs, their education, family lineage, known associates, and organizations they belong to is the essential information to evaluate in the due diligence scenario. This process credibly narrows the field of advocates to recruit for advocacy campaign positions;
- Coordinate grasstop and grassroots advocacy campaigns to increase support for a specific position. Decision-makers seek public approval. Thus, decision-makers are constructively impacted by organized public support for a particular outcome;
- Knowing the correct timing to tap into the ***political family***. Professional advocates understand their relationships and their utility in grasstop advocacy. The political imperative is not to waste capital on advocating for issues with diminishing returns because of missteps associated with how the ***political family*** is utilized. Effective advocates balance their need to win on an issue with maintaining a healthy relationship;
- Balancing pressure and persuasion. Advocacy efforts are action dependent. Decision-makers look for consensus at public meetings and events; and,
- Being transparent in the advocacy campaign. Effective advocates are clear about their intentions. Advocates do not risk losing trust and credibility with decision-makers who find their efforts "fake" or misleading in some way.

For example, advocates are wise to utilize grasstop advocacy to generate support from the top down associated with protecting the condor from extinction. In this case, scheduling grasstop representatives to meet with FWS officials result in government and NGO being aligned to protect and increase the endangered condor's population. Jointly recruiting a prominently known wildlife conservation group further enhances the power of the group and thus, the likelihood of achieving the campaign's objectives. In addition, other audiences and prominent members of the conservation community are influenced to accept the government's decision. The powerful coalition of government and private sector stakeholders that result from this grasstop example is optimal to ensure the condor's population is revitalized.

"Having the ear" of a decision-maker means that there are a number of influential advocates that have joined together in recommendations worthy of action.

Grassroots Advocacy

Another mechanism for delivering information to government officials and issue stakeholders is through a grass roots advocacy campaign. Grassroots differs from grasstops in that grassroots advocates do not have access to a "political family" to which they can discuss issues with. Grassroots campaigns build coalitions of citizens that share a common interest or goal. Campaign leaders disseminate information to the public encouraging them to contact their local government official to support a specific idea or cause. The more public support a grassroots campaign can generate, the more likely it is that a government official will take notice and act on an issue. General public concern and desire for change is credited as being the most effective to succeed in winning a change in an implementing a new policy or program.

For example, a California condor conservation group begins to hand out fliers on a busy street in San Francisco intended to provide general information about the issue. The flier contains quick statistical facts and figures that highlight protecting and expanding the declining condor population. The flier also advertises the next scheduled public hearing on the condor protection plan. As awareness and participation in the campaign begins to grow more citizens attend public hearings and voice their positions on condor breeding. This results in local government leaders utilizing more of their resources to ensure the consensus communicated by the American public is adopted and acted on by the elected and appointed officials.

Grassroots campaigns are focused on bringing awareness to issues. Grassroots advocates utilize all forms of communication to reach the American public. These communication mechanisms range from fliers being handed out on street corners to those walking by or mass e-mail or traditional mail campaigns. Phone calls, issue correspondence s, and public demonstrations are all in a grassroots advocate's arsenal of techniques.

Grant Proposals/Grant Preparation

Principles of Effective Grant Writing

Professional advocates assist qualifying organizations respond to Federal grant solicitations. The government uses grants to finance authorized projects and programs to improve public services and stimulate the economy. Grants are also utilized to support a range of other initiatives including but not limited to innovative research, endangered species recovery projects, and analysis of public policy alternatives.

Successfully applying and being selected for a grant award is a "cottage industry" for grant writing advocates. Effective grant writers demonstrate the following characteristics:

- Comprehend the culture, priorities, and role of the granting agency;
- Experienced following written and verbal steps associated with preparing grant applications;
- Experienced writing clear, concise, transparent, and peer-reviewed information as specified and outlined in solicitations;
- Experienced utilizing the appropriate words, phrases, terms, and abbreviations recognized by agency and stakeholder professionals;
- Knowledgeable of deadlines and their significance;
- Knowledgeable of the process by which proposals are reviewed, scored, and awarded inclusive of the factors grant reviewers view as most important;
- Knowledgeable of the agency's policy objectives and political imperatives; and,
- Knowledgeable of each phase of the grant process:
  - Pre-announcement phase – communication is free flowing between the advocate and the granting agency as no solicitation is published. Career government officials welcome ideas and specific inquiries;
  - Announcement phase – inquiries and requests for information associated with the detailed instructions published as a part of the solicitation are welcome. Agency staff addresses questions that clarify the formal process and requirements for appropriately responding to the solicitation;
  - Review Phase – communication is limited to the agency's questions of applicants and is generally published and available to all applicants; and,
  - Award Phase – the award decision is public. The agency provides the terms and conditions associated with the grant award.

Dos and Don'ts of Grant Writing

All grant opportunities are unique. Grant writers must carefully address the requirements associated with the grant process. It is the responsibility of grant writing advocates to demonstrate their qualifications and expertise in their written proposals and presentations.

Grant review boards seek proposals that articulate purposeful action statements. For example, a grant opportunity focused on protecting endangered species will focus on innovative breeding approaches for the California condor, The grant proposal articulates methods to reduce human interaction within condor habitat. The grant's objective is to determine and propose one specific action that will result in the establishment of a condor Refuge to include a breeding research facility. The advocate, familiar with the objectives of the granting agency, included an action plan within the grant that specified the size of the facility, the acreage to be acquired for the refuge and the benefits versus risks of the action plan toward achieving the objective. The grant proposal that does not clearly address the objective and discusses alternatives that are less direct and measureable relative to goal attainment would be evaluated as insufficient for funding. How the financial award will be applied must be both clear and transparent. The review panel should be perfectly clear as to what activity the grant will fund.

Again, if the applicant advocate responds to a federal grant solicitation to reduce human interaction with condors by constructing a new California condor breeding and incubating laboratory was submitted, the proposal would fail because its' action plan did not result in goal attainment as the previous grant proposal did.

The applicant advocate must prepare their materials to the specifications provided by the granting agency in their instructions. Regardless of the benefit of a proposal, applications that do not address each factor in the solicitation fail if it skips factors the applicant advocate does not believe are important to their proposal.

Knowing the Audience

Effective grant writers understand how to prepare solicitation responses. They understand the grant review process. A successful grant award requires the writer to demonstrate that their response to the agency's solicitation will achieve the agency's articulated goals.

An effective grant writing advocate gains experience with the granting agency's priorities by researching previously awarded grants and their methodologies to ensure that the information and services can be provided within the timeframe and budget outlined in the solicitation.

The advocate must also understand the political environment associated with the solicitation. For example, the grant writer should consider perspectives inclusive of all stakeholders concerned about the condor population. This includes the White House's and the granting agency's perspectives. The response to the agency's solicitation must incorporate the history, experience, and pertinent information encompassing each stakeholder's position.

Loan Guarantee Applications

A loan guarantee is a Federal financing program advocates provide technical support for applicants seeking funding. A number of federal departments including Agriculture, Treasury, DOE, DOI, and Commerce offer Loan Guarantee Programs (LGP). Under the LGPs, the government backs loans to private entities for projects that are too risky for commercial financing. The government program finances more risky projects to advance the demonstration of new or innovative technologies consistent with a statute's intent. For example, DOE offers loan guarantees to finance innovative renewable energy projects that might not otherwise be cost-competitive relative to conventional energy projects. These programs are designed to bridge the gap between first-of-a-kind technology and commercial or industrial-scale deployment in the marketplace. Once that gap has been bridged, new technologies become proven, less risky, and commercially financeable.

The most important difference between the LGP and commercial loans is how each views and accounts for default risk. Commercial banks choose how much risk they are willing to take and specify financing criteria accordingly. These criteria considerations include value and liquidity of collateral, forecasted cash flow, and even categories of industry. If the borrower does not meet the criteria, the bank simply chooses not to make the loan. If a borrower does meet the criteria, the bank establishes an interest rate based on the historical default rate of loans that met similar criteria, and adds a premium to cover overhead costs and profit margin. This model works for banks because they diversify their portfolio of loans hedging risk profiles from different types of loans against each other. Commercial lenders do not believe market driven circumstances will arise that impact all loan related risk profiles at the same time. Their business model is specifically designed to minimize portfolio risk while returning a reasonable profit.

The private sector loan process differs from the commercial process is other ways, such as:

- The government does not seek to make a profit from its loan portfolio;
- The government loan program is designed to advance specific policy outcomes by statute; and,
- The government's loan requirements bear a higher risk profile and portfolio of loans than commercial loans by design.

The government manages its risk through a mechanism called credit risk subsidy. To determine the credit risk subsidy amount, the government calculates project-specific expected costs of a default by estimating the probability of that loan defaulting and multiplying it by the estimated cost in the event of a default. The government then charges the borrower this amount up front before guaranteeing the loan against default.[3] A commercial bank issues the loans based on the government's guarantee. Charging an interest rate determined by congress. In theory, the credit subsidy payment to the government provides a fund to protect the American taxpayers in the event a loan defaults and the government is required to act on its guarantee.

The following table outlines other differences between government-guaranteed loans and commercial loans:

	Loan Guarantee Program	Commercial Loan
Fees	Includes a non-refundable application fee, facility and maintenance fees apply if loan is granted, and charges for the use of evaluating consultants and credit subsidy costs.	Includes origination fee, packaging and construction loan fees, and closing cost fees if a loan is granted.

[3] Project specific expected cost of default (PECD) = Probability of loan defaulting (PbLD) X estimated cost to government for default (ECGD). PECD = PbLD X ECGD

	Loan Guarantee Program	**Commercial Loan**
Average Application Timeline	Average time from application to issuance 12-36 months.	Average time from application to issuance 1-3 months.
Risk Level	High	Low
Payment Terms	Up to 30 year repayment plans.	Up to 20 year repayment plan.
Cost Sharing	Yes	No
Default Liability	The Department of Treasury	100% Borrower
Loan Priorities	Priorities of LGP evolve with articulated priorities of the President's Administration.	Types and industry categories for loans are not prioritized. However, certain banks specialize in an industry category in its lending practices.
Interest Rate Calculation	Interest rates are below market rate and are similar across projects - not necessarily reflective of project risk level.	Interest rates calculated based on historical default rates of similar loans, plus a premium to cover bank expenses and a profit margin.
Loans in Default	Credit subsidy cost process designed to use collected fees to cover losses from loan defaults. The riskier the loan the higher the credit subsidy cost number as part of the initial fee structure.	Banks do not loan to companies they believe have a high chance of default. They set their interest rates to a level that covers the average amount loss in loans in default.
Compliance Costs	LGP is considered a "Federal action" and requires federal compliance with NEPA[1] and other applicable Federal statutes. These requirements result in greater fees, time, and labor for compliance.	Not required to meet unique federal compliance requirements beyond those that impact the entire nation's banking operations.
Preferred Loan Recipient	Fund "project companies" that seek to complete a specific project or program.	Loan to all qualified companies without any preferences toward specific projects.
Effects on Additional Funding Opportunities	Does not exclude the receiving company from using other non-federal incentive programs.	Eligibility for loan may be impacted by additional outside funding being received.

The loan guarantee process consists of three basic parts:

1. Application process;
2. Negotiation process; and,

120

3. Issuance and reporting process

Benefits of the Loan Guarantee program include:

- Relatively low cost of capital compared to other types of debt;
- The loan could be used as the cost sharing match for other funding opportunities; and,
- Loans provide terms of up to 30 years.

Drawbacks of the loan Guarantee program include:

- Non-refundable fee structure payable by applicants that have no assurance their application will be successful;
- A 20% equity component at a minimum;
- A more conservative due diligence/negotiation process resulting in a two to three year timeframe often not suitable for projects needing immediate funding;
- Long term debt may not be the most effective approach for a particular project; and,
- Projects are selected through a competitive process.

Effective loan guarantee advocates utilize similar characteristics attributed to those responding to federal solicitations:

- Knowledgeable of the eligibility requirements associated with the borrowing agency;
- Knowledgeable of the budget requirements and supporting documents required for the specific loan application;
- Knowledgeable on how to effectively communicate the financial needs of the borrower essential to the loan guarantee applications;
- Knowledgeable of the loan guarantee process and the loan granting decision-makers;
- Knowledgeable of public borrowing agencies' criteria required in financial documentation preparation;
- Seeking support from private and public sector stakeholders; and,
- Seeking the most up-to-date, transparent, and meaningful financial data.

The following is an example of how an effective advocate engages in Loan Guarantee Applications. The application is for the National Wildlife Refuge (NWR) to receive a $100,000,000 loan guarantee to build a habitat refuge for the California condor through the US Department of the Interior's Office of Indian Energy and Economic Development-Division of Capital Investment.

The advocate will first determine if the project is eligible for the LGP through the following determinations:

Chapter 9: Utilize Effective Message Delivery Mechanisms

1. The borrower must be either a federally recognized Tribe, an individual member of a federal recognized tribe, or an entity that is at least 51% owned by members of a federally recognized tribe;
2. The owner must have at least 20% tangible equity in the project being financed; and,
3. The project must benefit the economy of a reservation or tribal service area.

An advocate works with the NWR and DOI to collect the required documentation demonstrating their eligibility. Some professional advocates are specialized in the processes associated with filing the required documents such as:

1. A request for Loan Guarantee;
2. The Loan Guarantee Agreement;
3. The Assignment of Loan;
4. The Notice of Insured Loan;
5. The Loan Insurance Agreement;
6. The Notice of Default;
7. The Claim for Loss; and,
8. The Interest Subsidy Report.

Each of these instruments used effectively and objectively by the advocate assists the NWR achieve their goals. NWR's goals are written to align with the requirements of the Loan Guarantee Program. The goals benefit the reservation's economy. NWR will achieve their goals by providing a facility resulting in land preservation, environmental preservation, and the protection of condors. The goals also include temporary and long-term employment. Further, local tribal members are incentivized to invest in their community. Finally, the goal of protecting the condors by applying their cultural and traditional rituals is assured.

The Loan Agreement document is the most important delivery mechanisms. The document articulates specific parameters NFW must follow in order to remain eligible for financing throughout the duration of the Program. Further, it specifies actions the borrowing organization must complete inclusive of reporting requirements.

Data is made available to the agency as well as the business plan. The advocate often works with a local qualified lending institution to finalize the official loan guarantee request application.

The Division of Capital Investment within DOI guarantee up to 90% of an eligible loan. Thus, if NWR defaults on its debt to DOI and is unable to fulfill the requirements of the loan, the government agrees to reimburse them up to 90% of the unpaid principal and accrued interest due on the loan. When this occurs, the lender assigns its rights to the government, and the government becomes the new lender.

Writing Effective Issue Correspondence

Issue correspondences are common in presenting government decision-makers and other stakeholders with issue analyses and relevant information on issues. Effective advocates use this instrument to influence the decision-making process by sharing new information, status updates, and maintaining relationships.

A formal issue correspondence has specific metrics and follows a specific format. It should be printed on the organization's stationary and begin with a salutation such as:

- Dear Sir or Madam;
- Dear Mr./Mrs. Johnson; or,
- Dear (professional title) Name of Recipient.

The issue correspondence should end using these salutations:

- Respectfully yours, or yours faithfully, if you do not know the name of the person; or,
- Yours sincerely, if you know the name of the recipient.

The issue correspondence should also include:

- Your address;
- The address of the recipient; and,
- The date.

The opening paragraph of the issue correspondence should state the purpose of the correspondence. It should clearly identify what the issue correspondence is intended to accomplish.

The second paragraph, or the body of the issue correspondence, should provide supporting information regarding the topic and purpose of the issue correspondence. This portion of the issue correspondence should be concise and provide evidence and justifications as to why the issue correspondence is being penned.

The concluding paragraph should restate the position of the writer or the organization, and also summarize what is expected of the recipient such as requesting further information, requesting that a decision be made on an issue, or guidance on next steps.

There are numerous types of issue correspondence utilized by the advocacy community, examples include:

- Inquiry;
- Order;
- Refusal;

- Acceptance;
- Follow up or cancelation;
- Compliance;
- Complaints;
- Requests; and,
- Confirmation.

Each type of issue correspondence should follow the format outlined above and invoke the "Seven C's" of communication:

1. **Completeness** – Is a comprehensive presentation of information;
2. **Conciseness** – Is not redundant and all information is relevant to the issue;
3. **Consideration** – Outlines the benefits for the audience;
4. **Concreteness** – Is specific to its provisions of fact and figures;
5. **Clarity** – Is precise, concrete, and the vocabulary is easily understood by the other stakeholders;
6. **Courtesy** – Is respectful and appreciative to the decision-maker or stakeholder; and,
7. **Correctness** – Is peer reviewed to insure grammer is correct and data and facts have been doubled checked before sending.

An example of an effectively written and prepared issue correspondence is shown in Figure 9.6.

Figure 9.6

March 1, 2016

The Honorable Jane Dorsett,

U.S. House of Representatives

Washington, D.C. 20515-4501

Re: HR 2188

Dear Representative Dorsett,

I am writing this issue correspondence to express support of HR 2188. I urge you to vote in favor for this legislation. As you know, it is a top priority for the Condor Conservation Group that not only the condors be protected from extinction, but all wildlife.

More than 40% of your constituents have contacted the FWS office to address the declining condor population. This legislation is the best policy alternative to revitalize the condor population. You have been elected by your constituents with the expectation that their voices are heard, and that the will of the people be implemented.

Not only is the condor on the endangered species list, and not only is the FWS tasked with protecting the wildlife on that list, the people from your district have generated grassroots and grasstops campaigns to bring awareness of the issue and the support of HR 2188 to the entire state of California.

It would be my pleasure to meet with you personally to discuss HR 2188 and our objectives as an organization. Please inform me a time we could meet or that you have taken action on this item already. My contact information can be found below

Respectfully,

John Doe

Condor Conservation Group
1234 Conservation Ave.
Bitter Creek California 23394
Office: (555) 555-1234
Email: Johnd@CCG.com

Figure 9.6 addresses:

- The Congresswoman correctly;
- Her support of the proposed legislation;
- Why she supports the proposed legislation;
- Her position as it relates to the Condor Conservation Group's mission;
- The concerns of the constituents in the Congresswoman's Congressional district;
- The opportunity for a solution on behalf of the Congresswoman;
- The opportunity for the advocate and Congresswoman to meet face-to-face before the proposed legislation is up for vote in the House;
- Notification to send correspondence that the issue correspondence was received by the representative's office; and,
- Contact information for the advocate, including: name, address, e-mail address and telephone number.

Writing Effective White Papers

Whitepapers are compelling and informative instruments for decision-makers. They educate them about new content and are a credible delivery mechanism. Whitepapers differ from other written delivery instruments by providing a high level of valuable technical detail about the issue. White papers include in-depth how-to guides, visual aid diagrams, mathematical formulas pertinent to relevant industry issues, and other accredited research documents published by industry experts. For optimal impact content must be current, engaging, educational, and litigable. Thus advocates who effectively use whitepapers are persuasive, authoritative, and provide high level analytical skills. When an advocate's position is reliable and valuable to decision-makers, whitepapers become a functional asset for decision-makers to rely upon. These highly technical presentations provide decision-makers with:

- Reliable research from industry experts;
- Case study analysis, testimonials, technical reports, legislation;
- Graphics, charts, and diagrams;
- Plain and succinct language;
- A focus on benefits; and,
- Innovative and practical knowledge.

The following are necessary components for effective whitepapers:

- Incorporate graphics that use graphs or charts;
- Delay presenting the organization's or group's position while establishing expertise of the subject matter;
- Provide an analysis of the topic that can be applied generally to the impacted communities;
- Recognize the tone and knowledge base of the decision-maker. If the advocate knows the decision-maker is unfamiliar with the topic they provide significant details at the beginning of the paper;
- Observe grammatical and punctuation rules while maintaining a clear and logical flow; and,
- Make clear the call-of-action by describing how the specific expertise links the whitepaper to the issue.

Figure 9.7 is an example of an effective whitepaper.

Figure 9.7

Statement of the Issue:

Should the California condor continue to breed in the wild?

Background

- *The condor population has declined to levels resulting in various stakeholder requests that the government determine if status quo is the most effective strategy to prevent further decline and possible extinction.*
- *Experts report that hazards in the wild such as increased contact with power lines and wind farm energy operations, human encroachment, lead poisoning, and hunting are the major contributors to the decline.*

- *Authorities point out that the 180 condors in zoos are breeding. However, the breeding pattern of the remaining 230 condors in the wild is being disrupted by an increase in natural predators and a loss of prime habitat.*

Alternatives

1. Continue condor breeding in the wild;
2. Implement a captive breeding program; or,
3. Enhance breeding in the wild by removing environmental hazards through command and control regulations.

Issue Analysis

The conservation community asserts that condors can have difficulties breeding outside of their natural habitat and promote a wild breeding approach. They outline the following reasons:

- *Studies show death is common during capture due to the stress induced by the process of securing the bird;*
- *Condors have had difficulty breeding in captivity due to feeling "forced" to do so.*
- *Historically, breeding rates for captive birds are lower than that of naturally occurring pairs.*
- *The breeding rates for captive condors are negatively affected by the trauma and stress of the new habitat.*

Scientific experts assert that the most beneficial and efficient solution is the support of a controlled breeding environment such as a zoo. The budget estimate for this program is approximately $29 million. The most significant facts supporting this alternative are:

- *The captive breeding program involves 19 zoos throughout the continental United States, all of which have been identified as being appropriate for immediate transfer of condors;*
- *Utilizing the condor's ability to double clutch[4] results in the condor laying a second and sometimes a third egg. This increases the rate at which condors are hatched;*
- *Chelation treatment, an expensive and sometimes fatal treatment to remove lead and copper from the bird's blood system, will no longer be required as the threat of poisoning from toxic lead ammunition will be removed when the breeding birds are in captivity;*
- *Funding for the program will result in the construction of 12 new aviaries and the renovation of 16 existing aviaries; and,*

---

[4] Double clutching is the condor's ability to lay another egg after the first one fails to hatch. Wildlife handlers remove an egg from a nest and replace it with a mock egg. When the egg fails to hatch the condor lays another. The egg that is removed is incubated in a laboratory, hatched, and raised until its release into the wild.

- *Interagency collaboration between the Department of Agriculture, Department of Energy, Department of Interior, State and Local governments, and the NRA, continue to conduct rigorous evaluations of potential hazards and threats to the condor to determine the most effective approach for protecting the species.*

Writing Effective Emails

When writing in any media, professional advocates must consider their audience. Because emails can so readily be forwarded on, the audience may be much larger than your originally intended recipient. Consider the follow characteristics associated with emails when communicating with government officials and issue stakeholders:

Confidential or Personal Information – Email is a poor communication tool for conveying sensitive and personal information. When discussing advocacy strategies or proprietary business information use confidential means of communication such as hard copy issue correspondences. It only takes one recipient with poor judgment to hit the "forward" button.

Inability to Retract – Once an email has been sent, it is impossible to take back. Be sure that the information contained is polite, direct, and purposeful. Avoid using language that can be misconstrued or perceived to be offensive to the recipient.

Permanent Record – When considering the people in your audience, also consider that information technology experts have the ability to obtain emails that have been long since deleted from the sender or receiver's computers, tablets, or smart phones. Avoid discussing topics with government officials and stakeholders that you do not want to be on record.

Metrics for writing effective emails are as follows:

- Use the subject line – Government officials and private sector executives use the subject line to determine whether or not your messages are given any attention, or even opened. A common mistake is to use a vague or non-descriptive subject line. For example, rather than writing in the subject line "Working Lunch?" write the specific nature of the lunch meeting: "The Cali condor Study, follow up meeting." In addition, use the subject line to convey the level of urgency of your message: "Urgent: California condor analysis follow-up meeting." Do not leave the subject line blank; it is a sure way to get your message ignored or deleted;
- Separate points, separate emails – Each email should only discuss one point or one issue. Including multiple points in one message increases the likelihood that the recipient misses something important. Separate emails permit the recipient to address matters one at a time, thus, increasing the likelihood of a thoughtful response or follow-up action.

- Clearly state the response or action needed – State clearly what actions you expect from the government official or stakeholder. Emails are often read rapidly, and if they are unclear about what action needs to be taken, the effort could be meaningless and is likely to result in no action at all;
- Stay on Top of Your In-Box – Clear communication is essential to effective advocacy. If you want people to respond to your emails, respond to theirs. Email is so commonly used now that people rely on it and assume messages have been received. It is good policy to check emails at least twice per day. If you don't have time to respond in detail, let the sender know that. For example, "I received your question but will not be able to give it due consideration and respond until tomorrow afternoon." If you do not acknowledge receipt, the sender may assume you are ignoring them;
- Maintain formality – Because email is so common and quick to use, advocates and others often forget that emails are written documents and should be treated with the same care you would a memorandum to your boss. Do not utilize emoticons, text abbreviations or slang when emailing government officials and issue stakeholders;
- Unintended Emotion – Do not assume that someone should infer your emotion from an email. If you want your audience to know how you feel about an issue, be explicit, not subtle;
- Avoid the use of ALLCAPS – Typing in all CAPS sends an unintended message. Your readers will think YOU ARE YELLING AT THEM. This could jeopardize professional relationships; and,
- Describe email attachments – Attachments are a great way to pass documents along to others for quick review. The email should act as the cover note to the attachment. Mention the attachment in the email and explain its purpose. It is useful to highlight the main points of the attachment in your "cover" email.

An example of an effective email is found below:

Figure 9.8

FROM: Jim.Bird@CCG.org
TO: Jane.Dorsett@USRep.gov
SUBJECT: Policy Approach Presentation

The Honorable Jane Dorsett, please review the PowerPoint presentation slides attached to this email. Please provide any questions or comments you have in advance of the presentation so our staff can be sure those are addressed during the presentation scheduled for March 17th 2016 at 2:00pm at the Condor Conservation Refuge Conference Room in Brittle Creek, California.

You will notice that the analysis summarized in the presentation concludes that there is a strong correlation between public opinion in California, nationwide public opinion, and that of the other local government officials.

Thank you for your time, and I look forward to hearing from you before the March 17th Meeting.
Jim Bird
Senior Executive - Condor Conservation Group
ATTACHMENT 1 –Condor Policy Approach Presentation.ppt

Effective Use of News Outlets and Editorial Commentary Shows

At times professional advocates are required to address the American public directly through interviews with newspapers or magazines, radio talk shows, television talk shows, documentaries, or internet website interviews. Advocates sought after to appear on these shows are generally considered to be experts on their issue. All three categories of advocates fit the mold of someone that would positively address the subject issue to the public. The following metrics outline effective preparation and information delivery techniques utilized by the advocacy community:

- Know the facts, prepare in advance. When appearing on a talk show or interview it is essential that the advocate understands the information and can articulate the material clearly and concisely. Studying and reciting quick facts about the issue, and requesting that the interviewer or talk show production team provide a copy of the questions that will be asked before the recording;
- Remain flexible, and expect the unexpected. At times questions and answers can lead to other questions not communicated in advance. Having a thorough understanding of the material allows the advocate to communicate their message in ways they did not expect to. Remaining flexible and being able to deviate from the script without hassle will demonstrate to the audience and listeners that the advocate is an expert;
- Know the audience. This is an essential metric in all delivery mechanisms. When appearing on interview talk shows or radio shows the advocate must know the names of the people they are talking to, their position on the issue, and the position that their audience has on the issue. The advocate can prepare and interact according to the type of media outlet they are utilizing to communicate their message;
- Focus on the main points of the issue. To be effective an advocate must stay the course. Keep in mind the goals and objectives of the campaign when preparing answers or a script. Avoid going on tangents about unrelated issues and use the allotted time efficiently to address all the key talking points; and,
- Public forms such as these provide opportunities for professional advocates to gain support on issues of concern. They provide platforms that are unique and allow the public, government officials, and issue stakeholders to evaluate the issue in a context differently than they would in written reports. It also is provides a way to publically display the facts of the issue to individuals who may know nothing about the subject. When executed effectively the result is an increased amount of support and attention to the issue.

Delivering an Effective Speech

Delivering speeches and public speaking is a common delivery mechanism in the professional advocacy community. Speeches are designed to engage decision-makers and stakeholders, and present stated positions logically and with reliable evidence. Generally there are four types of speeches that are used in the advocacy community:

1. Informative;
2. Technical;
3. Persuasive; and,
4. Entertaining.

Different types of speeches should be used in different scenarios. Informational speeches educate decision-makers about a subject they did not know previously. They employ a balanced approach to presenting objective information to decision-makers and other stakeholders. Informative speeches are common to baseline and educator advocates.

Technical speeches provide instructional details to issue stakeholders and decision-makers. Similar to informative speeches, technical speeches educate the listeners about technical data about an issue. These generally follow a "step-by-step" template. Baseline, lobbying, and education advocates employ this type of speech when their audience is unfamiliar with a particular process.

Persuasive and entertaining speeches are frequently used by lobbying advocates. A persuasive speech spins information about the issue in order to spark emotion or excitement in the audience. These speeches intend to guide the audience into supporting a specific approach to an issue. They are intended to sway opinions and elicit change in their current position. An entertaining speech can be used to lighten the mood while subtly attempting to influence the decision-makers. Entertainment such as humor through storytelling is used to connect with the audience on a personal level. These speeches are used by lobbying advocates to build trust with decision-makers and improve the lobbying advocate's credibility.

Generally, effective speeches follow these metrics:

- Focuses on one idea or issue. Advocates present issue decision-makers and stakeholders with one issue and provides current and objective information associated with that issue;
- Follows the "problem-solution" model. The speech begins by addressing the reasons the issue needs attention. Then it prescribes possible solution(s) and provides evidence supporting the effectiveness of the solution(s);
- Contain background information, analysis of the issue, alternative approaches to a solution, an ask for a call to action, and concludes by summarizing the main points;Uses concrete words and illustrative examples to convey information;

- Provides evidence that clearly articulates the need for change to status quo. The strength of the speech is determined by how reliable the evidence is, how alternative approaches will be actualized, then impacts on the community's, benefits to stakeholders, and criteria for measuring success; and,
- Delivery is simplistic and elegant. The speaker should know the material so well that it is easily articulated.

To engage decision-makers and maintain their attention only include the most direct and influential points, provide supporting evidence, ask for a call to action and limit the speech to five (5) minutes. The most essential part of your speech is decision-maker feedback. While receiving this feedback advocates can gain a better understanding of how the decision-maker stands on an issue. Their comments and questions about the speech will provide insight into how the advocate should proceed.

Figure 9.9, spoken at an average talking speed, is an effective one minute speech introducing the event host, the topic of the speech, and what the audience can expect to learn from hearing the speech.

Figure 9.9

Thank you ladies and gentleman, and thank you Condor Conservation Group for hosting this event and allowing me to share some of the recent conclusions researchers have developed regarding the declining California condor population. The team at the Natural Wildlife Institute concluded that there are three alternative approaches that will most effectively revitalize condor populations. I will outline each of those alternatives, their projected impacts on condor populations, and estimated costs associated with each alternative. At the conclusion of this speech, you should be able to identify causes of condor decline, approaches to reversing the decline in populations, and avenues in which you yourself can be involved.

Components of an Effective Lecture

Advocates present lectures or participate in seminars to inform and educate decision-makers about specific subject matters. Lectures convey critical background information, theories, problems, and alternative solutions. Lectures benefit advocates as they provide:

- A forum to share new information;
- A controlled teaching environment;
- An opportunity to engage decision-makers and stakeholders;
- An opportunity to clarify misunderstandings; and,
- An opportunity to distribute unpublished or not readily available learning material.

The following are metrics associated with delivering effective lectures:Advocates must be adequately prepared. It is important to be familiar with the presentation environment; ensure audio-visual accessibility, and review talking points to ensure the prepared material is appropriate for the allotted time:

- Advocates prepare notes related to the implemented teaching style and are designed to effectively assist in the oral delivery. For example, a detailed outline, bulleted talking points, a tree or ven diagram should be tailored to ensure a clear delivery of information;Advocates begin with a brief summary of the key points being presented and conclude by restating of those key points. Throughout the presentation, periodically repeat the key points to remind decision-makers or other stakeholders. Make specific transitions between topics with transitional summaries linking current material to previously-learned content. Plan to discuss three to four major points in a fifty-minute lecture;
- Advocates design a lecture in ten-to fifteen-minute intervals. Change the pace to maintain interest. Actively engage decision-makers and stakeholders in learning activities such as a group brainstorming sessions and discussions, a multiple-choice quiz, or question and answer sessions;
- Advocates maintain regular eye contact with audience members and speak clearly using a conversational tone at an appropriate volume. Move around the room and express enthusiasm for the material being presented;
- Advocates utilize visual aids to stimulate, focus, and supplement the oral presentation;
- Advocates provide feedback to encourage participants to verbally share their thoughts or positions on the issue;
- Advocates provide the opportunity for feedback in written form following the lecture; and,
- Advocates provide an audio or video copy of the lecture to the public on their website or another easily accessible avenue.

Delivering Effective Testimony

Providing testimony allows the advocate the opportunity to formally convey their position on an issue that decision-makers are seeking to decide on. It provides expert, technical, operational, or other assessment-related information to the decision-makers. Testimony is requested as a response to Congressional investigations, inquiries, or oversight of federal programs and policies. It is designed to articulate the details and justifications for an advocate's proposed legislative initiative or position on an issue.

Testimony integrates the advocate's political, substantive, and institutional considerations on an issue. This is the advocate's only formal record provided to inform the members of the decision-making process. The advocate determines the testimony's content based upon the message they believe must be communicated to decision-makers prior to consideration of the issues, proposals, budget, etc. and is integral to the advocate's agenda.

Chapter 9: Utilize Effective Message Delivery Mechanisms

Testimony is transmitted in advance to the congressional committee with jurisdiction over the issue to be addressed. The various committees have their own unique rules and standards governing all aspects of the testimony, from preparation through the delivery of testimony before the committee.

The following is guidance on how to effectively prepare Congressional testimony:

- Always begin with a heading:
  - Testimony of **Your Name**;
  - Title of **Name of your Stakeholder Organization or Agency**;
  - Before the **House or Senate** and the **Name of Committee**; and,
  - **The Date**.
- After the heading, a one or two paragraph introduction is appropriate. This section should introduce the advocate. It should also state the advocate's position on the issue being addressed. It should clearly state the advocate's intent and expectations related to their testimony;
- Following the introduction, provide the background information deemed necessary to establish the basis for the position the advocate holds. It should also place the analysis on the issue in context. The background should be well documented and accurate with appropriate citations;
- Following the background, the most significant section of the issue should be analytically and systematically addressed. It is appropriate to quote sections of the bill or specific issues in the program so that the advocate's audience can easily follow the analysis, assertions, and arguments being made;
- This portion of the advocate's testimony is the most critical statement of the case being made or opposed in the statement;
- The advocate's statement and evidence (e.g., studies, surveys, news articles, and scholarly articles) must be compelling to decision-makers. Remember these are the advocate's only opportunity to develop and present uncontested arguments on the formal committee record; and,
- The conclusion must clearly state the advocate's desired outcome. Further, any summary of the most relevant rationale is also appropriate in the conclusion.

Effectively Answering Questions

Throughout their careers advocates will be required to address questions from stakeholders and decision-makers. It is crucial that advocates understand how to answer questions related to their issue. Effectively answering questions highly improves the asker's understanding of the issue, and also allows the advocate to clarify concepts and articulate an aspect of the issue in different terms. Answering questions effectively, confidently, and without hesitation demonstrates to the decision-maker that you have a clear understanding of your issue, and that your information is accurate and credible. Conducting the necessary background research and analysis of the issue provides the advocate with the answers they'll need to further explain the issue. Failing to properly prepare for interface with decision-makers jeopardizes their ability to gain support, educate, or influence the decision-making process in a constructive manner.

Three reasons decision-makers ask questions are:

- To gather information that they do not currently have and feel is relevant to their decision-making process.

Example: California Congresswoman from the district that contains the condor's habitat asks you "What is the probability that a captive breeding program will increase the condor's population?"

Answer:"The probability that the condor's will increase their population by 20% of the next 10 years is 70%."

- To build a record that is the decision-maker's position regardless of whether or not that position is supported by their office.

Example: California Congresswoman from the district that contains the condor's habitat asks you, "Do you understand that I ran my campaign on promises of increasing wind farms in our district?"

Answer: "Yes, I am aware of your position on renewable energy Congresswoman, and I am seeking to assist you in fulfilling those promises."

- To show support of or to oppose a program or initiative and to build a record that is consistent with their position.

Example: California Congresswoman from the district that contains the condor's habitat tells you, "I have previously voted in support of maintaining the populations of endangered species, do you believe that the captive breeding program will revitalize the condor population?"

Answer: "The facts have shown our organization that the captive breeding program has a 70% chance of increasing the condor population. That number indicates to us that an intervention approach, such as the captive breeding program, will positively impact the condor's population."

Chapter 10

EFFECTIVE COMMUNICATION CHARACTERISTICS

General Communication Types in Advocacy

This chapter focuses on the importance of each category of communication for professional advocates. It will provide guidance on how to effectively control and manage communication when engaging with government decision-makers and other stakeholders. Specifically, it will define metrics associated with:

- Effective written communication;
- Effective verbal communication; and,
- Effective nonverbal communication.

Effective communication is important for advocates because it provides another tool to employ when seeking to influence the decision-making process. Baseline, lobbying, and education advocates develop unique styles of communicating their messages, but follow common principles.

Three Track Interactive Communication with Government Officials

Effective advocates comprehend the different requirements for communication with career and political government officials. The requirements are associated with the official's roles and responsibilities. The complexity of applying communication metrics with the differing categories of government officials is defined by the three tracks delineated below. The first track is *technical* and *analytical*. The second track is *policy-laden* and *operational efficiency*. The third track is *political* and *philosophical*.

Advocacy experts provide objective and transparent data to government issue managers. The manager's imperative is to improve their understanding of issues and managerial challenges. The challenge is whether the government's decision improves the bottom line, whether it affirms status quo or operational updates. Meeting the first track challenge requires advocates to articulate technical and analytical conclusions associated with an issue to government decision-makers.

Advocates articulate varying policy alternatives to government policy wonks and operational managers seeking improved policy and operational alternatives. Often, these advocates must outline the alternative processes that assist career or political officials in their determination of what approach is most effective to address an issue. Policy, operational, and process related alternatives are intricate and can be difficult for government officials to clearly comprehend and address as they are bombarded with alternatives to current policy year after year. Nonetheless, they are required to examine all of the alternatives from varying perspectives. Even the most objective officials need help sorting through stakeholder arguments that confuse the outcome versus clarify the benefits of an alternative.

For example, the technical and analytical information provided by advocates of captive breeding was compared with information provided by various advocates who opposed captive breeding. The advocacy positions promoted by the other stakeholders were evaluated to provide government officials with an objective analysis of the proposals other stakeholder advocates bombarded government officials with. Both advocates' and government officials' objectivity required them to level the playing field and apply the same analytical criteria to evaluate the differing priorities associated with the alternatives. This is the pre-condition for the objective cost and benefit analysis of each alterative. Advocates empower government decision-makers when they ensure that a credible basis for evaluating each alternative including captive breeding is available. The challenge of addressing various stakeholder's policy and operational perspectives is almost impossible to evaluate without an analysis of this sort. The government typically cannot prepare such an analysis given the analytical resources required, the limited time to consider the alternatives, and the pressure from other stakeholders and their supporters to discount other alternatives. When government decision-makers are confronted and forced to consider all of these alternatives without any external analytical assistance, the outcome cannot be predicted. Professional advocates become essential to communicate with government decision-makers who are unable to conduct the depth of analysis required to discern which direction is best. Further, there is risk that this responsible and trustworthy advocate may even fail to be successful in attaining their preferred approach. These factors make this track the most important.

The final track requires advocates to demonstrate sensitivity to the government's partisan and institutional political perspective. It is critical that an advocate address a government official's best interests as a public servant. It is paramount that the advocate's communication addresses the challenges associated with an inaccurate philosophical belief or bias of the government official. Advocates must demonstrate to any government official that holds a specific position that it is neither factual nor practically justifiable. An advocate's sensitivity to partisan and institutional bias can only be overcome with indisputable, timely, and factual evidence. This is why the third track and its challenges are so important. This track most accurately addresses philosophical beliefs and biases.

The complexity of effectively communicating and applying communication metrics associated with the three tracks requires a unique understanding of the motivations, interests, and definitions of success held by government decision-makers.

Advocacy campaigns are always focused on changing the status quo. This requires influencing decision-makers to objectively consider changes advocates present. Advocates seek changes in the status quo based on new approaches or interpretations of existing statutes, regulations, and associated policies to achieve the specific objectives the advocate is seeking. Thus, communication with government decision-makers must comport with specific metrics demonstrated to be effective from the bottom of the government hierarchy to the top of the government hierarchy. There are varying perspectives that are institutional, emotionally significant *in-the-day*, or strictly philosophical internally or externally that advocates must be sensitive too. Advocates must employ a system of communication that government decision-makers view to be consistent with their best interests as public officials.

The Metrics of Communication with Government Decision-Makers

Advocates communicate with four categories of government decision makers. The first category is career issue managers. Career issue managers are members of the government's workforce that work to add to, update, and facilitate discussions on specific subjects of interest relative to their institution's objectives. Typically these are the mid-level officials that prepare RFPs, review grant proposals, and conduct policy, budget, and regulatory analysis. This group of officials is very influential as they report directly to senior executive decision-makers. This group may even be delegated the responsibility to make the decision. The second category is career senior executives. Career senior executives have been selected based on their demonstration of the knowledge, skills, and abilities (KSAs) required to make appropriate decisions. These individuals serve in executive positions and generally report directly to Presidential Appointees. The third is political senior executives. Political senior executives are also government executives whose role is to support the Administration's partisan ideologies and the associated approaches to issue resolution. The fourth is confirmed

Presidential Appointees. Confirmed Presidential Appointees have been selected by the President and confirmed by the Senate to direct policy development and manage priorities in government departments.

Obviously, there are statutory and regulatory rules governing communications and interaction between professional advocates and government officials. The communication metrics and the overlay of these metrics in communicating within and between the three tracks and four categories will assist you in applying effective communication methodology. Your understanding of the tracks, categories, and metrics will prove to be the basis for your performance. Advocacy methods are only as effective as you implement them.

Close examination of the communication metrics reveal that:

- Five of the communication metrics are exclusively political whether viewed through partisan lenses or both the career executive as well as the presidential appointee lens;
- Seven of the communication metrics are applicable to both career issue mangers as well as career senior executive decision-makers; and,
- Eight of the communication metrics are shared and applicable to each of the categories.

Whether career GS-13, 14, 15 issues managers, career senior executives,[1] political senior executives,[2] or presidential appointees,[3] an advocates' interaction and communication is based on their issue positions, role within an advocacy campaign, and articulated objectives. Effective communication is achieved when advocates and government employees interact in a transparent and goal oriented manner.

Political Only

The Executive Schedule is comprised of five schedules: Schedule I is the highest paid and are Presidentially Appointed Secretaries of each Department, Schedule II includes Deputy Secretaries, Schedule III includes Under Secretaries and CFOs, Schedule IV includes Assistant Secretaries and Administrators, Schedule V is the lowest executive level and includes Administrators and Associate Administrators.

1. **Partisan position and rhetoric/philosophical imperative** – All presidential appointees seek to change the status quo and to apply the political party's platform. The party's platform is a composite ideology and variables. Some government career officials are included in this category. Their inclusion is

---

[1] The Senior Executive Services (SES) consists of high level Federal jobs replacing GS-16, 17, and 18 of the General Schedule. There are two categories within the SES: Senior Level (SL) positions, or Scientific of Professional (ST) positions. There are approximately 640 SL and 470 ST positions allocated to several Executive agencies. One of the categories within the SES is Political both scientific and Professional (ST) positions. Further, there are Schedule C positions that are also non-career.

[2] See above note.

[3] Presidential appointees are compensated through the Executive Schedule and consist of five (V) levels or schedules.

due to their institution's demonstrated biases. They decide issues based on their institutional memory that is just as strong as a political party ideology;

2. **Meet and greet protocol/no agenda** – Every new Administration appoints Schedule C and other Presidential Appointees. While advocates know many of the appointees from the campaign, some are unknown to the professional advocacy community. Thus, the first interaction is to build trust and get to know the new leader. It is appropriate to simply meet with government officials with no agenda. This approach can establish credibility;

3. **Advocacy passive/little analytical support** – Many political appointees are true believers in a specific ideology and associated approach. Thus, an advocate must be patient and make their views known casually but accurately and consistently. Effective advocates communicate their position on the issue without discrediting the appointee's ideologically based position;

4. **Support Administration's position/reinforce with data and analysis** – The target for this communication pattern is to the Presidential Appointee. The objective is to arm the appointee with information that can be articulated to the career bureaucracy credibly resulting in some level of support to change status quo. Success is measured by the bureaucracy's willingness to change when presented with accurate and factual data;

5. **Enacted policy and budget/career opposition** – Advocates are successful in their advocacy to the Congress and seek to influence a biased career or political bureaucracy to adopt the enacted congressional position versus the institution's approach. Each year the bureaucracy argues to either increase or decrease funding on issues of concerns based on their institutional memory. Advocates capitalizing on the politically enacted imperative to force change.

Career Executive & Issue Managers

6. **Be detailed/analytical** – Advocates are expected to provide more information, data, and analysis to career issue managers and executives. The career service is the guardian of all information associated with issues the government is responsible for. Analysis on issues of substance were evaluated and examined by the federal executive branch departments, agencies, offices, and, committees. All advocacy materials must be comprehensive, and include analytics that support and corroborate the advocate's position on the issue;

7. **Articulate in detail/complete data sets** – Advocates must present their assumptions, data, and analysis in the most transparent and objective manner. Their justification must never be defensive. Decision-makers need to have the capability to be as detailed as an audience demands to support their position or address others in a constructive fashion;

8. **Oppose administration's position/reinforce with data analysis** – There are occasions when government career, and, perhaps political executives and issue managers oppose the career Administration's position. Advocates provide factual materials and balanced analysis to them. The objective, as always, is to enhance their knowledge achieving as much as their credible objectives as possible. The career bureaucracy is mindful that their political bosses have

limited time. They often use the data to keep issues alive or to compromise with administration officials as programs are implemented;

9. **Internal institutional support/reinforce institutional analysis** – Advocates piggy back the government's institutional knowledge to add, update, and reinforce the bureaucracy's past and operational direction on specific issues coinciding with their interest. The analysis must be articulated in a manner that enhances the institution's understanding of the issue;

10. **Institutional position/external analytical support** – Advocates must perform and provide new analysis to government officials whenever possible. Again, this opportunity arises when the government's or advocate's positions are mutual. This metric is particularly valuable when the private sector is seeking a grant or contract. The results stemming from completing the scope of work amplifies the institution's position;

11. **Interagency position of support/internal and external career support** – When advocates are aware that other government agencies and decision-makers are in-sync with their position, providing updated evidence and a stronger justification to other stakeholder agencies and articulating the need for interagency deliberations is the basis for this metric;

12. **Consensus budget and policy enacted/presidential opposition** – If the President opposes the budget and underlying policy; advocates that articulate the president's position become popular with the political executives and perhaps, even some career officials. This is an issue that advocates enhance their trustworthiness and strengthen their credibility with government executives;

Issue Managers and Career and Political Executives

13. **Be clear/concise** – Advocates that articulate clear, accurate, and concise information are valued by all government officials. They are more likely to achieve their desired outcome given their approach;

14. **Summarize/high level** – Advocates that summarize their position inclusive of the most important data and analytical information are the most effective. The key to applying this metric is speaking the stakeholder's special language demonstrating their depth; this makes the continuing dialogue with government officials more likely;

15. **Summarize/policy priorities** – Advocates that can summarize policy imperatives in an articulate, clear, accurate manner, are most effective;

16. **Initiate relationship/seek information** – Advocates build credibility over time by providing objective, goal oriented advocacy materials. This allows the advocate to obtain and convey information informally or "off the record" improving their ability to gain support for their specific issue or cause;

17. **Use credible analysis/strengthen relationship** – Advocate's continued use of credible analyses demonstrates loyalty and commitment to achieving desired goals and objectives. Success is measured by the acceptance and continued use of the advocate's service to the political or career executive;

18. **Consensus budget and policy enacted/ resolve differences with regulation** – Advocates seek the support of career and political executives to bring change to the status quo by providing information and relevant analysis that supports the development and implementation of new regulatory actions;

19. **Consensus enacted policy and budget/external opposition** – Advocates supporting a position which opposes congressional enacted policy or budgetary requirements must provide objective and factual advocacy materials. The materials must justify the best course of action and compel the political and career official to believe that reversing prior decisions is the best approach for the American taxpayer; and,

20. **Consensus institutional and administrative position/external support** – Advocates that provide external support through provision of the most current and accurate information that reinforces the agency's institutional memory are critical to the decision-making process. Understanding each agency's position as it relates the Administration's help advocates develop effective advocacy materials.

Government decision-makers consider information that becomes available to them during the decision-making process. Successful advocates effectively manage delivery of verbal, nonverbal, and written information to decision-makers. They know that failure to appropriately manage how, when, and what information is injected in the process could put their objectives at risk. The combination of the three categories of communication with decision-makers is critical to the outcome on issues of concern.

The channel or medium chosen to convey information to the decision-maker is another key factor. Different channels have different levels or *"richness"* ranging from high to low. Information rich channels convey more nonverbal information.

Channels that provide high levels of information *richness* include: face-to-face conversations, videoconferencing, and telephone conversations.

Channels that provide a medium level of information *richness* are: emails, text-messages, and blogs.

The channels that provide a low level of information *richness* are: formal written documents and spreadsheets.

The logic associated with the aforementioned analysis of channel influence is accepted as a standard within the professional advocacy industry. Face-to-face interactions are the most effective way to convey information. There are many different aspects in face-to-face discussions that reinforce messages, perspectives, and factual information being conveyed. It is also accepted that formal written documents result in low information *richness* because the human element is not present. Verbal dialogue forces our minds to engage with others. Additionally, nonverbal actions assist with communicating messages based on the discussion and participants read of the body language. Decision-makers cannot read the tone of documents or associate nonverbal cues that reinforce the main points. Thus, matching the channel of conveyance with the advocate's message objectives and information is critical.

Effective Written Communication

Written communication differs from verbal communication in that a written instrument does not occur in real time. Further, written instruments are generally collaborative efforts and are developed over time. They are edited and re-edited to ensure that the messaging is as concise and accurate as possible. Written instruments are targeted to individuals, groups, or entire organizations. The 6 metrics for ensuring effective written communication follow:

1. Conduct adequate background research to ensure you understand the audience;
2. Ensure clarity in conveyance of the issue and analysis of policy alternatives;
3. Use rhetoric known to the issue stakeholders -- especially decision-makers;
4. Avoid redundancies;
5. Be transparent; and,
6. Proofread to ensure there are no grammatical errors or unwanted statements.

Each written instrument has a role in an advocacy campaign. Some instruments are focused on providing substantive background research bearing on the issue followed by educating stakeholders. Some instruments are intended to raise alternatives to issues and present them to relevant stakeholders.

Once decision-maker or stakeholder preferences are known, the instrument and delivery mechanisms are selected.

Finally, editing and proofreading is critical. This process is frontloaded in the sense that most of the work should be done before the actual instrument is written.

Beyond the formal written instruments, there are other less formal instruments from emails to inter/intra office memos. Following these pointers will make your argument stronger, more coherent and more influential:

- **Identify your primary readership** – Is your audience lay members of the public, government decision-makers, media outlets, or staff within your own organization? A document written for one may not be effective with another. Their levels of understanding, ability to affect change, and amount of interest will vary and a well-crafted advocacy document will reflect that by speaking in terms that are familiar to them;
- **Determine the appropriate channel of delivery** – The media offers a range of outlets to deliver information to stakeholders whether, specialists or non-specialists. There is an opportunity to showcase scholarly articles, Internet postings, or utilize simple email communication in an advocacy campaign. The discerning factor is which is best to connect with stakeholders;

- **Construct a clear message that they will understand** – Advocacy documents are most persuasive when focused on a single governing idea, or central message. The instrument should define the advocate's objectives and any requests of the decision-maker or stakeholder made by the advocate;
- **Be persuasive** – Determine how your objectives align with those of the stakeholder's or government decision-makers; and,
- **Change or modify their mindsets** – Consider the religious, political, economic or institutional paradigms of the stakeholders. Such mindsets can be addressed directly by providing substantive analysis and genuine understanding of the stakeholder's perspectives.

Effective Verbal Communication

Advocates must possess superior verbal communication skills in order to perform successfully before government decision-makers and other issue stakeholders. Face-to-face interaction is the best opportunity for a professional advocate to demonstrate the proper temperament, knowledge, accuracy, and commitment in an issue-oriented advocacy campaign. There are situations in which verbal communication is preferred over other forms of communication.

Written communication is most appropriate when advocates are just articulating facts, arguments for the public record, and delivering non-urgent messages. Written approaches are also more appropriate for articulating more complex and comprehensive explanations of issues that do not require immediate feedback. On the other hand, verbal communication is more appropriate when advocates are conveying their personal passion and commitment, are more transparent and do not need for the arguments to be part of the permanent public record. Additionally, when the timing to influence decision-makers is more urgent, or immediate feedback is required to ensure that the simple and easy messages do not get confused or misinterpreted, verbal communication is a priority.

Thus, the distinguishing factors governing when to use verbal versus written or other styles of communication must be considered in every circumstance involving advocacy on an issue.

It is important to note that verbal communication permits advocates to use their tone and nonverbal skills jointly to emphasize their commitment and passion around the issue being advocated. Varying the volume and speed of one's speech can only be employed during a verbal presentation. On the other hand, written communication is formulated to be clearer, more concise, and thus influential in ways that a verbal approach is not.

STANDARD METRICS OF VERBAL COMMUNICATIONS

The metrics that follow are standard for any verbal presentation:

1. Address decision-makers and other issue stakeholders by name to develop personal relationships;
2. Compliment decision-makers and their institutions by articulating why previous decisions were incrementally justified to establish the logic for the next incremental decision you are advocating;
3. Ensure that your statements are focused, simple, and concisely articulated;
4. Focus statements only on the main points of your argument; and ensure that counter-positions are disputed or discredited within the body of your main points;
5. Listen to the decision-makers' and stakeholder's feedback as the basis of improving your arguments;
6. Establish your expertise as an authority on the issue of concern by including your credentials in the presentation;
7. Outline the scope of your issue analysis for the decision-maker before launching into focused arguments;
8. Focus your arguments to accurately lead decision-makers to question the logic of opposing alternative perspectives on the issue;
9. Quickly re-summarize the logic and reality of your arguments following the explanation of major points;
10. Anticipate questions from decision-makers and other stakeholders when making verbal arguments;

OVERLAPPING COMMUNICATION METRICS

Though some of the following metrics overlap with metrics of other communication approaches, the following metrics can never be overemphasized:

11. Know the level of formality required of your presentation to facilitate governmental agency deliberations, including forums in which senior/mid-level or executive analysts are primary participants in the issue campaign;
12. Canvass decision-makers to determine whether visual aids are appropriate when advocating for an issue. Sometimes charts, maps, PowerPoints, and photographs improve a presentation. But other times, they confuse or decrease your decision-maker's focus of the issue;
13. Be persuasive by connecting the issue with the decision-maker's role and mandate. This often requires repeating important points with different, but directed rhetoric;
14. Seek to impact the decision-maker's mindset by showing your emotion, passion, and commitment using arguments that are positive, constructive, and realistic;

METRICS GOVERNING THE USE OF VISUAL AIDS

15. Do not obstruct visual aids by positioning them to your left;
16. Introduce visual aids to decision-maker to reinforce their importance to clarity in your presentation;
17. Ensure there is consistency between the visual aid and your oral presentation;
18. Remember the visual aid is a supplement that must not supplant your verbal articulation;
19. Remember complex visual aids will confuse and distract decision-makers and other stakeholders; and,
20. Do not read from the visual aids because eye contact with the decision-makers will be lost.

Verbal Presentation Delivery Tips

- Practice your verbal presentation prior to the meeting or forum where you will present your message;
- Prepare to be questioned by decision-makers by brainstorming with colleagues prior to your presentation;
- Know your allotted time to present your perspective on the issue. A rule of thumb is that 2000 words per 10 minute time span is considered average. Failure to heed this tip is likely to result in a loss of the decision-maker's attention; and,
- Indicate that you will provide answers to questions where you are not knowledgeable following the session.

Verbal communication has the unique advantage of offering advocates the opportunity to appeal to stakeholders by genuinely expressing their commitment and "Human" passion for their perspective. Advocates connect issue arguments with the actual decision-maker and sometimes the faces of other stakeholders. Face-to-face interaction brings the issue to life rather than just written positions and justifications.

Advocates demonstrate their authenticity and credibility through verbal communication. Authenticity is not an ascribed status; rather, it is something attributed by stakeholders. Thus, one should always be cautious so that authenticity is not perceived as phony or just doing a job. This perspective results in lost credibility and human genuineness.

Demonstrating actual authenticity requires individual management and control. Advocates consider stakeholder's personality traits and anticipate the information needed to advocate successfully. These learned behaviors shape how to direct and manage an advocacy campaign. The environment and social situation dictates what parts of the advocate's personality need to be displayed in order to convey their message. To do this, advocates must have a strong understanding of self, their decision-makers or stakeholders, and the organization they are communicating with. Advocates need to present the appropriate aspects of their personality to develop trust and authenticity with government decision-makers. This allows advocates to be selective and consistent in the presentation of perspectives and policy alternatives. Authenticity and credibility depend on the assurance that the verbal communication is consistent with the objectives of the advocacy campaign.

Advocates can help build credibility through self-disclosure. They must share information about themselves in efforts to reach common ground with decision-makers and stakeholders. Generally, their stakeholders will listen attentively to someone they can relate to. In order to achieve this, advocates must focus on learning the stakeholder's history on the issue and the decisions that led the issue's current status.

Nonverbal Communication

Nonverbal communication is information conveyed without verbal or written communication. Decision-makers are attentive to nonverbal cues. Nonverbal cues are influential in conveying one's emotion/passion on an issue of concern.

There are ten nonverbal cues:

1. **Facial expressions** – Convey positive or negative inclination associated with the issues being discussed. This includes how engaged one is when participating or listening to other perspectives. Facial expressions are understood even when there are language barriers. Happiness, sadness, anger, and fear are conveyed easiest;

2. **Gestures** – Movement of the body and hands to communicate a perspective without the use of words. Again, gestures are sometimes deliberate, but can also be coincidental;

3. **Paralinguistic** – These are factors such as tone, loudness, inflection, pitch, which impact how messages are received;

4. **Body language and posture** – Communicate attitude and emotion. For instance, slouching, crossed arms, and looking down indicate a negative attitude or disagreement; whereas, direct eye contact and an open demeanor conveys positive attitudes and often concurrence;

5. **Active listening** – Communicate interest and engagement. Lean in and focus your eyes, ears, and energy into the conversation. Demonstrate respect and appreciation for your decision-maker taking the time to meet with you;

6. **Space** – This is the distance between individuals engaged in a meeting or when addressing a group. Depending on the meeting environment an intimate distance is between 1 and 2 feet commensurate with a one-on-one meeting versus 2 to 4 feet commensurate with meeting around a conference table. When addressing a group or forum the distance might range from 5 to 25 feet commensurate with a stage and dais setting or a witness table and committee dais setting;

7. **Eye gaze** – Honesty, confidence, and security can be evaluated based on the direction of eye contact. Shifty eyes and an inability to maintain eye contact

is seen as an indicator of deception or selfish intent;

8. **Touch** – From hug therapy[4] to a purposeful touch or jab, an appropriate touch can convey commitment, intensity, and passion attached to an issue. Negative and inappropriate touches are pinches, squeezing, punching etc. Further, sex differences also play a role in how people utilize touch to communicate. Women tend to use touch to convey care, concern, and nurturance. Men are more likely to use touch to assert power or control over others;

9. **Appearance** – Dress and appearance are evaluated by decision-makers. Appearance can alter physiological reactions such as social judgments and interpretations. Culture also influences how appearance is judged. Certain social norms set expectations for decision-makers. They expect an advocate to look professional e.g. suit, dress shirt, and tie. Appearance can also communicate a level of preparedness. Having a sloppy appearance jeopardizes an advocate's credibility. Poor hygiene or inappropriate attire further damages an advocate's communication of their intended message; and,

10. **Situational awareness** – Reading the nonverbal cues of others improves your ability to respond appropriately. Inappropriate responses demonstrate a lack of competency and confuse those engaged in the discussion.

Nonverbal communication plays an important role in how advocates convey information to government decision-makers and stakeholders, and how decision-makers interpret the actions of advocates. What a person verbally articulates along with his or her expressions, appearance, and tone of voice conveys the entire message to the recipients.

Dr. Albert Mehrabian, a research psychologist who studies nonverbal communication, concludes that 97% of the information individuals convey is nonverbal; while only 7% is communicated verbally. Further, he concludes that 38% is vocal and 55% is facial nonverbal communication. These findings reinforce the importance of nonverbal attributes. Our automatic nervous system constantly sends signals facilitating nonverbal communications. Advocates must manage their nonverbal cues so that the decision-maker's or stakeholder's automatic responses are favorable.

---

[4] Keating, K., & Noland, M. (1983). Hug therapy. Minneapolis: CompCare.

Chapter 11

TRUST BUILDING CHARACTERISTICS

This chapter discusses the importance of developing and maintaining mutual trust relationships with decision-makers and other stakeholders in the advocacy process. There are transparent and ethical approaches that must be applied in order to build strong, trustworthy, and credible relationships between professional advocates, government decision-makers, and other issue stakeholders. Thus, the objective of this chapter is to discuss the importance of adherence to the lessons articulated throughout this book, and the conceptual, philosophical, and practical principals underlying the value of building strong trust relationships between the professional advocacy community and government decision-makers.

Social psychologists articulate two main approaches to understanding trust. The first is a dispositional (person-centered) view. Trust entails general beliefs and attitudes about the degree to which other individuals are likely to be reliable, cooperative, or helpful in daily-life contexts.

Second the dyadic (interpersonal) where, trust is a psychological state or orientation of an actor (the truster) toward a specific partner (the trustee) with whom the actor is in some way interdependent (that is, the truster needs the trustee's cooperation to attain valued outcomes).

Trust is a function of properties of the self (I), the specific partner (you), and the specific goal in a current situation (to do X).[1]

THE TRUST EQUATION

Trust is also a bilateral relationship. Government officials evaluate the trustworthiness of the professional advocates. Professional advocates evaluate the trustworthiness of government officials that receive proprietary and other sensitive information from them. The issue is how the government uses such information in the government's decision-making process. The following equation, known as the trust equation[2], has been expanded upon from its original model and defines the conceptual value of trust and general relationships, but specifically trustworthiness in the government's decision-making process.

Government decision-makers must continuously evaluate whether and when to expand their baseline resources and institutional memory by incorporating the information and analysis provided to them by professional advocates. The key factor for government decision-makers and other government issue stakeholders is the extent to which substantive and issue specific contributions advocates provide improve the quality and applicability of government decisions. Professional advocates must also trust government officials who receive information from company or industry advocates that would negatively impact competition between companies or US industry vs. international competitors. Thus, trustworthiness is defined when the parties demonstrate that their contributions reflect the characterizations associated with equation variables.

(C) CREDIBILITY (5) + (Rs) RESPECT (5) +(R) RELIABILITY (5) + (E) EXPERTISE (5) + (I) INTIMACY (5) / (S) SELF INTEREST (1) = TRUST (25)

The equation's variables are defined as follows:

1. **Credibility** – Must be characterized by a transparent presentation of accurate information supporting issue alternatives for decision-makers; also, clarity associated with the advocates intent when seeking to influence decision-makers. Likewise, government recipients of proprietary or competitively sensitive information must maintain confidentiality requested by advocates;

2. **Respect** – Must be demonstrated towards government decision-makers and other issue stakeholders whether they support the advocate's preferred alternative or not. Likewise, government officials must be respectful and objective toward all issue stakeholders;

---

[1] Simpson, Jeffery. *Psychological Foundations of Trust*. University of Minnesota. Current Directions in Psychological Science. Volume 16 –Number 5, 2007.

[2] The Trust Equation is based on the work of Charles H. Green, noted author and trust expert. Charles H. Green, David Maister, and Robert Galford co-authored the best selling business book *The Trusted Advisor* in 2000.

3. **Reliability** – Must be characterized by consistent and accurate issue analysis presented to decision-makers at all times. Likewise, government officials must maintain analytical integrity and sourcing of data internal to the government's decision-making processes;

4. **Expertise** – Must be characterized by an advocate's comprehensive command of the subject matter inclusive of knowledge characterizing opposing alternatives and other positions during presentations to decision-makers and stakeholders. Likewise, government officials must be transparent in articulating gaps in their expertise and understanding of information presented to them;

5. **Intimacy** – Must be characterized by genuineness in the delivery of the issue analysis as well as the rationale for recommendations reflecting both sensitivity and respect toward other stakeholders and government officials involved in the decision process. Likewise, government officials must be direct in communicating what can and cannot be shared during the process with professional advocates; and,

6. **Self interest** – Must be characterized by transparency in the disclosure of the advocate's self-interests. This must be juxtaposed with a demonstrated understanding of the decision-maker's statutory, regulatory, and operational requirements for achieving successful outcomes within the government's mission. This includes ensuring that government officials are well informed and have credible analysis of the alternatives that facilitate equitable decision-making associated with issues. Likewise, government decision-makers must articulate where their institutional data base conflicts with industries' or analytical impacts counter-intuitive to industries' analysis.

Government officials must communicate that their goal is always to improve the delivery of goods and services and to enhance the quality of life for the American public.

Each variable of the equation is measured on a numerical performance scale ranging from 1 to 5 regardless as to whether the application is to government stakeholders receiving information or advocates receiving information from the government:

1. No characterization;
2. Characterization below stakeholder expectations;
3. Characterization representing stakeholder expectations;
4. Characterization exceeding stakeholder expectations; and,
5. Characterization exceeding stakeholder expectations for balance, substance, and comprehensiveness.

The self interest variable is measured on the same scale of 1 to 5, notwithstanding differing criteria:

1. Characterized by complete transparency and disclosure of interests;
2. Characterized by some straightforwardness with factual disclosure of interests;
3. Characterized by limited and subjective disclosure of interests;

4. Characterized by biased and "spun" disclosure of interests; and,
5. Characterized by being self-serving and misleading in the disclosure of interests.

The extent to which stakeholders perform within the parameters of the performance scale when applying the characteristics related to each variable enhances a government or advocate stakeholder's ability to balance their evaluation and associated trust.

Trust Metrics

The following metrics outline how the professional advocacy community builds trust with government decision-makers and how government officials build trust with advocates and the American public:

1. **Meet personally to identify subject issues** – Advocates and government decision-makers, when meeting personally, gain a greater understanding of their respective decision criteria. Government officials rely on their institutional perspective as the issue baseline for status quo. Advocates provide government decision-makers with the materials and analytical support necessary to justify change. During in-person meetings, verbal articulation and body language is critical to accurately evaluating how invested one is in their current position on an issue. The government's issue position versus the advocate's must consider an analysis of alternatives.

    This metric is applicable to both of the professional advocacy community and government officials alike. Meeting face-to-face with issue stakeholders facilitates both parties' capability to gather intelligence and provide the most up-to-date and accurate information to one another;

2. **Conduct appropriate research on the government's priorities and other issue stakeholders** – Advocates and government officials must demonstrate their respective commitment to improve the government's delivery of services and the quality of life of the American public. The goal is to motivate issue stakeholders to be open to change when there is compelling evidence. Advocates present alternative approaches, and address why their alternatives positively and constructively impact a governmental policy or program. Finally, decision-makers must address their assessment of each stakeholder's positions or perspectives associated with their impact on the government's decision-making process;

3. **Develop issues from each position perspective** – Advocates and government decision-makers must evaluate each alternative approach to an issue and ensure that there is both transparency and full disclosure in the decision-making process. Written and verbal presentations must be clear and should never blame the government for maintaining status quo; rather, the objective is

to utilize new information and analysis to articulate the reasons for adopting a new approach that improves the cost/benefit and cost efficiency for American taxpayers.

4. **Articulate a path forward that is positive and improves the quality of life for the American public** – Advocates and government officials must be committed to the proposition that changes in government policy benefit the public's quality of life. Support for a change from status quo requires a comprehensive justification and quantification of benefits compared with other credible alternatives. Clear statements regarding what will be accomplished must be addressed in accurate and concise language. Government officials are entrusted by the American public to make rational improvements using objective information. They are responsible for ensuring that enacted policy is in the public's best interest; and,

5. **Issue stakeholders clearly explain what is at stake if status quo continues** – This addresses each aspect of the issue including social, economic and political implications to government decision-makers. If a decision-maker is to justify a change, interagency stakeholders must take into consideration the stakes and risks associated with maintaining status quo. To facilitate the change, government decision-makers must consider the needs of the public and evaluate the information they receive from advocates objectively. This promotes trustworthy and ethical interactions between all parties.

Each professional advocate's campaign begins because new information has highlighted issues associated with the status quo of a governmental policy or program. This metric recognizes the stakeholder's position and demonstrates to them the potential to facilitate winning strategies and produce issue resolution alternatives.

The Principles of Trust

The core component of building positive relationships between advocates and government decision-makers is a mutual demonstration of trustworthiness. Trustworthiness relies on an advocate's ability to add value and government officials to be objective throughout the decision-making process. Stakeholders both evaluate each others' core beliefs, values, and principles when deciding whether an appropriate environment exists to address the issue of concern.

Government officials and advocates apply the trust metrics and tenants of the equation as the following principles of trust are realized:

1. **Stakeholders demonstrate sincerity in their approach** – Stakeholders accomplish objectives in the best interest of the American Public. Their mutual focus is the credibility of substantive arguments juxtaposed with the articulated

objectives associated with the issue. A relationship based on financial gain and the preservation of one's self-interest eventually dissolves;

2. **Listen attentively and share information** – All stakeholders must know that they are both heard and understood based on the merits of their respective positions. Again, honesty, openness, and transparency are the credo of the stakeholders. Open lines of communication via email, phone calls, written correspondences, and the participation in personal meetings so information flows easily, frequently, and in a timely manner;

3. **Use a collaborative approach and work together to accomplish objectives**– Whether a professional advocate, government decision-maker, or a stakeholder in the issue of concern, it is important that all participants in the advocacy campaign work together towards a common goal. This encourages trust and provides meaning for everyone to support throughout the advocacy campaign;

4. **Clearly communicate the expectations of your advocacy efforts** – Issue stakeholders and government decision-makers create clear goals and objectives to guide their advocacy campaigns. This ensures all parties are aware of each other's expectations and position. Each group is provided with adequate feedback to ensure the most beneficial result;

5. **Be transparent** – Transparency between government decision-makers and advocates facilitates healthy, trustworthy, and productive outcomes. Government decision-makers and the advocacy community rely on each other to provide accurate and peer reviewed information; and,

6. **Build a relationship; do not make a deal** – Relationships between advocates and government decision-makers are long lasting. Issues often evolve over time and stakeholders are in constant need of new information to ensure the policies and programs implemented are in the best interests of the American public.

TRUST EQUATION APPLIED

In order to validate the value of the equation to government decision-makers, the following examples are applied to the six variables and the California condor issue related analyses and alternatives discussed in preceding chapters.

> ### Baseline Advocate
>
> When an advocate for the California condor community addressed the government's inter-agency committee to provide information associated with the decrease in the California condor population, three alternatives to address the decline were presented: continue the condor breeding program in the wild, initiate condor captive breeding, or breed in the wild removing environmental hazards. The advocate's presentation was balanced, credible, and responsive to the government decision-makers questions and concerns. Based on the quantitative and qualitative evidence and analysis presented, government decision-makers considered new and unique aspects of the analyses in order to supplement, improve, and balance their decision-making process. The government's decision-maker measured the advocate's performance on the equation scale as follows:
>
> $C(5)+Rs(5)+R(5)+E(5)+I(5) / S(1) = Trust\ Score$
> $5+5+5+5+5/1 = 25$
>
> *The Baseline Advocate trust score is 25.*

The score validates that the baseline advocate focused on each of the alternatives. Further, the baseline advocate did not show support for one alternative or another. As a result, the numerical scale validates that the baseline advocate met the expectations of the government decision-maker. Further, the advocate could not be criticized for failing to be balanced in presenting information associated with the other alternatives. Finally, the advocate demonstrated sensitivity to other stakeholder positions as well as the government's institutional perspective. Collectively, the trust level is high.

Lobbying Advocate

When a lobbying advocate for the California condor community addressed the concerns of government executives involved in the condor protection program and the associated decision-making process, information associated with the decline in the California condor population was provided. The lobbyist's emphasis was to present compelling arguments to support a captive breeding program which would result in an increase in the condor's population. The lobbyist intent was to reinforce the benefits of captive breeding over the other alternatives while the discussion of the other alternatives was factual, their high costs and disadvantages were emphasized. The quantitative and qualitative evidence supporting the captive breeding program were both factual and transparent. The lobbyist also articulated why captive breeding was superior to the other alternatives. Finally, the lobbyist reinforced the cost/benefit of captive versus other alternatives. The advocate also described the successes and cost efficient budget experienced in similar captive habitat programs associated with reproduction of other endangered bird populations. However, no evidence associated with successes in other breeding approaches was presented. The government decision-maker measures the lobbyist's equation score as follows:

$C(4)+Rs(5)+R(4)+E(5)+I(5) / S(1) = Trust Score$

$4+5+4+5+5/1 = 23$

The lobbying advocate's trust score is 23.

Lobbying advocates seek to influence decision-makers towards one specific alternative. To enjoy a trust relationship with decision-makers, lobbyists must be transparent and disclose their biases and self-interests to government decision-makers and other stakeholders. If decision-makers are suspicious that the information provided does not represent an appropriate balance with information validating other alternatives, the trust is diminished. As is evident in this example, the equation performance scale is decreased because the lobbyist did little to balance the information presented. The only comprehensive presentation is the lobbyist's preferred alternative.

Education Advocate

When an education advocate for the California condor community addressed the government's biological experts, the results of their research to address variations in condor population impacts spanning 10 years were presented. The advocate opined that the decline in condor population was due to inclement weather, a reduction in natural food sources, and natural predators. The advocate's presentation followed strict adherence to research protocols and was submitted to peer review. In the delivery of the findings, there was no bias or position taken on the alternatives. Further, the advocate's presentation articulated the expertise and lack of concern associated with any of the government's potential decisions for future breeding of condors.

C(5)+Rs(5)+R(5)+E(5)+I(5) / S(1) = Trust Score

5+5+5+5+2/1 =25

The education advocate's trust score is equal to 25.

An education advocate informs and equips decision-makers and stakeholders with accurate, up-to-date, and objective information to facilitate the decision-making process. The example above demonstrates an education advocate meeting the expectations of decision-makers.

Government Decision-maker

Upon attending a committee meeting on the subject of the California condor declining population, the government decision-maker is trusted by the American Public to evaluate the information provided to them and make a decision. The evaluation process begins before the committee hearing. Over time, the government decision-maker has spoken to and met personally with stakeholders presenting various positions on what they believe is the best course of action to support the condor population. They evaluate the peer-reviewed information provided to them and reflect on their experiences with the advocacy communities. They objectively review the expert qualitative and quantitative information provided on the issue. The government official determination is based in the American public's best interest and one alternative is selected and announced to the public. The announcement articulates what policy implementation plans the FWS has decided on that will support efforts to increase the condor's declining population.

C(5)+Rs(5)+R(5)+E(5)+I(5) / S(1) = Trust Score

5+5+5+5+2/1 =25

The government decision-maker's trust score is equal to 25.

BASIS OF TRUST SCORES

The differences in trust scores reflect the manner and substance of data and information the advocate provides to government decision-makers and how the government official uses the information that is provided to them. Obviously, full and balanced disclosure inclusive of the sources and analysis delineating the relevance of the information improves the trust score.

Baseline advocates present a balanced, accurate, and clear analysis of each alternative. As a result their manner, substance, analysis, and transparency are reflected in their trust score. Government decision-makers are best served by baseline advocates when each alternative is comprehensively analyzed and each variable of the trust equation is applied and measured as articulated in the performance scale.

The most effective lobbying advocate ensures full disclosure with decision-makers based on straight forward communication of their interests, facts reinforcing each alternative, and credible analysis and delivery vehicles for decision-makers by which their perspective is reinforced. Obviously, any perceived lack of honesty or transparency increases the self interest variable lowering the overall score.

Education advocates differ from baseline and lobbying advocates in that their motivation and self interest leads them to research, uncover, and analyze the issue as comprehensively as possible within time parameters. They are also motivated to seek their colleague's validation and report their findings regardless of opposing views or political/situational preferences. As a result, their presentation of transparent and objective information is most important.

One of the most important actions for a decision-maker's evaluation of an advocate's trustworthiness is their previous experiences. As critical as the advocate's performance in presenting of information. Finally, decision-makers deem certain variables more significant than others. For instance, if there is a pre-existing relationship between the decision-maker and the advocate, the decision-maker's trust score will be biased based on whether the relationship was judged good or bad. The variables in the equation are useful to gauge trustworthiness in these circumstances.

Be mindful that any increase in self interest associated with deception, or the presentation of inaccurate information, decreases the trustworthiness of all professional advocates. When properly juxtaposed, the advocate that demonstrates the most transparency, honesty, openness, and respect given the decision-maker's role in the process is likely judged the most trustworthy. Advocates and government officials driven by self interests have a low trust/success ratio when applied to their interface with stakeholders.

Trust is based on the professional relationship between advocates and government decision-makers. The trust level is dictated by an advocate's earned credibility, validity and reliability of the information provided in the decision-making process along with characterizing respect to others and the system while providing full disclosure of any self serving interests of the advocate. Over time, as advocates and government officials apply the variables in the trust equation, opposing stakeholders and government decision-makers increase their perceived trustworthiness ratings.

Chapter 12

Public Demand Characteristics

Determining the Public's Perception

This chapter examines how public perception impacts the professional advocacy community and the government's decision-making apparatus. The public views the government and government decision-makers, negatively. Decision-makers often receive requests for information (FOIA) and inquiries concerning issues of interest during and after the decision-making process from the public. The public is suspicious about the information the government relies on to make decisions associated with changes to policies and regulations. To combat this, government decision-makers must utilize the most objective, current, and up-to-date information to justify any changes to the status-quo.

Generally, there are three aspects of the public's impact on public policy that we know to be accurate:

1. The public, overall, holds congress and government decision-makers in low esteem; demonstrated by the fact that in 2014 the public's approval rating of Congress was an average of 14%;[1]

---

[1] http://www.politifact.com/truth-o-meter/statements/2014/nov/11/facebook-posts/congress-has-11-approval-ratings-96-incumbent-re-e/. Report averaged the results of five different polls: Fox News, CBS News, CNN/ORC, ABC News/ Washington Post, and NBC News/Wall Street Journal.

2. The public, overall, trusts their congress person to protect the interests of their district or state enough that in 2014 the house and senate saw at 95% reelection rate[2]; and,

3. The public, overall, is the single most influential factor in facilitating changes in public policy.

A 2012 study conducted at Michigan State University published in the journal of *Interest Groups & Advocacy* aggregated information from 268 sources and reviewed the history of domestic policy making across 14 domestic policy issue areas from 1945-2004. The study concluded that the most commonly credited form of influence on domestic policy issues is general support and lobbying by advocacy organizations.

The study concluded that interest groups or representatives and organizations that are part of the professional advocacy community are involved in significant policy enactments quite often.

Figure 12.0

	Interest Groups Credited for the Change	Percentage of The Total Significant Actions
Significant New Laws Passed	279	54.80
Significant Executive Orders	31	41.30
Significant Administrative Agency Rules	35	39.30
Significant Judicial Decisions	46	36.80

Policy historians credit public interest groups and their representatives with playing a significant role in government decision-making. Interest group activities are often the most significant factor in successful advocacy campaigns. This is particularly relevant when combined by public events, media coverage, inter-agency meetings or deliberations,and the support of specific policymakers.

The following tables repors how interest groups and their representatives support policy changes. Specific organizations and coalitions are often cited as influential in policy deliberation.

---

[2] http://www.politifact.com/truth-o-meter/statements/2014/nov/11/facebook-posts/congress-has-11-approval-ratings-96-incumbent-re-e/. In 2014, 373/386 incumbents in the House were reelected, and in the 2014 Senate election 23/26 incumbents won reelection.

Figure 12.1

Tactic	Percentage of Policy Enactments Associated With Tactic
General Support	22.15
Congressional Lobbying	16.08
Constituent Pressure	9.37
Report Issued	9.11
New Group Mobilizes	6.08
Group Switch Sides	3.16
Protest	2.91
Resource Advantage	1.65

Figure 12.2

Tactic	Percentage of Policy Enactments Associated With Type of Influential Group
Advocacy Group	33.8
Business Interest	19.75
Academic	10.63
Professional Association	6.58
Union	6.2
Think Tank	1.9
Foundation	1.27

The two polls below illustrate the uphill battle that government decision-makers face when justifying a decision to the public. The public believes that the government relies on biased information provided by special interest groups. The result is the public's low approval rate associated with governance.

Figure 12.3

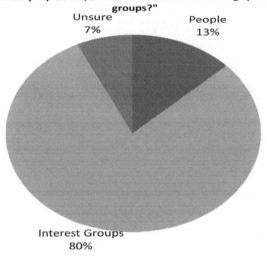

"Do you think most members of Congress are more interested in serving the people they represent, or more interested in serving special interest groups?"

Figure 12.4

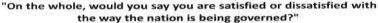

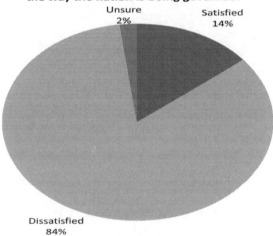

"On the whole, would you say you are satisfied or dissatisfied with the way the nation is being governed?"

The public is influenced by focus groups and polling data which the media reports and *spins* in order to heighten public awareness on high profile or controversial issues within the government's area of responsibility.

Thus, the public often has the wrong perspective. Professional advocates monitor the media's *spin* and perspective on significant public policy issues relevant to their objectives. They use the media's *spin* and focus group and poll data when it coincides with their point-of-view. Professional advocates also initiate grassroots campaigns and organize public relation's (PR) events to highlight their perspective on issues. Thus, public perception, colored by both events and the media has an impact on advocacy campaigns. The most dynamic evidence of the point is the effectiveness of grassroots advocacy campaigns and influence of the media on the general public.

A grassroots campaign utilizes local citizens' collective actions to effect change at local, regional, national, and international levels. These campaigns are bottom-up, rather than top-down movements. Advocates use PR events to mold media coverage. This dovetails with the media's perspective in an advocacy campaign.

Government decision-makers gauge many of their deliberations against the same polls and media stories that advocates do. Polls are often developed by professional advocates and financed by their clients seeking a particular outcome. This publication uses illustrative polls in our examples to state the point.

While the government denies that public perception is the significant driver impacting public policy and actions the government is responsible for, it is clear that the public's perception is a significant factor. Political considerations in the government's decision-making on issues and actions are often driven by the public's opinion. The impact of the public's perspective is evident when government decision-making is evaluated; especially, when elected or high profile Presidential appointees are involved and communicating decisions.

Polls consistently conclude that the American public believes that government decision-makers should pay closer attention to their views and their opinions on issues. The question is whether the public's knowledge of significant issues is objective and expert enough to result in effective public policy.

Figure 12.5

*If the leaders of our nation followed **the views of the public** more closely, do you think the nation would be better off, or worse off than it is today?*

	Postgraduate	College Grad	Some College	High School or less
Better Off	62%	69%	73%	78%
Worse Off	35%	24%	21%	17%
No Difference	3%	7%	6%	5%

Figure 12.6

*If the leaders of our nation followed **the views of public opinion polls** more closely, do you think the nation would be better off, or worse off than it is today?*

	Postgraduate	College Grad	Some College	High School or less
Better Off	44%	57%	57%	72%
Worse Off	47%	36%	35%	25%
No Difference	9%	7%	8%	3%

Figure 12.7

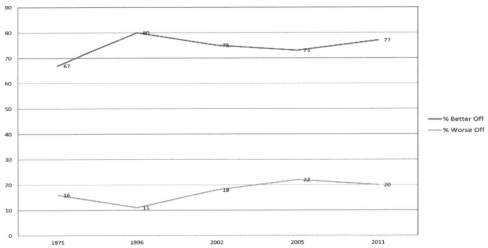

Polls measure the public's perception of the government, the professional advocacy community, and the companies and industries which comprise the private sector.

The following chart demonstrates that the American public does not understand the U.S. industry sectors role in the decision-making process; further, that government takes the brunt of the public's frustration:[3]

Americans Rate Computer Industry Best, Oil and Gas Worst. Frank Newport. August 16th, 2012. Gallup. http://www.gallup.com/poll/156713/americans-rate-computer-industry-best-oil-gas-worst.aspx

Figure 12.8

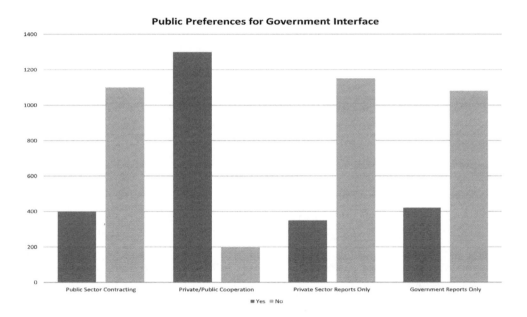

However, this poll is an indicator that the public does not realize that much of the professional advocacy sector is retained from the industries held in higher esteem than the government. Further the public does not know that professional advocates are retained to influence the government on industries' behalf. The public's lack of knowledge about the influence of professional advocacy community is unfortunate but a reality associated with the public policy development process.

Government decision-makers embrace the role of the professional advocacy community due to its provision of information, data, and analysis the government does not have. Government officials stated purpose is to improve the provision of government services and the public's quality of life.

The public is also unaware that government officials evaluate the objectivity of professional advocates' contributions to the decision-making process. This reality clearly improves government decision-makers' policy development process and ensures that the public's view of the U.S. industries is considered as they evaluate policy alternatives. Again, the government needs the most current analysis and information associated with issues they must address. In many cases, the information they need the most can only be provided by professional advocates familiar with an industry's unique issues. Information provided by subject matter experts from the industry sector is critical to ensure that the government's decisions encompass the unique needs/challenges of the impacted industries.

Similarly, effective government decision-makers evaluate the public's perspective and expectations to consider whether their input reinforces industry's position or challenges it. This is accomplished by releasing data and analysis that support the government's decision when it is contrary to the industry's perspective. The government develops its own information by funding experts or innovations in the private sector to conduct analyses on potential solutions. Decision-makers also analyze the politics of issues they are responsible for. This often assists them in the explaination of unpopular decisions to the American public thus outflanking advocates who attempt to leverage the process. When this occurs, the government typically makes the right decision. Independent data point out that members of Congress often vote based on significant campaign contributions mixed with credible advocacy materials. As discussed earlier, voters believe their own congressional representative is ethical, honest, and productive; however, voters believe the Congress as a whole is not. This belief often provides the Executive Branch with leverage over the Congress. This is most obvious when Congress opposes one of the President's priorities and loses to the President in the court of public opinion. When the President is able to prevail in a showdown with the Congress, his leverage with the public is obvious. This leverage is actualized by polls that conclude that 63% of likely voters believe Congress is performing poorly.

A Gallup poll from 2011 suggests that the public sometimes supports the government's decision-making that challenges their perspective that industry is more trustworthy than government decision-makers. This poll indicates that the public believes industry has too much power vis-a-vis the government. The poll asked the question below and the nationwide results are outlined in the Figure 12.9.

Figure 12.9

"Please indicate whether you think these entities have too much power, about the right amount of power, or not enough power."

Perceived Power of Major U.S. Societal Entities			
	Too Much	About Right	Not Enough
	%	%	%
Lobbyists	71	13	8
Major Corporations	67	21	9
Banks	67	23	8
Federal Government	58	30	9
Labor Unions	43	28	24
State Government	34	49	15
The Court System	34	49	14
Organized Religion	25	46	24
Municipal Government	22	53	21
The Military	14	53	28

Figure 12.10[4]

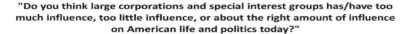

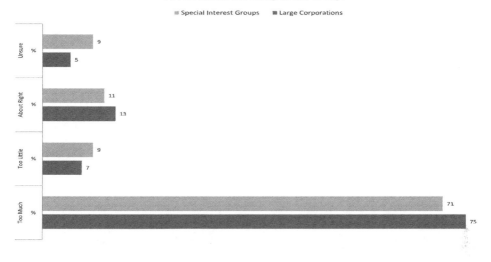

"Do you think large corporations and special interest groups has/have too much influence, too little influence, or about the right amount of influence on American life and politics today?"

While public trust in the government remains near historic lows, recent surveys reinforce the conclusion that only 24% of the public indicate they trust the government in Washington "always or most of the time".[5] Furthermore, the graph below confirms the trend of the decline of trust over the last 15 years. This mistrust of the government is associated with the public's perspective that special interests represented by lobbyists are too influential and the government's performance is unsatisfactory as a result.

Figure 12.11

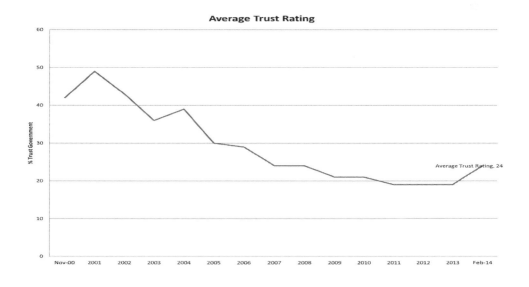

4 http://www.gallup.com/poll/147026/americans-decry-power-lobbyists-corporations-banks-feds.aspx
5 http://www.people-press.org/2014/11/13/public-trust-in-government/

Chapter 12: Public Demand Characteristics

Numerous polls cite the public's low opinion of government and lobbyists.[6]

Figure 12.12

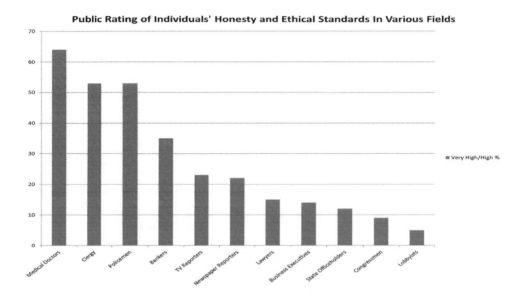

Baseline Advocacy

A baseline advocate working with the government's career staff often assists in developing policy alternatives to improve existing programs and/or provide solutions for failing government programs.   This type of advocacy campaign often goes unnoticed as it is categorized as routine interface between government officials and professional advocates; not as advocacy defined by the public. In this circumstance, those career officials are advocating and benefiting from up-to-date and comprehensive information. The information when evaluated often justifies changes to the status-quo. This approach ensures that their agency or department's performance improves sufficiently to justify stable or increased funding for the next fiscal year. Because this advocacy approach is not understood outside of the advocacy community, the public's allegations of bias against government decision-makers is not deserved but real in the public's eye nonetheless. Thus, baseline advocates helping to develop policy alternatives do not receive the brunt of what the public perceives as poor performance and bias.

---

[6] Lobbyists Debut at Bottom of Honesty and Ethics List. http://www.gallup.com/poll/103123/lobbyists-debut-bottom-honesty-ethics-list.aspx

For example, condor conservation advocates conducted a poll to determine how the public perceives the efforts that the Fish and Wildlife Service (FWS) have put towards protecting the California condor and its habitat. The results of the poll can be seen in Figure 12.13.

Clearly, the public believes that the FWS has performed inadequately at protecting the condor. Only 10% believe that the actions taken thus far are acceptable and are willing to support them. 80% of respondents believe that government actions are inadequate, or at least believe they can be improved.

Figure 12.13

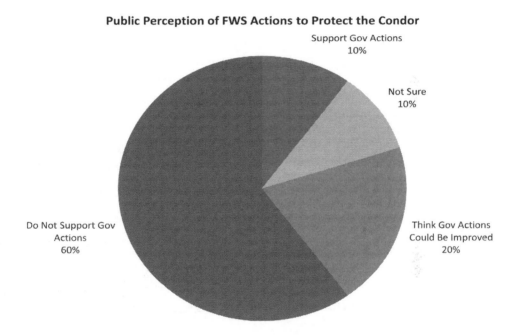

Public Perception of FWS Actions to Protect the Condor

Support Gov Actions 10%

Not Sure 10%

Do Not Support Gov Actions 60%

Think Gov Actions Could Be Improved 20%

Due to the public's protest and ranker over the decline of the condor population, the Assistant Secretary of the Department of Interior issued a memo that requests the FWS develop policy alternatives that will result in increasing the population of the California condor. This is a direct and political response to support change in the government's approach. Advocates who testify at hearings, organize grassroots support, and advertise about the plight of the condor provide strong fuel and mold media coverage to support the condor's protection and programs facilitating condor breeding. The result is to compel the FWS to take immediate action. This situation leverages the public's perspective to support the advocate's position to change the government's existing program or *status quo*.

Notwithstanding the advocate's objective, the FWS benefits by evaluating credible alternatives presented by baseline advocates. As emphasized earlier, baseline advocates collect the most up-to-date and accurate data available to develop policy options that meet the public's imperative. The data used to support the baseline advocate's policy alternatives are balanced and comprehensive. Experts conducted studies focused on the impact that lead poisoning has had on condor breeding in the wild, studies on the impact on condor habitat, impacts from wind farm accidents, analysis of the impacts of breeding statistics when condors are captive, or when the government promulgated condor specific environmental regulations or acquired additional habitat. The result is a better understanding of the condor's plight leading to an informed decision on the best approach to increase its population.

Baseline advocates must always address the American public's negative and biased perception of the government. They must also distinguish themselves as non-lobbyists. Occasionally, they work with the media to present the positive and constructive evaluation of issues by the government. They also often assist the government spin its response so the public has a more positive perception of both the government and correctness of the government's action. This is accomplished when advocates work the government's core of experts and managers. It is essential that government officials are educated on the objective and positive alternatives available to them. The government often contracts with qualified consultants or awards grants to develop corroborating evidence to the information that the government relies on from their *institutional memory*. Where the objectivity and comprehensive analysis can be associated with the government's decision-making process, the public's poor view of the government is neutralized. The policy alternatives proposed must be balanced and comprehensive, otherwise the public's perception of government bias would be justified. Even if the public does not have the knowledge to evaluate the objectivity, credibility, comprehensiveness, and value of the partnerships between the public and private sector experts, government decision-makers do. The interface between advocates and government officials is often the key variable for sound decision-making.

Figure 12.14

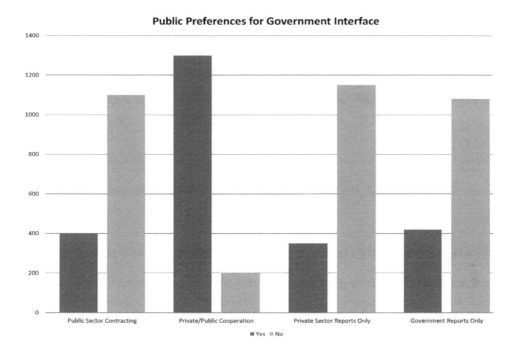

The poll above[7] represents how the public prefers government decision-makers receive information related to policy decisions that lead to the sustainability of the condor.[8] One can conclude from this example that members of the public believe their interests are best represented when the private and public sector work together on issues.

Lobbying Advocacy

Lobbying advocates can improve their standing with the public as well as their relationships with government decision-makers. The key is adopting the ethics and transparency metrics associated with their advocacy campaigns. As the polls suggest, even lobbying advocates that have proven to be ethical and honest among their counterparts and peers continue to fight an "*up-hill*" battle against negative public perception.

For example, the San Diego Zoo's CEO reads the Assistant Secretary's memo regarding the California condor issue. The Zoo hires a lobbying advocate with a relationship with the Assistant Secretary to make the case for moving condors from the wild to the Zoo. The lobbyist conducts their own public poll and identifies the following results:[9]

[7] Poll is illustrative to the point.

[8] The poll utilizes the following 4 questions: (1)Do you prefer the government only contract the private sector through grants and research to conduct studies on the condor to make their policy decision? (2) Do you prefer the government work alongside the private sector to gain insight into various stakeholder positions to make their policy decision? (3) Do you prefer the government only use information provided by the private sector regarding the condor issue to make their policy decision? (4) Do you prefer the government use only the data and reports they have conducted themselves relative to the condor to make their policy decision.

[9] Poll is illustrative to the point.

Figure 12.15

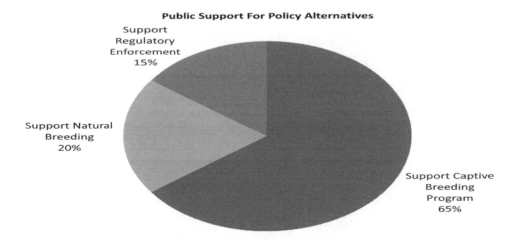

The lobbyist's objective is to make the case that if the government orders the condor into a captive breeding program it would result in an increase in the condor population. The lobbyist's emphasis would not be to present a balanced presentation toward the other two viable alternatives. Lobbyists that are ethical in representations to the government will be especially transparent in delineating the cons of the captive breeding program. By presenting the cons of the program, the other alternatives could be accurately addressed.

The lobbyist, using public polling results, will likely target the media and apply a grassroots methodology to recruit average citizens and friends of the zoo to build public support and apply constructive pressure on the government. Remember, the lobbyist's objective is to win the issue, notwithstanding the viability of the other two alternatives. The lobbyist was honest and transparent in the admission that the other alternatives were not fully explained nor subjected to a cost/benefit analysis. In this case, the lobbyist was invisible to the public; there was grassroots support from media stories highlighting the benefits that captive breeding was effective.

When the government decision-makers weighed the public's perceptions, the benefits of the captive breeding alternative, and compared them with the costs/benefits of the other alternatives, the decision was captive breeding. The lobbyist provided compelling data and analysis to formulate the government's public statement. The biases were masked by the emphasis and spin associated with the captive breeding program. Public perception associated with the government's action was positive and the Assistant Secretary's credibility was also validated.

Education Advocacy

Education advocates qualify as experts based on academia's consensus criteria. These advocates apply their expertise to address the substantive issues that is a part of any credible alternative. Both baseline and lobbying advocates use data and analysis developed by the expert education advocates. Education advocates do not focus on a specific alternative, rather they focus on specific issues bearing on alternatives.

Figure 12.2 illustrates that professionals and education advocates are viewed differently from lobbyists. Education advocates are accepted by the public as experts. As such they are perceived differently and not vilified because they are biased.

The public's perception of education advocates is more positive. The public judges an advocate's credentials and expertise. The public believes that the factual conclusions attributed to an expert's research are more credible than another stakeholder's position on a comprehensive alternative.

For example, the Assistant Secretary's staff's Ornithologist is an expert. Thus, an Ornithologist's study on the condor, such as the illustrative one detailed below, would be relied upon when the government reports or testifies on an issue.[10] The Ornithologist's conclusion that the most successful breeding environments for California condors is in captivity would be significant to government decision-makers.

Figure 12.16

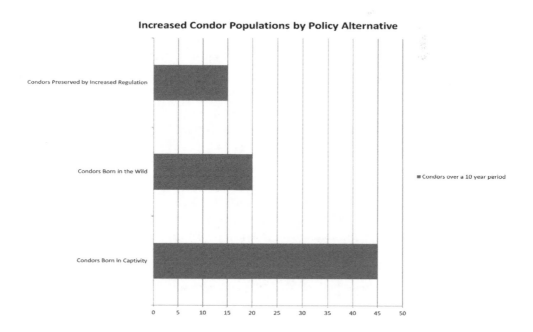

_____
[10] This study is illustrative to the point.

Conversely, if the same Ornithologist reported or testified that the most successful breeding environment was in the wild, that result would be similarly significant. Unless the Ornithologist crosses the line to articulate their bias for the wild or captive breeding alternative, their role in the decision-making process is considered ethical and honest by the public. Thus, the education advocate's role is only to present their expert conclusions on issues to government decision-makers. The public and the decision-makers gain new knowledge and understanding through the eyes of an expert, and are therefore equipped to make a better decision.

Government Decision-makers

Government decision-makers are impacted by public perception. In this example, the California condor issue was the result of a grassroots campaign organized by advocates. The lobbyist advocate utilized the media and organized local citizens around a singular alternative sought by their client. However, baseline advocates developed new information and alternatives in a balanced approach. This approach did not narrowly focus on a singular solution. Education advocates performed credible research studies focused on the controversial issues involving condor breeding. However, none of the alternatives were recommended by the education advocate. All of these approaches and categories of advocacy can occur simultaneously and benefit the government's decision-making process.

As discussed earlier, the Assistant Secretary tasked the FWS to evaluate and recommended a decision which would be viewed by the public as appropriate and credible. The government's senior management ensures that the career bureaucracies as well as program decision-makers understand how to gauge public perception and judge the public's role in decision-making. The training on how to evaluate the public role and apply it in decision-making is specialized. For instance, training on how to use issue specific studies, how to judge polls and television ratings, and other "how to" like presentations is utilized. Further, there is mandatory course work, such as leadership and participation in selected external groups representing both pro and con positions. All of this is to ensure sensitivity to public expectations and make decisions reflecting the interests of the American public.

In this example, the FWS reports to the Assistant Secretary's Office that it is their recommendation that the federal government proposes and implements a captive breeding program. FWS recommends an approach to the staff of the Assistant Secretary. The staff's recommendation is based on a balanced and comprehensive policy analysis. The review materials are diverse and comprehensive. Thus, even bias from advocates or other stakeholders is taken into account during the decision-making process. The advocates in the condor matter considered all of the external and internal variables prior to the Assistant Secretary's final decision and public announcement. In our example, the program secured funding for a captive breeding program designed to increase the California condor population; all of which is consistent with the approaches discussed in previous chapters.

Benefits to the Public

Advocacy is necessary for the success of the government's decision-making apparatus. A benefit is derived by informing public representatives about what issues the public has concerns for. Moreover, through this awareness, it places pressure for continued or new support and funding from the federal government. Absent, it can mean that even the best intended and most thoroughly analyzed policies may not receive the level of support necessary for federal implementation ultimately under serving the public.

Advocacy also makes significant contributions to the democratic process. It assists the government in the development of public policies that are accountable to public interest and concern. Advocacy encourages the mobilization of citizen's involvement and is often seen as a cornerstone of a democratic culture.

Advocates distill the abundance of information relating to public policy issues. Although political and career officials have support staff, they have limited time and resources to research and analyze all information relating to a particular issue. Baseline, lobbying, and education advocates gather information, review and analyze data, and explain the advantages and disadvantages of various policy alternatives expediting the decision-making process. Additionally, advocacy campaigns save public funds. The work conducted by advocates to solicit and collect data, garner public opinion, and organize detailed analysis is privately funded and often serves to the benefit of educating decision-makers on issues of public interest.

Chapter 12: Public Demand Characteristics

Chapter 13

Advocacy Directory

This chapter provides a diverse listing of organizations that advocate varying perspectives on public policy issues to the government. Their intent is to influence public policies and associated issues through baseline, lobbying, and education advocacy activities.

I. **BOUTIQUE CONSULTING FIRMS SPECIALIZING IN ADVOCACY**
    – These are companies that are staffed by experts in specific practice areas. The experts are both experienced and academically trained in their area of specialty. Their unique skill set requires a thorough understanding of analytical methods and substance included in presentations intended to influence the government's decision-making process.

    1.   The Brattle Group

Address: 1850 M St. NW, #1200, Washington, DC 20036

Phone: (202) 955-5050

The Brattle Group provides clients with answers to complex economic, regulatory, and financial questions. Brattle advises corporations, law firms, and governments around the world.

2. The Chartis Group

Address: 120 East 23rd St. Fifth Floor, New York, NY 10010

Phone: (877) 667-4700

Founded in 2001 with the mission to materially improve the delivery of healthcare in the world. The Chartis Group is the largest national advisory services firm dedicated to the healthcare industry. The firm is comprised of 250 senior healthcare professionals and consultants who apply a deep knowledge of healthcare economics, markets, clinical models, technology and organizational dynamics to help clients achieve unequaled results.

3. Eagle Hill Consulting

Address: 241 18th St. Suite #615, Arlington, VA 22202

Phone: (703) 229-8600

A family-run, woman-owned company, Eagle Hill Consulting serves clients in three distinct sectors: financial services, public service, and communications, media and technology.

4. Green Strategies

Address: 816 Connecticut Ave NW, #200, Washington, DC 20006

Phone: (202) 328-1123

Green Strategies provides its client base with decades of experience working inside and with key decision makers within the environmental and energy worlds. Green Strategies helps clients build strategies and relationships to create value and solve problems.

5. Insight Sourcing Group

Address: 5555 Triangle Pkwy NW, #300, Norcross, GA 30092

Phone: (770) 446-9890

Founded in 2002, Insight Sourcing Group is a consulting firm that focuses exclusively on strategic sourcing and procurement. Led by alumni of some of the world's top consulting firms, including the likes of Accenture, Deloitte and McKinsey. Around half of the firm's clients are in the private equity industry, where Insight Sourcing Group has developed a reputation for its ability to improve valuations.

      6.   Jabian Consulting

Address: 14643 North Dallas Pkwy, Suite 620, Dallas, TX 75254

Phone: (855) 452-2426

A local consultancy with offices in Atlanta, Dallas and Charlotte. The firm was founded in 2006. Jabian focuses on the big picture challenges, including business strategies, customer interaction, human capital management, operational excellence, and technology optimization and execution.

      7.   Scott Madden Management Consultants

Address: 3495 Piedmont Road, NE Building Ten, Suite 805, Atlanta, GA 30305

Phone: (404) 814-0020

A management consulting firm that operates in four main practice areas: energy, grid transformation, clean tech and sustainability, and corporate and shared services as well as contracts with the federal government.

II. CONSULTING FIRMS SPECIALIZING IN ADVOCACY – These firms have an experienced workforce that assist issue stakeholders on a wide variety of topics and industry sectors. The companies are specialized in working with both the private sector and government defined needs.

      1.   Accenture

Address: 1629 K St. NW, Washington, DC 20006

Phone: (703) 947-2000

A multinational management consulting, technology services, and outsourcing company which has also developed a federal services practice. Accenture Federal Services delivers solutions that help federal agencies seize opportunities to deliver public service for the future. Clients trust their staff to help them address the growing complexity of mission and citizen demands. With 5800 dedicated U.S. employees, Accenture Federal Services helps agencies shatter the status quo, achieve enduring efficiencies, and deliver results that matter to their missions and the country. Accenture

Federal Services is a long-time and trusted partner in the federal community. Every cabinet level agency in the United States—and 30 of the country's largest federal government agencies—has worked with Accenture Federal Services to achieve meaningful outcomes and high performance.

2. Booz Allen Hamilton

Address: 901 15th St. NW, Washington, DC 20005

Phone: (202)898-3310

Has a marketing and public affairs department with years of federal experience in obtaining federal contracts.

3. Deloitte Consulting, LLP

Address: 80 M St. SE, Suite 610, Washington, DC 20003

Phone: (202) 777-1230

A British multinational professional services firm headquartered in New York City in the U.S. Deloitte is one of the "Big Four" and the second largest professional services network in the world by revenue and largest by the number of professionals. Deloitte provides audit, tax, consulting, enterprise risk and financial advisory services with more than 225,400 professionals in over 150 countries. The company currently has a total of 46 global member firms and in FY 2015, earned a record $35.2 billion USD in revenues.

4. Ernst & Young

Address: 1101 New York Ave NW, Washington, DC 20005

Phone: (202) 327-6000

A multinational professional services firm headquartered in London, United Kingdom and is the third largest professional services firm in the world by aggregated revenue in 2014. The organization operates as a network of member firms which are separate legal entities in individual countries. It has 212,000 employees in over 700 offices around 150 countries in the world. It provides assurance (including financial audit), tax, consulting and advisory services to companies.

5. Pricewaterhouse Coopers (PwC)

Address: 1301 K St. NW, #800W, Washington, DC 20005

Phone: (202) 414-1000

A multinational professional services network. It is the largest professional services firm in the world. PwC understands the challenges facing government officials. From defining effective requirements to measuring accountability and performance, PwC's consultants are trusted advisors to the public sector. PwC delivers advisory services that support the government's move toward a more citizen-centric, performance-based delivery model. As the public sector strives to meet the demands of its citizens, changes are required in developing and supporting department-wide strategies, managing risk and compliance, and harnessing business intelligence and analytical capabilities. PwC's advisory professionals bring direct hands-on knowledge of public sector standards for systems, internal controls and financial reporting.

6. KPMG

Address: 1801 K St. NW, Suite 12000, Washington, DC 20006

Phone: (202) 533-3000

A professional service company, being one of the Big Four auditors, along with Deloitte, EY and PwC. Its global headquarters is located in Amsterdam, the Netherlands. KPMG employs 162,000 people and has three lines of services: audit, tax, and advisory. Its tax and advisory services are further divided into various service groups. The name "KPMG" was chosen when KMG (Klynveld Main Goerdeler) merged with Peat Marwick.

III. **Research Institutes at Leading Universities** – These organizations are usually federally funded and supplemented with privately funded research dollars depending on the issues the institute specializes in. Their peer review products provide valuable objective data analysis for government decision-makers and other issue stakeholders.

1. Massachusetts Institute Technology (MIT)

Address: 77 Massachusetts Ave, Cambridge, MA 02139

Phone: (617) 253-1000

Founded in 1861 MIT is a private research university. Its research institutions include Picower Institute for Learning and Memory, MIT Kavli Institute for Astrophysics and Space Research. The Picower Institute for Learning and Memory is an independent research entity within MIT's School of Science. Picower Institute consists of a diverse array of brain scientists who are dedicated to unraveling the mechanisms that drive the quintessentially human capacities to remember and learn, as well as to explore related functions like perception, attention, and consciousness. Their research ranges from explorations of the most basic biological interactions of genes and proteins to in-depth examinations of cellular and systemic mechanisms.

The MIT Kavli Institute for Astrophysics and Space Research (MKI) is an interdepartmental center that supports research in space science and engineering, astronomy, and astrophysics. MKI plays a leading role in the design, construction, and utilization of instruments placed aboard space vehicles launched by NASA or other agencies..

2.   University of California at Los Angeles (UCLA)

Address: 695 Charles E Young Dr S, Los Angeles, CA 90095

Phone: (310) 825-5061

UCLA is widely known for supporting its research institutes and centers with over $1billion in funding since 2010. The university currently boasts over 350 research labs, centers, and institutes. From the beginning UCLA has made some of the world's greatest discoveries, from the invention of the internet, to reporting and classifying the first AIDS case in 1981.

3.   John Hopkins University

Address: 3400 N Charles St. Baltimore MD, 21218

Phone: (410)-516-4624

John Hopkins University is the nation's first research institute. There are many research opportunities at JHU that offer a variety of opportunities in exciting fields of research. The universitie's Silcio O. Conte Center, which is located at the Maryland Psychiatric Research Center (MPRC), provides students opportunities to conduct neuroscience research in preclinical and clinical laboratories, participate in a didactic lecture series, ethics discussions with faculty, literature journal club, and career development seminars.

4.   Texas A&M University

Address: 400 Bizzell St. College Station, TX 77840

Phone: (979)845-3211

Texas A&M provides much needed extensive research on the agricultural issues of today. Currently, there are 13 research centers with over 1,700 employees, over 500 of which are doctoral-level scientists. The researchers at A&M strive to maintain a traditional connection to farming and ranching, while developing crops with enhanced nutrition, discovering innovative renewable energy resources, and implementing new methods to improve air and water quality. This vast research organization serves all 254 counties in Texas and has 15 facilities around the state.

5. Princeton University

Address: 87 Prospect Ave, 3rd floor, Princeton, NJ 08544

Phone: (609) 258-3000

Princeton University contains over 75 research institutions across the following area which include Engineering and Applied Science, Humanities, Natural Sciences, Social Sciences. Their research facilities include the Small Molecule Screening Center, Survey Research Center, Mirco/Nano Fabrication Laboratory to name a few.

6. California Institute for Technology (CALTECH)

Address: 1200 E California Blvd, Pasadena, CA 91125

Phone: (626) 395-6811

Caltech research facilities are known for their scientific inquiry. The university has a variety of research centers currently active that cover multidisciplinary topics. Its Engineering department and Applied Science field offer many exciting research opportunities

7. Yale University

Address: New Haven, CT 06520

Phone Number: 203-937-3802

Along with being one of the most prestigious Universities in the nation, Yale also is one of its leading research institutes. Their leading research institute includes the Arts, Humanities and Social Sciences, Medical & Health Sciences, Science & Engineering.

8. Cornell University

Address: Ithaca, NY 14850

Phone Number: (607) 254-4636

Cornell University has over 150 research centers, institute, laboratories, and programs. These programs span across an extensive array of topics which includes energy, global labor, neuroscience , cancer, social justice, nutrition, sustainability and many more.

The university boasts two national research centers, Cornell High Energy Synchrotron Source (CHESS) and Cornell NanoScale Facility (CNF).

9.   Georgia Institute of Technology

Address: North Ave NW, Atlanta, GA 30332

Phone Number: (404) 894-2000

Georgia Tech is home to 13 diverse core research areas. The areas range from Bioengineering and Bioscience to Robotics and systems.

10. Emory University

Address: 201 Dowman Dr. Atlanta, GA 30322

Phone number: (404) 727-6123

The university is home to the Woodruff Health Sciences Center, and the Yerkes National Primate Research Center, which specializes on research based in its school of medicine, nursing, and public health. Through its multidisciplinary studies they also have the Institute for Advanced Policy Solutions along with the Emory/Georgia Tech Predictive Health Institute.

IV. **THINK TANKS** – A body of experts that base their advice and ideas on specific political or economic issues that are based on credible and balanced analysis on issues of concern to government decision-makers and issue stakeholders.

1.   American Enterprise Institute for Public Policy Research

Address: 1150 17th St. NW, Washington, D.C. 20036

Phone: (202) 862-7177

AEI is a private, nonpartisan, not-for-profit institution dedicated to research and education on issues of government, politics, economics and social welfare. AEI's purpose is to serve leaders and the public through research and education on the most important issues of the day. AEI research is conducted through seven primary research divisions: Economics, Foreign and Defense Policy, Politics and Public Opinion, Education, Health, Energy and the Environment and Society and Culture.

2.   American Foreign Policy Council

Address: 509 C St. NE, Washington, DC 20002

Phone: (202) 543-1006

For over three decades, the American Foreign Policy Council (AFPC) has played an essential role in the U.S. foreign policy debate. Founded in 1982, AFPC is a 501(c) (3) non-profit organization dedicated to bringing information to those who make or influence the foreign policy of the U.S. and to assisting world leaders with building democracies and market economies. AFPC is widely recognized as a source of timely, insightful analysis on issues of foreign policy, and works closely with members of Congress, the Executive Branch and the policymaking community. It is staffed by noted specialists in foreign and defense policy, and serves as a valuable resource to officials in the highest levels of government.

3.   Arms Control Association

Address: 1313 L St. NW, Suite 130, Washington, DC 20005

Phone: (202) 463-8270

Since 1971, the Arms Control Association (ACA) is proud to have played a part in advancing and securing major arms control and nonproliferation successes that have helped avoid bad situations from becoming much worse. The Arms Control Association has shown it can deliver authoritative information, ideas, and analysis that help shape the public policy debate in Washington, across the U.S., and around the world.

4.   Asia Society Policy Institute

Address: 1300 I St. NW, Suite 400E, Washington, DC 20005

Phone: (202) 833-2742

Asia Society is the leading educational organization dedicated to promoting mutual understanding and strengthening partnerships among peoples, leaders and institutions of Asia and the U.S. in a global context. Across the fields of arts, business, culture, education, and policy, the Society provides insight, generates ideas, and promotes collaboration to address present challenges and create a shared future.

Founded in 1956 by John D. Rockefeller 3rd, Asia Society is a nonpartisan, nonprofit institution with headquarters in New York, centers in Hong Kong and Houston, and offices in Los Angeles, Manila, Mumbai, San Francisco, Seoul, Shanghai, Sydney, Washington, DC and Zurich.

5.   Atlantic Council of the U.S.

Address: 1030 15th St. NW, Washington, DC 20005

Phone: (202) 778-4952

The Atlantic Council promotes constructive leadership and engagement in international affairs based on the Atlantic Community's central role in meeting global challenges. The Council provides an essential forum for navigating the dramatic economic and political changes defining the twenty-first century by informing and galvanizing its uniquely influential network of global leaders. Through the papers they write, the ideas they generate, and the communities they build, the Council shapes policy choices and strategies to create a more secure and prosperous world.

6. Brookings Institute

Address: 1775 Massachusetts Ave NW, Washington, DC 20036

Phone: (202) 797-6000

An American think tank based on Embassy Row in Washington, D.C. One of Washington's oldest think tanks, Brookings conducts research and education in the social sciences, primarily in economics, metropolitan policy, governance, foreign policy, and global economy and development. In the University of Pennsylvania's *2014 Global Go To Think Tanks Report*, Brookings is ranked the most influential think tank in the world.

7. Carnegie Council on Ethics and International Affairs

Address: Merrill House, 170 East 64th St. New York, NY 10065

Phone: (212) 838-4120

Articles from Ethics & International Affairs, our peer-reviewed journal, are used in hundreds of classrooms in dozens of countries around the world. Carnegie Council's resources are featured in the international textbook World Politics: Trends & Transformation, used by over 200 colleges in 20 countries. The website is part of the U.S. Library of Congress collection of Public Policy Internet Materials. The Global Ethics Network connects educators and students from 113 countries, and includes theGlobal Ethics Fellows representing universities across five continents. Their weekly TV series, Global Ethics Forum, airs on several public television stations and on YouTube.

8. Carnegie Endowment for International Peace

Address: 1779 Massachusetts Ave NW, Washington, DC 20036

Phone: (202) 483-7600

A foreign-policy think tank with centers in Washington, D.C., Moscow, Beirut, Beijing, and Brussels. The organization describes itself as being dedicated to advancing cooperation between nations and promoting active international engagement by the United States. Founded in 1910 by Andrew Carnegie, its work is not formally associated with any political party. In the University of Pennsylvania's 2014 Global Go To Think Tanks Report, Carnegie is ranked the third most influential think tank in the world, after the Brookings Institution and Chatham House.

9. Cato Institute

Address: 1000 Massachusetts Ave NW, Washington, DC 20001

Phone: (202) 842-0200

An American libertarian think tank headquartered in Washington, D.C. It was founded as the Charles Koch Foundation in 1974 by Ed Crane, Murray Rothbard, and Charles Koch, chairman of the board and chief executive officer of the conglomerate Koch Industries. In July 1976, the name was changed to the Cato Institute. Cato was established to have a focus on public advocacy, media exposure, and societal influence.

10. Center for Defense Information

Address: 1779 Massachusetts Ave NW, #615, Washington, DC 20036

Phone: (202) 332-0900

The Center for Defense Information (CDI) is a nonprofit, nonpartisan organization based in Washington, DC. It specializes in analyzing and advising on military matters. CDI was founded in 1971 by an independent group of retired military officers including Adm. Gene La Rocque and Adm. Eugene Carroll. Formerly, CDI operated under the umbrella of the World Security Institute. In 2012, the World Security Institute closed, and CDI merged with the Project On Government Oversight (POGO). In addition, POGO continued the publication of *The Defense Monitor*.

11. Center for Global Development

Address: 2055 L St. NW, Fifth Floor, Washington, DC 20036

Phone: (202) 416-4000

The Center for Global Development (CGD) works to reduce global poverty and inequality through rigorous research and active engagement with the policy community to make the world a more prosperous, just, and safe place for us all.

The policies and practices of the rich and the powerful—in rich nations, as well as in the emerging powers, international institutions, and global corporations—have significant impacts on the world's poor people. CGD aim to improve these policies and practices through research and policy engagement to expand opportunities, reduce inequalities, and improve lives everywhere.

12. Center for Strategic and Budgetary Assessments

Address: 1667 K St. NW, Suite 900, Washington, DC 20006

Phone: (202) 331-7990

The Center for Strategic and Budgetary Assessments (CSBA) is an independent, nonprofit public policy research institute established to promote innovative thinking and debate about national security strategy, defense planning and military investment options for the 21st century.

CSBA's goal is to enable policymakers to make informed decisions in matters of strategy, security policy and resource allocation.

13. Center for Strategic and International Studies

Address: 1616 Rhode Island Ave NW, Washington, DC 20036

Phone: (202) 887-0200

Center for Strategic and International Studies is a bipartisan, nonprofit organization headquartered in Washington, D.C. The Center's 220 full-time staff and large network of affiliated scholars conduct research and analysis and develop policy initiatives that look to the future and anticipate change.

14. Center for the Study of Intelligence

Address: 1000 Colonial Farm Rd. McLean, VA 22101

Phone: (703) 482-0623

A division within the Central Intelligence Agency whose main duties included:

- The CSI publishes key documentary collections from the Cold War and conduct oral history projects. It produce monographs on CIA history and the history of intelligence and provides support for the State Department's Foreign Relations of the United States.

15. Council on Foreign Relations

Address: 1777 F St. NW, Washington, DC 20006

Phone: (202) 509-8400

The Council on Foreign Relations (CFR) is an independent, nonpartisan membership organization, think tank, and publisher. Each of these functions makes CFR an indispensable resource in a complex world.

16. East-West Institute

Address: 110 Maryland Ave NE, #511, Washington, DC 20002

Phone: (202) 544-9345

The East-West Institute works to reduce international conflict, addressing seemingly intractable problems that threaten world security and stability. They forge new connections and build trust among global leaders and influencers, help create practical new ideas, and take action through our network of global decision-makers. Independent and nonprofit since their founding in 1980, they have offices in New York, Brussels, Moscow, San Francisco and Washington, D.C.[1]

17. Eisenhower Institute

Address: 818 Connecticut Ave NW, #800, Washington, DC 20006

Phone: (202) 628-4444

Honoring the legacy of Dwight D. Eisenhower, the Eisenhower Institute is a distinguished center for leadership and public policy that prepares the successor generations to perfect the promise of the nation.

18. Heritage Foundation

Address: 214 Massachusetts Ave NE, Washington, DC 20002

Phone: (202) 546-4400

An American conservative think tank based in Washington, D.C. The foundation took a leading role in the conservative movement during the presidency of Ronald Reagan, whose policies drew significantly from Heritage's policy study Mandate for Leadership. Heritage has since continued to have a significant influence in U.S. public policy making, and is considered to be one of the most influential conservative research organizations in the U.S.

---

[1] See http://www.eastwest.ngo/about

19. Hoover Institute

Address: 1399 New York Ave NW, #500, Washington, DC 20005

Phone: (202) 760-3200

An American public policy think tank and research institution located at Stanford University in California. Its official name is the Hoover Institution on War, Revolution, and Peace. It began as a library founded in 1919 by Republican Herbert Hoover, before he became President of the United States. The library, known as the Hoover Institution Library and Archives, houses multiple archives related to Hoover, World War I, World War II, and other world history.[2]

20. International Crisis Group

Address: 1629 K St. NW Suite 450, Washington, DC 20006

Phone: (202) 785-1630

The International Crisis Group is an independent, non-profit, non-governmental organization committed to preventing and resolving deadly conflict.

21. Institute for Policy Studies

Address: 1112 16th St. NW, #600, Washington, DC 20036

Phone: (202) 234-9382

A think tank based in Washington, D.C. It has been directed by John Cavanagh since 1998. The organization focuses on U.S. foreign policy, domestic policy, human rights, international economics, and national security. The IPS is one of the five major, independent think tanks in Washington.

22. Lincoln Institute of Land Policy

Address: 113 Brattle St. Cambridge, MA 02138

Phone: (617) 661-3016

A think tank based in Cambridge, Massachusetts that was founded to promote the economic ideas of Henry George known as land value tax and Georgism, but the foundation now focuses more generally on the use, taxation, and regulation of land. It

---

[2] According to the *2014 Global Go To Think Tank Index Report* (Think Tanks and Civil Societies Program, University of Pennsylvania), Hoover is #19 (of 60) in the "Top Think Tanks in the United States."

conducts research and policy evaluations, holds conferences, provides education and training, supports demonstration projects, and publishes books and reports on policy issues relating to land. Its mission is to improve the quality of public debate about land by integrating theory and practice, and by providing a nonpartisan forum for the discussion of related issues.

23. National Bureau of Asian Research

Address: 1301 Pennsylvania Ave NW, #305, Washington, DC 20004

Phone: (202) 347-9767

An American nonprofit, research institution based in Seattle, Washington, with a branch office in Washington, D.C. The organization's mission is to inform and strengthen Asia-Pacific policy. Nationa Bureau of Asian Research (NBR) brings together specialists, policymakers, and business leaders to examine economic, strategic, political, globalization, health, and energy issues affecting U.S. relations with East, Central, Southeast and South Asia and Russia. Richard J. Ellings is the current president. Funding for NBR's research comes from NBR itself, foundations, corporations, government departments and agencies, and individuals. NBR undertakes a small amount of contract work for public and private sector organizations.

24. Nixon Center

Address: 1615 L St. NW, #1250, Washington, DC 20036

Phone: (202) 887-1000

Former President Richard Nixon established The Center for the National Interest in 1994 to serve as a voice for strategic realism in U.S. foreign policy. As he said at the time, "the U.S. has won the Cold War, but it has not yet won the peace." Today, the Center seeks to stimulate debate, promote public understanding of U.S. foreign policy and international affairs, and define principled yet pragmatic policies to advance America's national interest in the complex world of the twenty-first century.

25. Progressive Policy Institute

Address: 1200 New Hampshire Ave NW, #575, Washington, DC 20036

Phone: (202) 525-3926

A non-profit, 501(c) (3) organization that serves as a public policy think tank in the United States, founded in 1989. It styles itself as promoting the ideas of "New Democrats," covering a wide range of issues and describes itself as centrist. Its founder and current president is Will Marshall, who writes on foreign policy, defense, national service, globalization, trade policy, and cultural issues. Its chief economic strategist is Michael Mandel, who writes on innovation, growth, and regulatory policy.

26. RAND Corporation

Address: 1200 S Hayes St. Arlington, VA 22202

Phone: (703) 413-1100

An American nonprofit global policy think tank originally formed by Douglas Aircraft Company to offer research and analysis to the U.S. Armed Forces. It is financed by the U.S. government and private endowment, corporations including the health care industry, universities and private individuals.[3] The organization has expanded to work with other governments, private foundations, international organizations, and commercial organizations on a host of non-defense issues. RAND aims for interdisciplinary and quantitative problem solving via translating theoretical concepts from formal economics and the physical sciences into novel applications in other areas, that is, via applied science and operations research. Michael D. Rich is president and chief executive officer of the RAND Corporation.

27. U.S. Institute of Peace

Address: 2301 Constitution Ave NW, Washington, DC 20037

Phone: (202) 457-1700

Institute of Peace is an independent, nonpartisan institution established and funded by Congress to increase the nation's capacity to manage international conflict without violence.

28. World Economic Forum

Address: 3 East 54th St. 18th Floor, New York, NY 10022

Phone: (212) 703-2399

The World Economic Forum, committed to improving the state of the world, is the International Organization for Public-Private Cooperation. The Forum engages the foremost political, business and other leaders of society to shape global, regional and industry agendas.

Established in 1971 as a not-for-profit foundation and is headquartered in Geneva, Switzerland. It is independent, impartial and not tied to any special interests. The Forum strives in all its efforts to demonstrate entrepreneurship in the global public

---

[3] See http://www.rand.org/about/clients_grantors.html#industry

interest while upholding the highest standards of governance. Moral and intellectual integrity is at the heart of everything it does.

V. **LAW FIRMS SPECIALIZING IN ADVOCACY** – These firms have expanded their legal practice to focus on seeking legislative and administrative changes to assist their clients in achieving specific objectives. They are typically staffed by a specialized workforce that includes executive leadership admitted to the state bar associations.

1. Akin Gump, Strauss Hauer & Feld, LLP

Address: 1333 New Hampshire Ave NW, Washington, DC 20036

Phone: (202) 887-4000

Akin Gump's bipartisan public law and policy practice comprises over 70 lawyers and other professionals who practice exclusively on legislative, policy, and regulatory matters, including many former members of Congress and other lawyers with considerable experience in government service, many of whom also engage in outside political activities in both major U.S. political parties. These former members of Congress and political operatives are able to effectuate the best outcomes for their clients.

2. Baker Botts LLP

Address: 1299 Pennsylvania Ave NW, #1250, Washington, DC 20004

Phone: (202) 639-7700

Baker Botts lawyers help clients identify important regulatory considerations, develop strategies to address regulatory issues, and implement strategies to achieve their clients' business goals. As a global law firm, they have represented officers, directors and corporations in regulatory matters before various federal and state agencies in the U.S. and internationally. Their counseling experience includes providing advice on matters involving FCPA, OSHA and regulatory acts pertaining to various agencies, antitrust, international trade, governance and compliance, energy and climate change, securities regulation and enforcement, environmental permitting, fiduciary operations and investor relations.

3. DLA Piper

Address: 500 8th St. NW, Washington, DC 20004

Phone: (202) 799-4000

Provides clients with the strategies necessary to manage crises and create opportunities. DLA advocates before legislative and executive branch decision-makers as well as independent federal agencies. DLA also has a federal law and policy group focused on achieving client's federal objectives. DLA employs a cross-disciplinary approach because the path to success frequently is not linear, but one that requires carefully coordinated efforts in different forums. DLA believes that legislative and administrative advocacy is a skill that is quite distinct from defending an enforcement action or seeking to overturn a recently promulgated rule or regulation.

4.   Greenberg Traurig, LLP

Address: 2101 L St. NW, #1000, Washington, DC 20037

Phone: (202) 331-3100

Home to a multidisciplinary team of lawyers and governmental affairs professionals with strategic experience helping companies of all sizes to navigate the federal government. They focus on governmental affairs, federal procurement, global trade and investment, health and FDA business, litigation, government contracts, antitrust, insurance recovery and advisory, energy, telecommunications, real estate, intellectual property, representation of foreign governments, and national defense and homeland security. Their clients range from the federal defense sector to energy, telecommunications and health care companies, which we represent before government agencies, regulatory bodies, Congress and the courts. GT's D.C. attorneys are also involved in handling a wide range of corporate and finance work for clients in these industries.

5.   Hogan Lovells, LLP

Address: 555 13th St. NW, Washington DC 20004

Phone: (202) 637-5600

Has the objective to help clients achieve a competitive advantage and minimize regulatory risk. Hogan's Government Regulatory practice utilizes the skills of lawyers across the U.S., Europe, and Asia who have significant experience in heavily regulated public sectors. Hogan's team of lawyers are from around the world and some have held leadership positions in public service, including former members of the U.S. House of Representatives, the European Commission, and the Legislative Affairs Commission of the Chinese National People's Congress. Hogan has also added staff that has experience as lobbyists, or has counseled for virtually every major world regulatory body. Hogan understands the nexus of business and government and guides clients through the growing array of regulatory issues.

6.   Holland & Knight, LLP

Address: 800 17th St. NW Suite 1100, Washington, DC 20006

Phone: (202) 955-3000

Holland's lawyers and professionals have developed strong professional relationships on a bipartisan basis in Congress, the executive offices of the White House, and key executive agencies. They provide a comprehensive understanding of the federal policy and regulatory process. The Federal Practice Team generally takes the lead on public advocacy projects.

    7.   K&L Gates

Address: 1601 K St. NW, #1, Washington, DC 20006

Phone: (202) 628-1700

The K&L Gates policy group operates at the intersection of public policy, law, and business. At its founding few law firms had lobbying practices, the K&L policy group has grown from a single lobbyist to become the largest of any fully integrated global law firm.

    VI. NON-PROFIT ORGANIZATIONS (NPOs) – A nonprofit organization is a business entity that is granted tax-exempt status by the Internal Revenue Service.

NPOs Advocating for Community Outreach

    1.   Alexandria Domestic Violence Intervention Project

Address: 301 King St. Alexandria, VA 22314

Phone: (703) 746-HELP

The Domestic Violence Intervention Project (DVIP) is dedicated to promoting safe and healthy relationships through community coordination. DVIP addresses arrest, prosecution, victim advocacy, treatment, education, and training. The goals of DVIP are to coordinate and monitor the response of the legal system and the community to family violence incidents in Alexandria, Virginia.

    2.   Becky's Fund

Address: 5 Thomas Circle NW, Washington, DC 20005

Phone: (724) 518-1169

Becky's Fund works to fight against Domestic Violence and make individuals aware of its danger through fostering awareness, encouraging advocacy, promoting activism and creating support systems. Volunteers support the organization through fundraising, event planning, administrative support, and activism.

3. Calvary Women's Shelter

Address: 1217 Good Hope Rd. SE, Washington, DC 20020

Phone: (202) 678-2341

Women who come to Calvary find more than a safe place to live and basic needs like nutritious meals. Calvary also provides women educational programs, employment opportunities, personal support from case managers, mental health services, addiction recovery support and much more. With a strong emphasis on resident involvement, collaboration with other agencies, and excellence in management, Calvary strives to provide the best possible services to women in need in our community.

4. Catholics for a Free Choice

Address: 1436 U St. NW, Suite 301, Washington, DC 20009

Phone: (202) 332-7995

CFFC is an independent non-profit organization engaged in policy analysis, education, and advocacy on issues of gender equality and reproductive health. It is also an international educational organization that supports the right to legal reproductive health care, especially to family planning and abortions. CFFC also works to reduce the incidence of abortion and to increase women's choices in childbearing and child-rearing through advocacy of social and economic programs for women, families, and children.

5. Community Bridges

Address: 620 Pershing Drive, 2nd floor, Silver Spring, MD 20910

Phone: (301) 585-7155

Community Bridges empowers diverse girls to become exceptional students, positive leaders, and healthy young women. They accomplish this through academic skill building, conflict resolution, creative exploration, health and prevention, leadership and community action, outdoor discovery, and team building.

6. Maryland Vietnamese Mutual Association (MVMA)

Address: 8121 Georgia Ave, Suite 503, Silver Spring, MD 20910

Phone: (301) 588-6862

MVMA is a non-profit organization that serves the needs of low-income immigrant families and seniors. MVMA works to empower the Vietnamese American community to live healthy, happy, successful lives by providing direct services to families with school-aged children, isolated seniors, and new immigrants. Direct services focus on family relationships and education, healthcare and access to government services, and naturalization. Students are needed for assistance with mentorship, web design, grants, office support, and special events planning/staffing. Knowledge of Vietnamese is useful for other tasks like transportation, visiting seniors, research & surveying, teaching English, and interpretation/translation.

    7.   Vietnamese-American Community Service Center

Address: 2437 15th St. NW, Washington, DC 20009

Phone: (202) 667-0437

The center helps to empower the Vietnamese community and integrate them into mainstream American culture we offer many resources for the family, for both adults and children. The center has an after-school program called the Safe Place for Learning (SPL) program, where children receive assistance with academics, learn computer skills, and socialize. Many neighborhood and social awareness workshops for parents are offered. Finally, Youth Mentoring Program (YMP) for our most at-risk youth is available.

NPOs Advocating for Criminal & Social Justice

    1.   Capitol Area Immigrants' Rights Coalition (CAIR)

Address: 1612 K St. NW, Suite 204, Washington, DC 20006

Phone: (202) 331-3320

The mission of CAIR Coalition is to serve as the primary source of legal assistance for detained immigrants (adults and children) in the D.C. metropolitan area and to strengthen and support the work of our Coalition members. We work with community groups, pro bono attorneys, volunteers and immigrants from DC, Virginia and Maryland to ensure that all immigrants are treated with fairness, dignity and respect for their human and civil rights.[4]

    2.   Coalition for Juvenile Justice (CJJ)

---

[4] See http://www.caircoalition.org/what-we-do/

Chapter 13: Illustrative Advocacy Directory

Address: 1319 F St. NW, Suite 402, Washington, DC 20004

Phone: (202) 467-0864
The Coalition for Juvenile Justice (CJJ) envisions a nation where fewer children are at risk of delinquency; and if they are at risk or involved with the justice system, they and their families receive every possible opportunity to live safe, healthy and fulfilling lives. CJJ is a nationwide coalition of State Advisory Groups (SAGs) and allies dedicated to preventing children and youth from becoming involved in the courts and upholding the highest standards of care when youth are charged with wrongdoing and enter the justice system.

3. Court Service and Offender Supervision Agency

Address: 633 Indiana Ave NW, Washington, DC 20004

Phone: (202) 220-5300

CSOSA's mission is to increase public safety, prevent crime, reduce recidivism, and support the fair administration of justice in close collaboration with the community. In the District of Columbia, eighty percent of pretrial defendants are released to the community and approximately 70 percent of convicted offenders serve some portion of their sentence in the community. As such, CSOSA's effective supervision of pretrial defendants and convicted offenders provides a crucial service to the courts and paroling authority and is critical to public safety.

4. DC Books to Prisons

Address: 1500 16th St. NW, Washington, DC 20036

Contact: btopdc@gmail.com; www.dcbookstoprisoners.org

Since 1999, DC Books to Prisons Project has provided free books to prisoners around the country. We also develop and support local prison libraries. Our work is done solely by concerned volunteers on donated time and resources. Unlike some programs, we do not limit requests for books to a particular geographic area or demographic group; therefore, we receive a tremendous number of requests. Yearly, we send out close to 4,000 packages containing over 10,000 books. These packages go to prisoners in 150 different prisons in all 50 states. Pack books Wednesday evenings between 5:30pm and 9:00pm.

5. The Equal Rights Center

Address: 11 DuPont Circle NW, Suite 450

Phone: (202) 234-3062

The ERC began as the Fair Housing Council of Greater Washington in 1983. Although the organization was founded with a focus on discrimination in housing, throughout the years, the organization's mission has grown and programs have expanded to encompass more programs and issue areas.

Joined by the Fair Employment Council of Greater Washington in 1999, the ERC expanded the scope of its programs to include discrimination in both the workplace as well as in public accommodations.

6. Families Against Mandatory Minimums (FAMM)

Address: 1100 H St. NW, Suite 1000, Washington, DC 20005

Phone: (202) 822-6700

Families Against Mandatory Minimums (FAMM) is a nonprofit, nonpartisan organization fighting for fair and proportionate sentencing laws that allow judicial discretion while maintaining public safety.

FAMM advocates for state and federal sentencing reform, and mobilizes thousands of individuals and families whose lives are adversely affected by unjust sentences to work constructively for change.

7. Mexican American Legal Defense and Education Fund

Address: 1016 16th St. NW, Suite 100, Washington, DC 20036

Phone: (202) 293-2828

MALDEF's mission is to foster sound public policies, laws and programs to safeguard the civil rights of the 40 million Latinos living in the United States and to empower the Latino community to fully participate in our society. MALDEF achieves its mission by concentrating its efforts on employment, education, immigration, political access, language, and public resource equity issues.

8. The Sentencing Project

Address: 1705 DeSales St. NW, 8th Floor, Washington, DC 20036

Phone: (202) 628-0871

The Sentencing Project works for a fair and effective U.S. criminal justice system by promoting reforms in sentencing policy, addressing unjust racial disparities and practices, and advocating for alternatives to incarceration. The Sentencing Project was founded in 1986 to provide defense lawyers with sentencing advocacy training and to reduce the reliance on incarceration. Since that time, The Sentencing Project has become a leader in the effort to bring national attention to disturbing trends and inequities in the criminal justice system with a successful formula that includes the publication of groundbreaking research, aggressive media campaigns and strategic advocacy for policy reform.

9. Young Ladies of Tomorrow

Address: 78 U St. NW, Washington, DC 20001

Phone: (202) 332-7184

This organization works directly with young women and girls that have experienced the juvenile justice system. The goal is to offer counseling, therapeutic recreation, job training, mentorship and provide other resources these ladies may need in order to reach their potential.

NPOs Advocating for Energy & Environment

1. African Wildlife Foundation

Address: 1400 16th St. NW, #120, Washington, DC 20036

Phone: (202) 939-3333

The leading international conservation organization that is focused solely on Africa. For over 50 years, they have worked to ensure the wildlife and wild lands of Africa will endure forever.

2. Clean Water Network

Address: 1200 New York Ave NW, #400, Washington, DC 20005

Phone: (202) 289-2395

Since 1992, the Clean Water Network has served as a place for groups working to tackle these challenges and protect our waterways to come together, share experiences and knowledge, and gain expertise and resources to work at the federal level and in their own backyards. A nationwide coalition of local, regional and national groups, the Network serves as a convener, working to ensure that organizers and advocates across the country have the resources and connections they need to effectively fight to protect the waterways we love and depend on.

3. Energy Advocates

Address: 1701 Pennsylvania Ave NW, Washington DC 20006

Phone: (202) 580-6532

Demonstrate their commitment to sharing the truth on energy issues specifically on economic, environmental, and matters of national security. Their goal is to raise public awareness and change the public's perception of the importance of the energy industry. Energy Advocates raise capital through donations and fundraisers.

4.   Green America

Address: 1612 K St. NW, Suite 600, Washington, DC 20006

Phone: (800) 584-7336

The vision of Green America is to harness economic power—the strength of consumers, investors, businesses, and the marketplace—to create a socially just and environmentally sustainable society. The organization works for a world where all people have enough, where all communities are healthy and safe, and where the bounty of the Earth is preserved for all the generations to come.

5.   GreenPeace

Address: 702 H St. NW, #300, Washington, DC 20001

Phone: (202) 462-1177

The leading independent campaigning organization that uses peaceful protest and creative communication to expose global environmental problems and promote solutions that are essential to a green and peaceful future. Greenpeace is the leading independent campaigning organization that uses peaceful protest and creative communication to expose global environmental problems and to promote solutions that are essential to a green and peaceful future. A group of thoughtful, committed citizens came together in 1971 to create Greenpeace.

6.   National Council for Science and the Environment (NCSE)

Address: 1101 17th St. NW, #250, Washington, DC 20036

Phone: (202) 207-0002

The National Council for Science and the Environment (NCSE) is a not-for-profit organization dedicated to improving the scientific basis of environmental decision-making. It seeks to be a bridge that spans the divide between science, its applications, and policy.

NCSE specializes in programs that foster collaboration between the diverse institutions and individuals creating and using environmental knowledge to make science useful to policies and decisions on critical environmental issues.

7. RiverKeepers

Address: 20 Secor Rd. Ossining, NY 10562

Phone: (800) 21-RIVER

Protect the environmental, recreational, and commercial integrity of the Hudson River and its tributaries, as well as safeguard the drinking water of nine million New York City and Hudson Valley residents.

NPOs Advocating for Healthcare

1. American Cancer Society (ACS)

Address: 555 11th St. NW, Washington, DC 20004

Phone: (202) 661-5700

The American Cancer Society (ACS) is the largest voluntary health organization in the U.S. advocating on behalf of cancer patients and survivors. Through the support of their contributions, more than 1.5 million lives have been saved in the US in the past two decades.

2. DC Diaper Bank

Address: 315 12th St. NE, Washington, DC 20002

Phone: (202) 656-8503

Works to ensure that babies and toddlers grow up healthy and safe with the diapers they need. Volunteers do everything from working in the warehouse to assisting with social media and marketing or holding diaper drives.

3. Family Health & Birth Center-Community of Hope

Address: 1413 Girard St. NW, Washington, DC 20009

Phone: (202) 407-7757

The Family Health and Birth Center (FHBC) is a full scope birth center providing prenatal, birth, postnatal, gynecological and primary health care to women and their families in NE Washington D.C. Volunteers assist with child care, translation services, administrative health clinic tasks and gardening.

4. International Rescue Committee (IRC)

Address: 8700 Georgia Ave Suite 500, Silver Spring, MD 20910

Phone: (301) 562-8633

The International Rescue Committee's Public Health Program provides physical and mental health services to the IRC's beneficiaries. The Public Health Program offers a variety of programming in public health awareness, access, and advocacy. They hope to find volunteers to assist with research of local health options, design curricula for and facilitate health promotion workshops, mentor refugee clients with specific health concerns, to translate/interpret, or to help compile educational materials or first aid kits, etc.

5. National Physicians Alliance (NPA)

Address: 888 16th St. NW, #800, Washington, DC 20006

Phone: (202) 420-7896

A national multi-specialty medical organization founded in 2005. NPA creates research and education programs that promote health and foster active engagement of physicians with their communities to achieve high quality, affordable health care for all.

NPOs Advocating for Human Rights

1. Africa Faith and Justice Network (AFJN)

Address: 3025 4th St. NE, Suite 122, Washington, DC 20017

Phone: (202) 817-3670

The Africa Faith and Justice Network (AFJN) advocates for responsible U.S. relations with Africa. AFJN stresses issues of peace building, human rights and social justice that tie directly into Catholic Social Teaching. AFJN advocates for USA policies that will benefit Africa's poor majority, facilitate an end to armed conflict, establish equitable trade and investment with Africa and promote sustainable development.

2. Africare

Address: 440 R St. NW, Washington, DC 20001

Phone: (202) 462-3614

Africare is a leading non-governmental organization (NGO) committed to addressing African development and policy issues by working in partnership with African people to build sustainable, healthy and productive communities.

3. The ARK Foundation of Africa

Address: 1002 Maryland Ave NE, Washington, DC 20002

Phone: (202) 832-5420

ARK strives to serve all East African children facing a daily struggle to survive. ARK and its program partners provide a range of comprehensive services, including: family counseling, financial support for grandparents caring for orphans and other vulnerable children, health education, nutrition information, food assistance, academic support and job training.

4. Arlington Academy of Hope (AAH)

Address: PO Box 7694, Arlington, VA 22207

Phone: (703) 609-6830

Arlington Academy of Hope is a nonprofit 501 organization based in Arlington, Virginia, in the United States. The organization seeks to help children in Uganda by providing access to education within their village communities.

5. Asian American LEAD (AALEAD)

Address: 2100 New Hampshire Ave NW, Washington, DC 20009

Phone: (202) 884-0322

Asian American LEAD's overarching goal is to increase the opportunities and ability of low-income Asian American children to move out of poverty and become successful, self-sufficient adults. AALEAD firmly believes that education is the key to meeting this goal. However, AALEAD understands that children need additional family, school, and personal supports, not just academic assistance, to succeed. Consequently, AALEAD uses a five pronged approach to youth development, offering each child after school intervention in a safe space, mentoring, family support and educational advocacy.

6. Association for Women in Development

Address: 666 11th St. NW, Suite 450, Washington, DC 20001

Phone: (202) 628-0440

Association for Women in Developmen is a non-profit, professional membership organization of women in development and gender and development (WID/GAD) researchers, practitioners, and policymakers committed to the full participation of women in forming a gender-equitable, just, and sustainable development process. AWID works to redefine development based on women's perspectives. It promotes research, policy, and practice to fully engage women in building a just and sustainable development process.

7.   Association for Women in Development

Address: 1200 New York Ave NW, Suite 650, Washington, DC 20005

Phone: (202) 326-8940

AWIS is a non-profit organization dedicated to achieving equality and full participation for women in science, mathematics, engineering, and technology. AWIS fosters the careers of women science professionals by facilitating networking among women scientists. AWIS also publishes a variety of materials to inform girls and women about science programs and women's issues, including the AWIS Magazine. AWIS also sponsors educational activities in schools and communities in addition to holding national conferences.

6.   Break the Chain Campaign

Address: 1112 16th St. NW, Suite 600, Washington, DC 20036

Phone: (202) 787-5245

Break the Chain Campaign seeks to minimize the effects of human trafficking, modern-day slavery and worker exploitation through comprehensive direct service, research, outreach, advocacy, training and technical assistance. The Campaign is committed to assisting migrant trafficked enslaved and exploited workers through the provision of: 1. Case management services offering access to legal, social, mental health, and medical referrals and assistance and 2. A multicultural center dedicated to providing a safe, supportive, and educational environment for trafficked, enslaved and exploited workers.

7.   Central American Resource Center of DC (CARECEN)

Address: 1459 Columbia Road NW, Washington, DC 20009

Phone: (202) 328-9799

CARECEN is a community based organization which offers legal, educational, housing, citizenship and civic participation programs to the Central American/Latino community. Volunteers help conduct citizenship classes, hold mock interviews, help fill out applications, lead field trips, facilitate discussions, and register voters.

8. Children's Defense Fund

Address: 25 E St. NW, Washington, DC 20001

Phone: (202) 628-8787

The Children's Defense Fund exists to provide a strong and effective voice for all American children, who cannot vote, lobby, or speak for themselves. CDF pays particular attention to the needs of poor and minority children and those with disabilities. The goal of CDF is to educate the nation about the needs of children and encourage preventive investment in children before they get sick, drop out of school, suffer family breakdown, or get into trouble.

9. Citizens for Global Solutions

Address: 418 7th St. SE, Washington, DC 20003

Phone: (202) 546-3950

Citizens for Global Solution mission to build political will in the United States in order to achieve their vision. They do this by educating the citizens about global interdependence, communicating global concerns to public officials, and develop proposals to create, strengthen, and reform international institutions such as the United Nations.

8. Crossroads Youth Opportunity Center (CYOC)

Address: 7676 New Hampshire Ave #411, Takoma Park, MD 20912

Phone: (301) 422-1270

Crossroads Youth Opportunity Center's Identity program provides programs for Latino youth in Montgomery County, Maryland to help them achieve a sense of confidence, connection, and control over their lives. Our goal is to reduce social and cultural barriers that hamper Latino youths' ability to participate fully in society's benefits and responsibilities.

9. DC Coalition Against Domestic Violence

Address: 5 Thomas Circle NW, Washington, DC 20005

Phone: (202) 299-1181

DCCADV is the District's leading voice on domestic violence public policy, systems coordination and reform. Partnering with and on behalf of our member programs, we: track and analyze legislative and systemic activity impacting victims and survivors of domestic violence; educate policy makers; conduct outreach and facilitate collaboration with community based organizations and stakeholders; lead advocacy efforts for funding for domestic violence programs and services; develop briefing papers, reports and other public materials, and; provide technical assistance and training on issues including confidentiality, domestic violence laws, barriers facing underserved populations including victims who are LGBT and victims with disabilities, and workplace policies and procedures. Volunteers can choose to help with policy, material distribution, outreach, and fundraising.

10. DC Rape Crisis Center

Address: 5321 1st Pl. NE, Washington, DC 20011

Phone: (202) 232-0789

The DC Rape Crisis Center is dedicated to creating a world free of sexual violence. The Center works for social change through community outreach, education, and legal and public policy initiatives. It helps survivors and their families heal from the aftermath of sexual violence through crisis intervention, counseling and advocacy. Committed to the belief that all forms of oppression are linked, the Center values accessibility, cultural diversity and the empowerment of women and children. Programs include helping adults recover from sexual violence, helping children recover from sexual abuse, accompanying survivors through the systems, educating the community, and training professionals. Volunteers are responsible for staffing our 24-hour crisis hotline and serving as an advocate at DC area hospitals (though primarily through Washington Hospital Center), in police stations, and in court.

11. District Alliance for Safe Housing

Address: 2639 16th St. NW, Washington, DC 20009

Phone: (202) 462-3274

At the District Alliance for Safe Housing, (DASH), they believe that all survivors of domestic violence and their families no matter what their situation, should have access to, and be welcomed into, safe housing and a wide variety of services that allows them to rebuild their lives on their own terms. Volunteers play a vital role in furthering the mission of DASH, by supporting programming and working one-on-one with our residents. They have a number of opportunities to volunteer including tutoring, Art Group, dance classes and monthly service learning trips.

12. Feminist Majority Foundation (FMF)

Address: 1600 Wilson Boulevard, Suite 801, Arlington, VA 22209

Phone: (703) 522-2214

The Feminist Majority Foundation (FMF) founded in 1987, is a cutting edge organization dedicated to women's equality, reproductive health, and non-violence. In all spheres, FMF utilizes research and action to empower women economically, socially, and politically.

13. Freedom House

Address: 1850 M St. NW, Floor 11, Washington, DC 20036

Phone: (202) 296-5101

Freedom House is an independent watchdog organization dedicated to the expansion of freedom and democracy around the world.

They analyze the challenges to freedom, advocate for greater political rights and civil liberties, and support frontline activists to defend human rights and promote democratic change. Founded in 1941, Freedom House was the first American organization to champion the advancement of freedom globally.

14. Guatemalan Human Rights Commission (GHRC)

Address: 3321 12th St. NE, Washington, DC 20017

Phone: (202) 529-6599

Guatemalan Human Rights Commission is an active organization strongly committed to solidarity in the international struggle for human rights in Guatemala.

GHRC works for systematic change; denouncing torture, forced disappearances, massacres and the role of the international community in human rights violations.

15. Hmong National Development, Inc.

Address: 1628 16th St. NW, Suite 203, Washington, DC 20009

Phone: (202) 588-1661

Hmong National Development, Inc. (HND) is a national non-profit organization dedicated to building capacity, developing leadership and empowering the Hmong American community. HND envisions a vibrant Hmong American community leading in educational achievement, economic development, civic engagement and social justice.

16. Human Rights Watch (HRW)

Address: 1630 Connecticut Ave NW, Suite 500, Washington, DC 20005

Phone: (202) 612-4321

This organization conducts regular, systematic investigations of human rights abuses in around 70 countries, including: the human rights of refugees and displaced persons. Their goal is to defend the freedom of thought and expression, due process, and equal protection of the law.

17. Immigration and Refugee Services of America (IRSA)

Address: 1717 Massachusetts Ave NW, Suite 200, Washington, DC 20036

Phone: (202) 797-2105

This organization provides refugee resettlement, immigration counseling, and other supportive services meant to ease the burden of transition both for the newcomers and the communities receiving them. Agencies provide asylum representation and advocate on behalf of the rights of immigrants and refugees.

18. International Labor Rights Forum (ILRF)

Address: 1634 I St. NW, Suite 1001, Washington, DC 20006

Phone: (202) 347-4100

International Labor Rights Forum is an advocacy organization dedicated to achieving just and humane treatment for workers worldwide. ILRF serves a unique role among human rights organizations as advocates for and with working poor around the world. The organization promotes enforcement of labor rights internationally through public education and mobilization, research, litigation, legislation, and collaboration with labor, government and business groups.

19. Just Associates (JASS)

Address: 2040 S St. NW, 3rd Floor, Washington, DC 20009
Phone: (202) 232-1211

Just Associates is an international feminist organization driven by the partners and initiatives of its regional networks in Mesoamerica, Southern Africa and Southeast Asia. JASS is dedicated to strengthening and mobilizing women's voice, visibility and collective organizing power to change the norms, institutions and policies that perpetuate inequality and violence, in order to create a just, sustainable world for all JASS equips activist leaders from all walks of life, promotes and sustains grassroots and local-to-global organizing, maximizes women's creative use of social media to amplify their visibility, and produces and publishes knowledge from practice.

20. Latino Economic Development Center (LEDC)

Address: 641 S St. NW, Washington, DC 20001

Phone: (202) 588-5102

Latino Economic Development Center's mission is to drive the economic and social advancement of low- to moderate- income Latinos and other underserved communities in the D.C. and Baltimore Metropolitan Areas by equipping them with the skills and tools to achieve financial independence and become leaders in their communities.

21. MAG America

Address: 1750 K St. NW, Suite 350, Washington, DC 20006

Phone: (202) 293-1904

Together with MAG (Mines Advisory Group), MAG America helps clear the remnants of conflict from some of the world's poorest nations, educate and employ local people, and helps provide solutions for those trapped by poverty and economic devastation through no fault of their own.

22. Mary House

Address: 4303 13th St. NE, Washington, DC 20017

Phone: (202) 635-9025

Mary House is a local nonprofit organization which works with immigrant and refugee families in the DC area. Mary House is open to all and many of the families are from foreign countries-including El Salvador, Mexico, Guatemala, Columbia, Bosnia, and Iraq.

23. National Association for the Advancement of Colored People

Address: 1156 15th St. NW, Suite 915, Washington, DC 20005

Phone: (202) 463-2940

The mission of the National Association for the Advancement of Colored People is to ensure the political, educational, social and economic equality of rights of all persons and eliminate racial hatred/discrimination.

24. National Black Justice Coalition

Address: 1725 I St. NW, Washington, DC 20006

Phone: (202) 349-3755

The National Black Justice Coalition is a civil rights organization of Black lesbian, gay, bisexual and transgender people and our allies dedicated to fostering equality by fighting racism and homophobia. The Coalition advocates for social justice by educating and mobilizing opinion leaders, including elected officials, clergy, and media, with a focus on Black communities.

25. National Coalition Building Institute (NCBI)

Address: 1730 Rhode Island Ave NW, Suite 203, Washington, DC 20036

Phone: (202) 785-9400

The National Coalition Building Institute (NCBI) is a nonprofit leadership training organization working to eliminate prejudice and intergroup conflict in communities throughout the world. NCBI's proactive approach begins with a corps of community leaders who are taught effective bridge-building skills to combat intergroup conflicts in various settings including schools, universities, foundations, correctional facilities, law enforcement agencies, government offices, and labor unions.

26. National Trust for Our Wounded

Address: 10001 Georgetown Pike #783, Great Falls, VA 22066

Phone: (703) 828-7848

The National Trust for Our Wounded™ (NTW) is a privately-financed 501(c)3 national fund dedicated to assisting America's Wounded and their families. NTW's Mission is to provide financial support to effective and successful 501(c)3 programs and services to ensure the full range of needs of the Wounded are being addressed, particularly those returning to rural areas and small towns.

27. Operation Understanding DC (OUDC)

Address: 3000 Connecticut Ave NW, Suite 335, Washington, DC 20008
Phone: (202) 234-6832

Operation Understanding DC is a year-long, intensive leadership development and multicultural education program for Washington-area African American and Jewish high school students, with the goal of developing a generation of leaders who will work to eradicate racism, anti-Semitism and all forms of discrimination, and to promote respect, understanding and cooperation within their communities.

28. Refugees International

Address: 2001 S St. NW, Suite 700, Washington, DC 20009

Phone: (202) 828-0110

Refugees International (RI) advocates for lifesaving assistance and protection for displaced people and promotes solutions to displacement crises. RI is an independent organization, and does not accept any government or UN funding. Timely responses to displacement crises can decrease vulnerability and improve the quality of life for those affected. Due to RI efforts, displaced people receive food, medicine, and education; families return home; and peacekeepers are sent to protect displaced people from harm.

29. South Asian Americans Leading Together (SAALT)

Address: 6930 Carroll Ave Suite 506, Takoma Park, MD 20912

Phone: (301) 270-1855

The South Asian American Leaders of Tomorrow (SAALT) is a national non-profit organization dedicated to ensuring the full and equal participation by South Asians in the civic and political life of the U.S. SAALT's goals are to: Provide a uniform and informed voice on issues affecting South Asians that relate to equality and civil rights, develop South Asian Coalitions that transcend religious, ethnic, or linguistic differences, to facilitate collective action and broader community change, and create opportunities for leadership, service, and volunteerism by South Asians in order to foster civic engagement.

30. Women for Women International

Address: 2000 M St. NW, Suite 200, Washington, DC 20036

Phone: (202) 737-7705

Women for Women International provides women survivors of war, civil strife and other conflicts with the tools and resources to move from crisis and poverty to stability and self-sufficiency, thereby promoting viable civil societies. Become an ambassador by committing to support women survivors of war by working locally throughout the year to raise funds and awareness for WfWI's programs and the countries in which they work.

31. Women Thrive Worldwide

Address: 1875 Connecticut Ave NW, Suite 405, Washington, DC 20009

Phone: (202) 999-4482

Women Thrive Worldwide advocates for change at the U.S. and global levels so that women and men can share equally in the enjoyment of opportunities, economic prosperity, voice, and freedom from fear and violence. Women Thrive Worldwide grounds their work in the realities of women living in poverty, partners with locally based organizations, and creates powerful coalitions to advance the interests of the women and girls they serve.

NPOs Advocating for Welfare & Socioeconomic Status

1. American Friends Service Committee

Address: 1822 R St. NW, First Floor, Washington, DC 20009

Phone: (202) 544-0324

The mission of the AFSC-MAR/DC Peace and Economic Justice Program is to bring together people to build a community where peace and social and economic justice prevail. They use the strengths of a Quaker base to listen to all voices, to diminish violence and to help create a community where each person's potential can be fully realized.

2. Back On My Feet DC

Address: 122 C St. NW, Suite 240, Washington, DC 20001

Phone: (202) 258-0832

Back on My Feet combats homelessness through the power of running, community support and essential employment and housing resources. Back on My Feet seeks to revolutionize the way our society approaches homelessness. Our unique running-based model demonstrates that if you first restore confidence, strength, and self-esteem, individuals are better equipped to tackle the road ahead and move toward jobs, homes, and new lives. For all in need, we aim to provide: practical training and employment resources for achieving independence; an environment that promotes accountability; and a community that offers compassion and hope.[5]

3. The Bethune-DuBois Institute

Address: 8630 Fenton St. Suite 910, Silver Spring, MD 20910

Phone: (301) 562-8300

Founded in 1986, The Bethune-DuBois Institute, a 501(c)(3) nonprofit organization, was established to sustain and magnify the educational legacies of two of America's greatest leaders, Dr. Mary McLeod Bethune and Dr. W.E.B. DuBois. Their examples and teachings emphasized personal leadership and the importance of education and training in solving public policy problems and in advancing the status and contributions of all African Americans in American society.

4. Center for the Advancement of Public Policy

Address: 1735 S St. NW, Washington, DC 20009

Phone: (202) 797-6245

CAPP is a non-profit organization dedicated to equity and accountability. CAPP fosters equitable, democratic, and humane management in government, corporations, and other organizations; it seeks the elimination of prejudice, sexism, and discrimination in the workplace and in society; and promotes democratic government through research, investigation, and education.

5. Center for Community Change

Address: 1536 U St. NW, Washington, DC 20009

Phone: (202) 399-9300

Center for Community Change mission is to build the power and capacity of low-income people, especially low-income people of color, to have a profound impact in improving their communities and the policies and institutions that affect their lives.

6. Center for Policy Alternatives

Address: 1875 Connecticut Ave NW, Suite 710, Washington, DC 20009

---

[5] See http://dc.backonmyfeet.org/

Phone: (202) 387-6030

Center for Policy Alternatives is a progressive, non-partisan, non-profit public policy center. CPA's mission is to champion women's economic agenda with a strong and united voice for a new economy that bridges class and racial lines. Its Women and the Economy Campaign seeks to translate the dialogue on women's equality from individual rights to economic potential and to reflect the priorities that bridge women across class and race.

7. Coalition for Smarter Growth

Address: 316 F St. NE, Suite 200, Washington, DC 20002

Phone: (202) 675-0016

Coalition for Smart Growth wants to ensure that transportation and development decisions accommodate growth while regenerating communities, providing more housing and travel choices, and conserving our natural and historic areas. Volunteer opportunities include event assistance, photography, filming, graphic design and web design.

8. Corporate Council on Africa

Address: 1100 17th St. NW, Suite 100, Washington, DC 20036

Phone: (202) 835-1115

The Corporate Council on Africa (CCA) works to strengthen and facilitate the commercial relationship between the U.S. and the African continent. CCA works closely with governments, multilateral groups and business to improve the African continent's trade and investment climate, and to raise the profile of Africa in the U.S. business community.

9. DC Employment Justice Center

Address: 1413 K St. NW, Washington, DC 20005

Phone: (202) 828-9675

The D.C. Employment Justice Center (EJC) protects and promotes the legal rights of low-wage workers in the DC metro area. To ensure that all workers are treated equally in the workplace, the EJC uses knowledgeable employment law attorneys and policy advocates to provide high-quality, free legal advice and assistance to low-wage workers and push for modifications in the workplace fairness laws. Volunteer opportunities include advocacy, workers rights clinics, administrative support, education programs.

10. Debt AIDS Trade Africa (DATA)

Address: 1400 Eye St. NW, Washington DC 20005

Phone: (202) 639-8010

Debt AIDS Trade Africa is an advocacy organization dedicated to eradicating extreme poverty and AIDS in Africa. The Washington, DC office works with political, media and faith leaders to raise awareness in the U.S. about the toll extreme poverty is taking in Africa and how lives can be saved and communities stabilized.

11. The Education Trust

Address: 1250 H St. NW, Suite 700, Washington, DC 20005

Phone: (202) 293-1217

The Education Trust is a non-profit Washington DC-based educational organization committed to closing the achievement gap that separates low-income students and students of color from other young Americans through advocacy and research. They especially focus on the work of schools and colleges most often left behind in education improvement efforts: those serving low-income, Latino and African American students.

12. Ethiopian Community Development Council, Inc. (ECDC)

Address: 901 South Highland St. Arlington, VA 22204

Phone: (703) 685-0510

Ethiopian Community Development Council, Inc. is a nonprofit agency providing cultural, educational, and socio-economic development programs in the immigrant and refugee community. They have a variety of programs including HIV education and prevention programs, breast cancer awareness, domestic violence prevention, employment assistance, a youth tobacco prevention project, financial services and small-business loans.

13. Fair Chance

Address: 2001 S St. NW, Washington DC 20009

Phone: (202) 467-2421

Fair Chance was founded in 2002 to guarantee that all children living in poverty have access to resources such as quality programs that will enable them to reach their future endeavors. Fair Chance believes that every child in the District of Columbia should be given the opportunity to succeed. Their mission is to strengthen the sustainability of nonprofit organizations and their leaders to change the lives of children and youth living in poverty.

14. Foundation Center

Address: 1627 K St. NW, Third Floor, Washington, DC 20006

Phone: (202) 331-1400

Established in 1956, Foundation Center is the leading source of information about philanthropy worldwide. Through data, analysis, and training, it connects people who want to change the world to the resources they need to succeed. Foundation Center maintains the most comprehensive database on U.S. and, increasingly, global grantmakers and their grants — a robust, accessible knowledge bank for the sector. It also operates research, education, and training programs designed to advance knowledge of philanthropy at every level. Thousands of people visit Foundation Center's website each day and are served in its five library/learning centers and at more than 450 Funding Information Network locations nationwide and around the world.

15. The Foundation for International Community Assistance (FINCA)

Address: 1110 15th St. NW, Suite 600, Washington, DC 20005

Phone: (202) 682-1510

Their mission is to support the economic and human development of families trapped in severe poverty. To do this, FINCA creates 'village banks': peer groups of 10 to 50 members, predominantly women.

16. Global Youth Partnership for Africa (GYPA)

Address: 1101 Pennsylvania Ave NW, Suite 601, Washington, DC 20004

Phone: (202) 756-4601

Global Youth Partnership for Africa (GYPA) is dedicated to fostering understanding, appreciation, and respect between young American and African leaders: tomorrow's global decision-makers. The Washington, DC office coordinates cultural exchange programs for American youth to travel to Africa and also directs educational and fundraising campaigns that raise awareness about HIV/AIDS, economic development, post-conflict reconstruction, and the use of sports to achieve social change.

17. Goodwill of Greater Washington

Address: 2200 South Dakota Ave NE, Washington, DC 20018

Phone: (202) 715-2638

DC Goodwill's mission is to transform lives and communities through the power of education and employment. They're building a community where people are empowered to achieve their fullest potential and rise to the highest level of personal successes. Since 1902, volunteers have been the spine of Goodwill's mission of assisting people with disabilities and disadvantages get jobs. They provide a volunteer packet that will help individuals learn about their agency and the work they do to benefit the community.

18. Green DMV

Address: 4409 South Capitol St. SW, Washington, DC 20032

Phone: (888) 625-4440

Green DMW was founded in 2007. Since its founding, they have developed successful programs to serve disadvantaged communities. Green DMV promotes sustainability in low-income neighborhoods as a pathway out of poverty. They believe that by helping underserved communities to realize the true benefit of clean energy, they can increase the vitality of small business community, educate the next generation on environmental stewardship, and strengthen the effectiveness of community stakeholders. They are fueled by the passion to ensure that the green economy is inclusive to all people.

19. Institute for Policy Studies

Address: 1112 16th St. NW, Suite 600, Washington, DC 20036

Phone: (202) 234-9382

The Institute for Policy Studies (ISP) strengthens social movements with independent research, visionary thinking, and links to the grassroots, scholars and elected officials. ISP empowers people to build healthy and democratic societies in communities, the U.S., and the world. Major areas of work include Global Justice, Peace and Security, Democracy and Fairness, among others.

20. InterAction

Address: 1400 16th St. NW, Suite 210, Washington, DC 20036

Phone: (202) 667-8227

InterAction is the largest alliance of U.S.-based international development and humanitarian nongovernmental organizations. InterAction convenes and coordinates its members so they can influence policy and debate on issues affecting millions of people worldwide and improve their practices. Students can reach a large array of service venues.

21. LIFT

Address: 1901 Mississippi Ave SE, Washington, DC 20020

Phone: (202) 450-2787

LIFT is a growing movement to combat poverty and expand opportunity for all people in the U.S. Their mission is to alleviate poverty in DC and our country for engaging our nation's college students in this effort. LIFT recruits and trains a diverse corps of undergraduates who make rigorous and sustained commitment to service while in school. This volunteer corps operates a national network of service centers, where they work side by side with low-income individuals and their families to find jobs secure safe and stable housing make ends meet through public benefits and tax credits and acquire critical support like healthcare and childcare.

22. Meridian International Center

Address: 1630 Crescent Place NW, Washington, DC 20009

Phone: (202) 667-6800

Meridian International Center is a non-profit institution that promotes international understanding through the exchange of people, ideas and the arts. Meridian offers a wide array of outreach, exchanges, and arts programs. They educate people of all ages about global issues, connect professionals from different countries and enrich the cultural perspective of audiences across the U.S. and abroad.

23. National Council of La Raza (NCLR)

Address: 1126 16th St. NW, Suite 600, Washington, DC 20036

Phone: (202) 785-1670

The National Council of La Raza is the largest national constituency-based Hispanic organization in Washington, DC for the Hispanic community with the goal to reduce poverty and discrimination and improve life opportunities for Hispanic Americans. Four major functions provide essential focus to the organization's work: capacity-building assistance; applied research, policy analysis, and advocacy; public information efforts; and special and international projects.

24. National Puerto Rican Coalition, Inc.

Address: 1444 I St. NW, Suite 800, Washington, DC 20005

Phone: (202) 223-3915

NPRC's mission is to systematically strengthen and enhance the social, political, and economic well-being of Puerto Ricans throughout the United States and in Puerto Rico with a special focus on the most vulnerable.

25. One DC

Address: 614 S St. NW, Rear Carriage House, Washington, DC 20001

Phone: (202) 232-2915

One DC's mission is to exercise political strength to create and preserve racial and economic equity in Shaw and the District. With volunteer opportunities in housing, income, wellness, and education, you can learn how to be the change and make the changes needed for justice and equity to be a reality in this city and this world.

26. Oxfam America

Address: 1112 16th St. NW, Suite 600, Washington, DC 20005

Phone: (202) 496-1180

Oxfam America is a non-profit organization that works to end global poverty through saving lives, strengthening communities and campaigning for change. They are an affiliate of Oxfam International.

27. Partners of the Americas

Address: 1424 K St. NW, Suite 700, Washington, DC 20005

Phone: (202) 628-3300

Partners of the America works together as citizen volunteers from Latin America, the Caribbean and the U.S. to improve the lives of people across the hemisphere on issues of agriculture, governance, gender equality, and youth.

28. Poverty and Race Research Action Council (PRRAC)

Address: 1200 18th St. NW, #200, Washington, DC 20036

Phone: (202) 906-8023

Poverty and Race Research Action Council is a non-partisan, national, not-for-profit organization convened by major civil rights, civil liberties and anti-poverty groups. The organization links social science research to advocacy work in order to address problems at the intersection of race and poverty.

29. Roots of Development

Address: 1325 18th St. NW, Unit 303, Washington, DC 20036

Phone: (202) 466-0805

The mission of Roots of Development is to build long-term, sustainable development. The organization is committed to development, not "dependency." Its focus is in Haiti. Its three roots are sustainable infrastructure, community businesses, and most importantly strengthening the community's capacity and skill set.

30. Vital Voices

Address: 1625 Massachusetts Ave NW, Suite 300, Washington, DC 20036

Phone: (202) 861-2625

This NGO's mission is to identify women leaders and empower them to be strong leaders in their community. The women are provided with resources and training to have the skill set to be advocates of social justice in their communities. Vital Voices is very involved in combating human trafficking and other violence that affects women.

VIII. **LEADING HISTORICAL ADVOCATES** – These positions are typically owned and operated by high profile individuals who have name recognition and credibility in their issues of interest. They typically have a proven track record of influencing the government decision-making process.

1. Al Gore

Address: One Bryant Park, 48th Floor, New York, NY 10036

Phone: (212) 584-3650

Former Vice President of the United States, the 2000 Democratic Party presidential nominee, and the co-recipient of the 2007 Nobel Peace Prize with the Intergovernmental Panel on Climate Change has been involved with the environmental activist movement for a number of decades. In 2004, Gore co-launched Generation Investment

Management a new London fund management firm that plans to create environment-friendly portfolios. Generation Investment will manage assets of institutional investors, such as pension funds, foundations and endowments, as well as those of "high net worth individuals," from offices in London and Washington, D.C.

2. Bill Clinton (Clinton Foundation)

Address: 1271 Ave of the Americas 42nd Floor, New York, NY 10020

Phone: (212) 348-8882

Former President Clinton established The Clinton Foundation. The money raised by the Foundation is spent directly on programs. Clinton's Foundation operate programs around the world each having a significant impact in a wide range of issue areas, including economic development, climate change, health and wellness, and participation of girls and women. The Foundations works with more than 30,000 American schools by providing kids with healthy food choices in an effort to eradicate childhood obesity; more than 85,000 farmers in Malawi, Rwanda, and Tanzania are benefiting from climate-smart agronomic training, higher yields, and increased market access; reduce more than 33,500 tons of greenhouse gas emissions annually through Foundation initiatives across the United States; over 400,000 people have been impacted through market opportunities created by social enterprises in Latin America, the Caribbean, and South Asia; through the independent Clinton Health Access Initiative, 9.9 million people in more than 70 countries have access to CHAI-negotiated prices for HIV/AIDS medications; 85 million people in the U.S. will be reached through strategic health partnerships developed across industry sectors at both the local and national level; and members of the Clinton Global Initiative community have made more than 3,400 Commitments to Action, which have improved the lives of over 430 million people in more than 180 countries.[6]

3. John Ashcroft

Address: 1101 Pennsylvania Ave Washington, DC 20004

Phone: (314) 863-70001

Former U.S. Attorney General, Governor and Senator John Ashcroft serves as founder and Chairman of The Ashcroft Law Firm. Together with the select group of seasoned, respected and experienced senior executives he recruited to join him—many of whom helped to lead the U.S. Department of Justice during a significant time in our nation's history—the Firm has earned a reputation for integrity and a track record for accelerating successful resolutions of even the most complex matters. Our unique approach blends precise legal analysis with business management expertise to serve all facets of our client's needs. With a focus on issues of integrity and corporate governance, the Firm

---

[6] See https://www.clintonfoundation.org/about

provides compliance advice, internal investigations, legal and consulting services to world-leading clients, including Fortune 500 companies, multi-national corporations and corporate executives.

4. Tom Foley

Address: 316 Bryan Hall, PO Box 645136, Pullman, WA 99164

Phone: (509) 335-3477

From October 2006 to January 2009, Foley was the U.S. Ambassador to Ireland, appointed by President George W. Bush. Foley served as Ambassador at a time when U.S. foreign policy was unpopular in Ireland. He directed his public diplomacy efforts mostly toward an improved understanding of U.S. foreign policy goals and shared interests with Ireland. Foley worked with Robert Tuttle, U.S. Ambassador to the U.K., and special envoy Paula Dobriansky to re-establish the devolved government in Northern Ireland under the Good Friday Agreement and to stimulate investment there. He was present in Belfast on May 8, 2007 when the new government of Northern Ireland was sworn-in. As Ambassador, Foley hosted a conference on green technology in Galway and another in Dublin on philanthropy, bringing together experts from the U.S. and their Irish counterparts. He was active in promoting cultural exchange by arranging visits from prominent Irish American artists and performers including Conan O'Brien and former U.S. Poet Laureate Billy Collins. The Thomas S. Foley Institute for Public Policy and Public Service was established at Washington State University in 1995 to honor Speaker Foley's more than 30 years of public service to both state and nation and as the 57th Speaker of the House of Representatives.

IX. **LOBBYING GROUPS SPECIALIZING IN ADVOCACY** – A lobbying firm is defined as a person or entity that has 1 or more employees who are registered as lobbyists on behalf of a client inclusive of a self-employed individual. They are particularly skilled at applying their knowledge, skills, and abilities to influence the government's decision-making process.

1. Alcalde & Fay

Address: 2111 Wilson Blvd #850, Arlington, VA 22201

Phone: (703) 841-0626

Drawing on the expertise of former members of the Executive Branch, Congress and Congressional staffs, Alcalde & Fay is able to provide efficient, effective representation of your views and input to federal decision-makers.

2.   Brownstein, Hyatt Farber Schreck, LLP

Address: 1350 I St. NW, #510, Washington, DC 20005

Phone: (202) 296-7353

Attracting the top professionals from around the country because to work at a high level on meaningful projects. The attorneys, policy consultants and staff here consistently find themselves ranked among the nation's best and brightest. In law. In politics. And in business.

3.   Capitol Hill Strategies

Address: 316 Pennsylvania Ave Washington, DC 20003

Phone: (202) 589-0002

Capitol Hill Strategies employs a close working relationship with clients in order to determine legislative goals, priorities, and vulnerabilities, as well as a consistent focus on long term implementation. In addition, it also employs face-to-face, everyday work on Capitol Hill, to be able to provide clients the advice, counsel, and congressional relationships necessary for success.

4.   Cassidy & Associates

Address: 733 10th St. NW, Washington, DC 20001

Phone: (202) 347-0773

Cassidy & Associates employs a full-time general counsel and outside counsel. Cassidy's clients are as diverse as high-tech entrepreneurs and groundbreaking start-ups to global brand names to national non-profits, universities and trade associations. The staff consists of professionals, both Republicans and Democrats, including former senior Congressional staff, Administration officials, retired military officers, scientists, and business executives.

5.   The District Policy Group

Address: 1500 K St. NW, Washington, DC 20005

Phone: (202) 842-8800

The District Policy Group is a team of lobbyists and public policy specialists who have advanced client interests before the legislative and executive branches of government at the federal and state levels. Our bipartisan team has extensive experience in government relations, advocacy, Capitol Hill policy and politics, federal agency rulemaking, grassroots organizing, social media and coalition building.

6. Gephardt Group

Address: 1333 Constitution Ave NE, Washington, DC 20002

Phone: (202) 546-0106

Led by former House Democratic Leader Dick Gephardt and leading strategist Tom O'Donnell, Gephardt's bipartisan team offers decades of policy, communications, and campaign experience to help clients set and carry out strategies to overcome legislative and regulatory challenges. Team members are top public policy and communications professionals from the House, Senate, and the Executive Branch. They have also served on corporate and non-profit Boards of Advisors, as Washington heads of Fortune 500 companies, and at leading trade associations.

7. Ogilvy Government Relations

Address: 1111 19th St. NW Suite 1100, Washington, DC 20036

Phone: (202)-729-4200

Ogilvy Government Relations' principals have bipartisan expertise on the full range of policy issues debated in Washington. Our principals effectively represent leading corporations, associations and institutions with their legislative and regulatory concerns. The blend of senior level former staffers and administration officials provide us the experience to develop winning government relations strategy campaigns and the ability to reach virtually every office on Capitol Hill and within The White House.[7]

8. Podesta Group

Address: 1001 G St. NW, Suite 1000, Washington, DC 20001

Phone: (202) 393-1010

Podesta has a bipartisan reach into both the executive branch and legislative and provides clients a deep, analytic-driven grasp on the issues and dynamics of the policy agenda. Podesta networks with decision-makers, recruits champions, leverages grassroots support, and builds coalitions to ensure the clients realize their advocacy goals.

---

[7] See https://www.ogilvygr.com/expertise/

9. Quinn Gillespie & Associates (QGA)

Address: 1133 Connecticut Ave NW, #500, Washington, DC 20036

Phone: (202) 457-1110

Quinn Gillespie & Associates (QGA) advises the nation's largest and oldest companies, as well as brand-new technology and consumer product startups. QGA has a strong reputation for tackling difficult challenges, including assisting companies, associations, and clients during their times of crisis. Our goal is to provide the best strategic advice and deliver a successful outcome time after time. While every challenge is unique, QGA's discipline and approach is a method that we've developed and been honing since our inception.

10. Williams & Jensen

Address: 701 8th St. NW, #500, Washington, DC 20001

Phone: (202) 659-8201

Focuses primarily on lobbying the firm's attorneys come from government service, having first worked in congressional or senate offices or other areas of the administration.

X. **GRASSROOTS ORGANIZATIONS** – These organizations vary in leadership structure, size, and specialties. The workforce is focused, location specific, and issue specific. These organizations are generally focused on specific advocacy campaigns and coordinate their activities with grassroots movements as they arise in the public domain. Rank and file membership is comprised of citizens who are vested in specific issues and are activists in their desire to influence the public policy process.

1. American Jewish World Service (AJWS)

Address: 1001 Connecticut Ave NW, Suite 1200, Washington, DC 20036

Phone: (202) 379-4300

American Jewish World Service (AJWS) is an international development organization motivated by Judaism's imperative to pursue justice. AJWS is dedicated to alleviating poverty, hunger and disease among the people of the developing world regardless of race, religion or nationality. Through grants to grassroots organizations, volunteer service, advocacy and education, AJWS fosters civil society, sustainable development and human rights for all people, while promoting the values and responsibilities of global citizenship within the Jewish community.

2. Americans for Democratic Action, Inc.

Address: 1625 K St. NW, Suite 210, Washington, DC 20006

Phone: (202) 785-5969

Americans for Democratic Action, Inc. is the nation's oldest liberal lobbying group. Its legislative priorities include economic policy, campaign finance reform, health care, anti-discrimination, civil rights, women's rights, and foreign and defense concerns. ADA is increasing its grassroots organizing capabilities including working with students across the country on local, state, and national issues.

3. Amnesty International

Address: 600 Pennsylvania Ave SE, Washington, DC 20003

Phone: (202) 544-0200

Amnesty International is a global movement of people fighting injustice and promoting human rights.

Work to protect people wherever justice, freedom, truth and dignity are denied. Currently the world's largest grassroots human rights organization, investigating and exposing abuses, educating and mobilizing the public, and helping to transform societies to create a safer, more just world. Received the Nobel Peace Prize for life-saving work.[8]

4. Bernie Sanders 2016 Presidential Run

Address: Bernie 2016, PO Box 905, Burlington, VT 05402

Contact: https://go.berniesanders.com/page/content/splash

This has been deemed by some as a grassroots campaign because of its focus on small donations, massive rallies, and other grassroots style politicking methods.

5. Free the Slaves

Address: 1320 19th St. NW, Suite 600, Washington, DC 20036

Phone: (202) 775-7480

---

[8] See http://www.amnestyusa.org/about-us

The mission of Free the Slaves is to end slavery worldwide. The organization believes that ending slavery is an ambitious–and realizable–goal. FTS combines original ideas of great research on the ground with grassroots movements, strategic thinking on how to leverage power and sharing the stories of slavery with the world.

6.   GlobalGiving

Address: 1110 Vermont Ave NW, #500, Washington, DC 20005

Phone: (202) 232-5784

A 501(c)(3) non-profit organization based in the U.S. that provides a global crowdfunding platform for grassroots charitable projects. Since 2002, more than 450,000 donors on GlobalGiving have raised more than $175 million to support more than 12,000 projects around the world.

7.   Grassroots Business Fund

Address: 1710 Rhode Island Ave NW, #1000, Washington, DC 20036

Phone: (202) 518-6865

The Grassroots Business Fund is a non-profit based in Washington, DC. It has field offices in Kenya, Peru, and India. Their mission is to build and support high-impact enterprises that provide sustainable economic opportunities to thousands of people at the base of the economic pyramid. These enterprises are grassroots business organizations in developing countries that empower large numbers of the poor as producers of income-generating commodities and products, as consumers of affordable goods and services, and as independent entrepreneurs. GBF actively supports enterprises throughout Latin America, Africa, India, and Southeast Asia.

The Grassroots Business Fund strives to create a world where economic opportunities reach everyone; their mission is to build and support High-Impact Businesses that provide sustainable economic opportunities to millions of people in low income communities. Business with operations in emerging markets have the potential to transform their economies and the standard of living in their communities, but often lack the resources and expertise to achieve success, scale, and reach sustainability. GBF partners with these businesses to deliver a distinctive blend of investment capital and business advisory services through 2 main vehicles working together: a private investment fund and a non-profit. Through the fund, GBF makes equity, mezzanine equity, mezzanine debt, and straight debt investments. These customized investment structures ensure that GBF's investment performance aligns with the businesses' performance. The fund delivers a form of capital suitable for long-term investment in businesses servicing low income communities. In tandem, the non-profit provides business advisory services to clients in the fund.

8. Grassroots Campaigns

Address: 1612 20th St. NW, Washington, DC 20008

Phone: (202) 797-9655

Grassroots Campaigns a self-styled grassroots organization that works on elections in the USA. Recently, Grassroots Campaigns worked on the Obama Campaign of 2012 and on Senate races in 2014 in Colorado, Kansas, and Iowa.

9. Grassroots DC

Address: 1227 G St. SE, Washington, DC 20003

Contact: liane@grassrootsdc.org

The mission of Grassroots Media DC is to provide basic computer and media production training to low-income and working-class residents of the Washington, DC Metropolitan Area and those who advocate on their behalf, and also to provide media coverage of issues that impact the underserved communities of the District of Columbia.

10. Grassroots Organization for the Well-Being of Seniors (GROWS)

Address: 6101 Montrose Rd. Suite 202, Rockville, MD 20852

Phone: (301) 765-3325

Grassroots Organization for the Well-Being of Seniors (GROWS) provides a platform for networking, education, advocacy, and public awareness for senior service professionals in the greater DMV area.

11. The Grassroots Project

Address: 727 15th St. NW, Suite 210, Washington, DC 20005

Phone: (202) 747-2931

The Grassroots Project serves to educate at-risk youth from Washington D.C. about HIV/AIDS awareness and prevention by utilizing Division I "student-athlete" role models. Founded in January 2009, The Grassroot Project is one of the first 501(c) (3) organizations to be designed, initiated, and managed completely by NCAA

Division I varsity athletes encompassing athletes from Georgetown University, George Washington University, Howard University and University of Maryland. We are also unique in our approach to HIV/AIDS prevention—instead of using a traditional education program that is lecture-based and taught by teachers or health educators, we use games that teach lessons and athletes as our messengers.

12. Grassroots Solutions

Address: 1725 Desales St. NW, Washington, DC 20036

Phone: (612) 465-8566

Grassroots Solutions provides consulting services in the areas of strategy, organizing, training, and evaluation.

13. Grassroots Targeting, LLC

Address: 707 Prince St. Alexandria, VA 22314

Phone: (703) 535-7590

Conduct voter research specific to client campaign or organization, starting with day-one strategic insights like vote goals and voter targeting that are unique to clientel. They use proprietary microtargeting methodology & predictive modeling to identify voters and their issues that matter most. They make data easy to understand and use with custom, interactive data visualization dashboards.[9]

14. Local Initiatives Support Corporation

Address: 1825 K St. NW, #1100, Washington, DC 20006

Phone: (202) 785-2908

Local Initiatives Support Corporation (LISC) equips struggling communities with the capital, strategy and know-how to become places where people can thrive.

Working with local leaders and investing in housing, health, education, public safety and employment - all basic needs that must be tackled at once so that progress in one is not undermined by neglect in another.

Bringing together key local players to take on pressing challenges and incubate new solutions. With them, they help develop smarter public policy. Theirtoolkit is extensive. It includes loans, grants, equity investments and on-the-ground experience in some of America's neediest neighborhoods.

---

[9] See http://www.grassrootstargeting.com/

15. National People's Action (NPA)

Address: 810 N Milwaukee Ave Chicago, IL 60642

Phone: (312) 243-3035

A network of grassroots organizations with a fierce reputation for direct action from across the country that work to advance a national economic and racial justice agenda. NPA has over 200 organizers working to unite everyday people in cities, towns, and rural communities throughout the U.S. through direct-action, house meetings, and community organizing.

16. National Environmental Trust

Address: 1200 18th St. NW, Ste 500, Washington, DC 20036

Phone: (202) 887-8800

A non-profit, non-partisan organization dedicated to educating the American public on contemporary environmental issues. Since 1995 (as the Environmental Information Center), NET has worked to promote strong, healthy, and safe environmental protection on issues including: food, air, drinking water safety, global climate change, public right-to-know policies, and endangered species protection. NET's public education campaigns combine research and analysis with effective grassroots efforts organizing media outreach to present the public with accurate, up-to-date information on environmental issues and related public policy debates.

XI. **BUSINESS ORIENTED ORGANIZATIONS** – These organizations focus their efforts on generating revenue for their shareholders. They are directed by a board of directors and an executive level workforce whose decisions determine the goals and objectives of the company or group of companies.

1. Business Roundtable (BTR)

Address: 300 New Jersey Ave NW, #800, Washington, DC 20001

Phone: (202) 872-1260

An association of chief executive officers of leading U.S. companies working to promote sound public policy and a thriving U.S. economy. Business Roundtable's CEO members lead U.S. companies with $7.2 trillion in annual revenues and nearly 16 million employees. BRT member companies comprise more than a quarter of the total value of the U.S. stock market and invest $190 billion annually in research and development – equal to 70 percent of U.S. private R&D.

Chapter 13: Illustrative Advocacy Directory

   2.   The Chamber of Commerce

Address: 1615 H St. NW, Washington, DC 20062

Phone: (202) 659-6000

The world's largest business organization representing the interests of more than 3 million businesses of all sizes, sectors, and regions. Members range from mom-and-pop shops and local chambers to leading industry associations and large corporations. They all share one thing—they count on the Chamber to be their voice when advocating change. The Chamber is set up to include local groups, state groups, and national groups.

   3.   Financial Services Forum

Address: 601 13th St. NW, #750S, Washington, DC 20005

Phone: (202) 457-8765

The Financial Services Forum is a non-partisan financial and economic policy organization comprised of the CEOs of 16 of the largest and most diversified financial services institutions with business operations in the U.S.

The purpose of the Forum is to pursue policies that encourage savings and investment, promote an open and competitive global marketplace, and ensure the opportunity of people everywhere to participate fully and productively in the 21st-century global economy. As a group, the Forum's member institutions employ more than 2 million people in 175 countries.

   4.   The Financial Services Roundtable (FSR)

Address: 600 13th St. NW, #400

Phone: (202) 289-4322

A financial services lobbying and advocacy organization. The Financial Services Roundtable (FSR) represents 100 of the largest integrated financial services companies which provide banking, insurance and investment products and services to American consumers.

   5.   Institute of International Finance

Address: 1333 H St. NW, #800E, Washington, DC 20005

Phone: (202) 857-3600

The Institute of International Finance is the global association for the financial industry, with close to 500 members from 70 countries. Its mission is to support the financial industry in the prudent management of risks; to develop sound industry practices; and to advocate for regulatory, financial and economic policies that are in the broad interests of its members and foster global financial stability and sustainable economic growth. Within its membership IIF counts commercial and investment banks, asset managers, insurance companies, sovereign wealth funds, hedge funds, central banks and development banks.

6.   Minority Business Enterprise Center

Address: 64 New York Ave NE, Suite 3152, Washington, DC 20002

Phone: (202) 671-1552

The Washington, DC Minority Business Enterprise Center (DCMBEC) is a business consulting development agency located in the Nation's Capitol. DCMBEC committed to increasing economic parity in performance between minority and non-minority companies. DCMBEC works with clients to improve their performance and profitability.

7.   National Small Business Association (NSBA)

Address: 1156 15th St. NW, #1100, Washington, DC 20005

Phone: (202) 293-8830

A nonpartisan organization including more than 150,000 small businesses across the country and is the nation's first small-business advocacy organization. Examples of advocacy efforts include the enactment of critical access to capital programs and important small-business tax deductions.

8.   National Women's Business Council

Address: 409 Third St. SW, Suite 210, Washington, DC 20416

Phone: (202) 205-6827

The National Women's Business Council is a bi-partisan, federal advisory council created to serve as an independent source of advice and policy recommendations to the President, Congress, and the U.S. Small Business Administration on economic issues of importance to women business owners. The Council's mission is to promote bold initiatives, policies and programs designed to support women's business enterprises at all stages of development in the public and private sector marketplaces -- from start-up to success to significance.

9. Securities Industry and Financial Markets Assn

Address: 1101 New York Ave NW, 8th Floor, Washington, DC 20005

Phone: (202) 962-7300

SIFMA brings together the shared interests of hundreds of securities firms, banks and asset managers. SIFMA's mission is to support a strong financial industry, investor opportunity, capital formation, job creation and economic growth, while building trust and confidence in the financial markets. SIFMA, with offices in New York and Washington, D.C., is the U.S. regional member of the Global Financial Markets Association (GFMA).

10. Small Business Majority

Address: 1101 14th St. NW, #1001, Washington, DC 20005

Phone: (202) 828-8357

A national small business advocacy organization, founded by small business owners to focus on solving the biggest problems facing small businesses. They actively engage small business owners across America to drive smart public policy and get entrepreneurs the resources they need to be successful.

11. U.S. Council for International Business

Address: 1400 K St. NW, #905, Washington, DC 20005

Phone: (202) 371-1316

An independent business advocacy group to promote free trade and help represent U.S. business within the United Nations. A primary objective is to expand the market access for U.S. products and services abroad. The organization is strongly in favor of open markets and sensible regulation.

12. The World Bank

Address: 1818 H St. NW, Washington, DC 20433

Phone: (202) 473-1000

The World Bank is a vital source of financial and technical assistance to developing countries around the world. We are not a bank in the ordinary sense but a unique partnership to reduce poverty and support development. The World Bank Group comprises five institutions managed by their member countries.

Established in 1944, the World Bank Group is headquartered in Washington, D.C. They have more than 10,000 employees in more than 120 offices worldwide.

XII. TRADE ASSOCIATIONS – These organizations are founded and funded by businesses that operate in a specific industry. They conduct their own research and analysis and provide information to both government decision-makers and other issue stakeholders.

1. American Bar Association (ABA)

Address: 1050 Connecticut Ave NW, #400, Washington, DC 20036

Phone: (202) 662-1000

A voluntary bar association of lawyers and law students, which is not specific to any jurisdiction in the U.S. The ABA's most important stated activities are the setting of academic standards for law schools, and the formulation of model ethical codes related to the legal profession. The ABA has 410,000 members.

2. American Financial Services Association (AFSA)

Address: 919 18th St. NW, Suite 200, Washington, DC 20006

Contact: info@afsamail.org

A trade association for the U.S. consumer credit industry. American Financial Services Association's 350 members include consumer and commercial finance companies, vehicle finance/leasing companies, mortgage lenders, credit card issuers, industrial banks, and industry suppliers.

3. Association of Corporate Counsel (ACC)

Address: 1025 Connecticut Ave NW, #200, Washington, DC 20036

Phone: (202) 293-4103

A global bar association that promotes the common professional and business interests of in-house counsel who work for corporations, associations and other private-sector organizations through information, education, networking opportunities, and advocacy initiatives. ACC generates the revenue necessary through advertising opportunities, fundraisers, and corporate dues.

4. Association of Government Relations Professionals (AGRP) Trade Associations

Address: 444 N. Capitol St. NW, #237 Washington, DC 20001

Phone: (202) 508-3833

Their mission is to enhance the professionalism, competence, and high ethical standards or public policy advocates through education, information exchange, and the ongoing advocacy of the Constitution's First Amendment right to petition government.

5.   Edison Electric Institute (EEI)

Address: 701 Pennsylvania Ave NW, Washington, DC 20004

Phone: (202) 508-5000

Represents all U.S. investor-owned electric companies. Its members provide electricity for 220 million Americans, operate in 50 states and the District of Columbia, and directly employ more than 500,000 workers. EEI is a leading advocate for public policy initiatives favorable to the IOU industry and works directly with government decision-makers to provide insight through the development of research and studies.

6.   National Association of Manufacturers (NAM)

Address: 733 10th St. NW, Washington, DC 20001

Phone: (202) 637-3000

The largest manufacturing association in the U.S., representing small and large manufacturers in every industrial sector and in all 50 states. Manufacturing has the largest national economic impact of any industry and as such has a very powerful voice and is a leading advocate for a policy agenda friendly to the manufacturing community.

7.   National Congress of American Indians

Address: 1516 P St. NW, Washington, DC 20005

Phone: (202) 466-7767

The National Congress of American Indians (NCAI) is the oldest, largest, and most representative organization of American Indian and Alaska Native tribal governments and individuals. NCAI's mission is to inform the public and the federal government on tribal self-government, treaty rights, and a broad range of federal policy issues affecting tribal governments.

8. Nuclear Energy Institute (NEI)

Address: 1201 F St. NW, Washington DC 20004

Phone: (202) 739-8000

Their mission is to foster the beneficial uses of nuclear technology before the Congress, the White House and executive branch agencies, federal regulators, and state policy forums. They proactively engage in communicating accurate and timely information while providing a unified voice on the global importance of nuclear energy and nuclear technology. NEI raises its capital through corporate donations and fundraising campaigns.

Chapter 14

LEARNING RESULTS FOR GOVERNMENT DECISION-MAKERS

A professional advocate's purpose is to ensure that public sector officials representing the American taxpayer have the most current, credible, and pertinent information on public policy issues. This is important so that decisions associated with changes in government policy or operations as well as selection of recipients awarded federal financial assistance are reinforced by that information and the associated analysis. This is the basis for improving the government's delivery of goods and services. Without this information and analysis, government decision-makers cannot justify changes in the approach to policy, statute, or regulation associated with issues that are part of the scope of the government's mission.

Government career and political executives are assisted in achieving their goals by professional advocates. It does not matter whether the advocate is in the baseline, lobbyist, or educator category. The information they provide is one of several sources of information and expertise that Government officials have at their disposal to discharge their responsibilities. The responsibilities include:

- Baseline performance requirements or position selection criteria applied during the hiring process;
- Specialized subject-matter training that they receive to improve their performance. The training is provided by departmental, government-wide or contracted training providers;
- Contracted non-governmental information-and service-providers;
- Transparent, ethical, and informal interactions with non-government professionals; and,
- Professional advocates from all categories. Career government executives as well as outside stakeholders carry out their responsibilities on the basis that the government is open to change for improved performance. Many argue that a career officials' perspective is that status quo is the safest position to pursue in implementing government programs and operations; however; this is not the position of this publication. Rather, the overwhelming majority of government executives are committed to taking whatever steps are required to improve government operations.

Changes of administration focus on issues which have developed in the public eye and are reinforced by media attention. The political process combines with the public's interest and the media's reporting to stimulate and motivate change. In many cases, the government awards grants and contracts to finance private sector experts' development of new alternatives and approaches.

Contracting out for government services and development of new and innovative ideas and programs is a significant portion of the budget each fiscal year. Congress routinely authorizes and provides some form of federal financial assistance to ensure that private sector expertise is available to improve government performance as new technologies, scientific knowledge, and practical experience become available. Even the competencies by which federal executives are evaluated are based on private sector performance models.

CASE STUDY AND SIMULATION OBJECTIVES

This chapter develops two case studies and simulations that are designed to assist both private sector advocates and public sector decision-makers expand their knowledge, skills, and abilities (KSAs). The cases and simulation require analysis and the evaluation of the most practical alternatives of issues. They are also a simulation of the realistic decision-making processes to address the nation's challenges. The cases integrate the roles of the private sector, the professional advocacy community, and the government's decision-making apparatus.

Learning results are only realized when government decision-makers gain experience digesting and effectively applying the information available to them.

The information provided within the case study is not solely based on factual sources; it is to support multiple roles' learning experiences. The sources provided in the cases do use the government's institutional memory, groundbreaking research, and analysis provided due to government-funded private-sector contractors and stakeholders work. The government decision-makers role is to ensure that the range of government responsibilities are decided and implemented in a cost-effective, publically-beneficial, and even-handed manner. By emphasizing learning results, officials seek to excel in attaining their position's performance requirements and associated competencies that their performance requirements are based on.

The manner in which government decision-makers balance and apply their institutional knowledge and diverse information presented by the private sector's professional advocacy community lead to the learning results that the California condor (condor) case study and simulation and the Shintech environmental justice interface with the government and community illustrates.

How best does a government executive utilize the information made available by the advocacy community?

CALIFORNIA CONDOR ISSUE: ROLES OF GOVERNMENT DECISION-MAKERS AND THE PROFESSIONAL ADVOCACY COMMUNITY

Statement of the Issue

The issue that simulation participants will focus on is the advocacy campaign applied by those in the professional advocacy community and the manner in which government decision-makers will use the information provided to them to decide how the government's policy toward protecting the California condor should be changed to provide more extensive, cost efficient protection.

Background

About the Condor

The California condor has the largest wingspan, 9.8 feet, of any North America bird and weighs up to 26 pounds, nearly the same as the Trumpeter Swan. The condor has a life span of up to 60 years in the wild and is classified as a scavenger because it feeds on large amounts of carrion, decaying flesh of dead animals. Today's California condor is the last surviving member of Gymnogyps species, and has no previously accepted subspecies. The condor is distinguished by black coloring with patches of white on the underside of the wings and a bald head. Its physical characteristics result in the exposure of its skin to the sterilizing effects of dehydration and solar ultraviolet light at high altitudes. Their critical habitat has been studied by a number of scientists framed by federally budgeted grants and contracts with private sector entities. The studies' findings are discussed throughout the case study.

Condors are a monogamous bird. Mated females are expected to lay one bluish-white egg every other year as early as January to as late as April. Some recent studies are documenting 30% fewer eggs are laid in the wild than in captivity. Condor eggs weigh 10 ounces and measure from 3 to 5 inches in length and 2.5 inches in width. The eggs hatch after 53 to 60 days of incubation by both parents. Though unproven, some condor experts believe condors' pair for life. The male and female take turns incubating the egg once it hatches, and for up to a year, they feed the offspring until it learns to find its own food.

The pairs prefer to nest in caves or on cliff clefts, especially ones with nearby roosting trees and open spaces for landing due to their large wing span. Since the young are able to fly after five to six months, but continue to roost and forage with their parents until they are in their second year, they need open and safe environments to grow. Condors roost in large groups and communicate with a combination of hisses, growls, and grunts as well as a system of body language, a skill-set that needs reinforcement while in captivity.

Condors live in rocky scrubland, coniferous forests, and oak savannas, which are near cliffs or large trees, used as nesting sites. Condor nest sites have mostly been discovered in mountain cliff caves. However, condors have also been known to nest in large cavities in the trunks of California's giant sequoia redwood trees. Individual condors have been known to travel up to 150 miles to feed on their preferred pick of cattle, pigs, and carrion.

Approximately 10,000 years ago, hundreds of condors lived on both coasts of North America. However, a dramatic range reduction occurred around that time. The reduction coincided with the extinction of large mammals in the wild that condors were known to feed on. By the time Europeans arrived in western North America, the condor's range was limited to a stronghold along the Pacific coast from British Columbia to Baja California. The condor population was plummeting due to its loss of habitat from human development and scarce food sources. Condor's reproductive rates declined from one every five years to one every nine years. Along with declining reproduction rates, the condor population was decreasing because of the increase in agricultural pesticides and hunting related lead poisoning from carcasses that condors feed on, as well as an increase from two hunting related deaths to five hunting related deaths per year documented in a 10 year study conducted by the FWS. The impact of these effects resulted in further range reduction in condor habitat where it is now focused mainly in southern California and parts of Arizona, Utah, and Nevada.

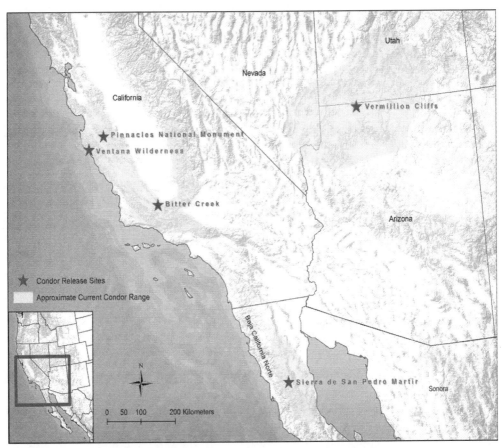

The Endangered Species Act: Statutory and Regulatory Requirements

The California condor has been listed as a Fully Protected Species under California state statute since 1953. The U. S. Department of the Interior's Fish & Wildlife Service (FWS) did not list the California condor as endangered under the authority of the federal Endangered Species Act (ESA) until March 11, 1967. Later, California listed the condor as endangered under the California Endangered Species Act on June 27, 1971. The federal government designated critical habitat for the California condor on September 24, 1976. The ESA provides conservation of the ecosystems upon which threatened and endangered species of fish, wildlife, and plants depend on.

Recovery programs are based on two over-arching goals that achieve the ESA's purposes: 1) recovery of endangered or threatened (federally-listed) species, and 2) conservation of species-at-risk, so that listing them may be unnecessary. Recovery programs achieve these goals through the minimization or abatement of threats that are the basis for listing a species as endangered. The ESA categorizes threats into the following five factors followed by their relevance to the condor's plight:

1. The present or threatened destruction, modification, or curtailment of a listed species' habitat or range; *documented to condor circumstance*;
2. Overutilization for commercial, recreational, scientific, or educational purposes; *not condor related;*
3. Disease or predation; *documented to condor circumstance*;
4. The inadequacy of existing regulatory mechanisms; *requires analysis for condor relevance; and,*
5. Other natural or manmade factors affecting a species' continued existence; *requires analysis for condor relevance.*

Following advocacy campaigns associated with the development of condor recovery plans, The Ridley-Tree Condor Protection Act (CPA) was enacted. Regulations in the CPA that pertain to the preservation of condor species are:

- 42 CFR 1.8008- No windmill will be constructed within a 30 mile radius of any condor breeding area. Enforcement - $2 million fine plus one year in prison;
- 42 CFR 2.8002- No hunter will be allowed to shoot lead bullets at either game or vermin within 50 miles of any condor breeding are. Enforcement - $500 fine plus 30 days in jail; and,
- 42 CFR 3.803- Cyanide or any other man made toxins used to kill vermin or scavengers is restricted from use within 75 miles of a condor's breeding area. Enforcement - $2000 fine plus 60 days in jail.

California's enactment of The Ridley-Tree Condor Preservation Act and associated regulatory restrictions angered California hunters who were already using non-lead ammunition (mainly steel and copper) for all big game hunting adjacent to the California condor range. They questioned a 2012 study by scientists at the University of California at Santa Cruz that concluded that "30% of blood samples taken from condors each year showed levels of lead high enough to pose significant health problems for condors and that 20% of condors required treatment to remove lead." However, the Center for Biological Diversity indicated that hunters could easily transition to non-lead ammunition. Their rationale was that adjustments to game tags and hunting in the area had been taking place for last five years. The condor population was believed to be stable.

The Listing and Critical Habitat Program (LCHP) provides protection under the ESA for foreign and domestic plants and animals when a species is determined to be threatened or endangered on the basis of the best available scientific information. This determination includes information crucial for recovery planning and implementation, and helps to identify and address the conservation needs of the species. This includes the designation of critical habitat. Without the legal protections afforded under Section 9 of the ESA that become effective upon listing, many species would continue to decline and become extinct.

The California Condor Wind Energy Work Group is a subgroup of the California Condor Recovery Team and appointed by the U.S. FWS as required by the Endangered Species Act. The purpose of the subgroup is to assist the U.S. FWS with recovery efforts. The process includes assessment and risk mitigation associated with wind energy activities within condor habitat. Wind energy has the potential to conflict with the recovery of the condor when projects are improperly sited and measures are not taken to minimize risks to condors. The U.S. FWS believes it is imperative to use the best scientific and technical guidance available to ensure that wind energy development proceeds without compromising California condor recovery.

Recovery efforts also implement actions for species near delisting or reclassification from *endangered* to *threatened* as well as actions that are urgently needed for critically endangered species. The Endangered Species Program participates in the Cooperative Recovery Initiative by combining resources with those of the National Wildlife Refuge System, the Partners for Fish and Wildlife Program, the Fisheries Program, the Science Program, and the Migratory Bird Program. A national, proposal-driven process to identify and implement the highest priority projects is conducted by FWS.

Condors in Captivity

In response to the significantly diminished condor population, the recovery program's strategy for condor breeding in captivity focuses on increasing reproduction in captivity; then, the release of healthy condors to the wild. This approach assumes minimizing condor death factors, protecting condor habitat, and implementing condor information and education programs for the public.

The table below highlights captive releases in 2013. SB# = Studbook #; SDZSP=San Diego Zoo Safari Park; WCBP=World Center for Birds of Prey; LAZ=Los Angeles Zoo. A successful fate indicates that the released condor was alive and remained in the wild population without having to be recaptured for 90 days following its initial release.

SB#	Sex	Hatch Date	Hatch Location	Transfer Date	Release Date	Fate
628	female	2-Jun-11	WCBP	21-Aug-13	20-Nov-13	Successful
632	female	21-Jun-11	LAZ	30-Oct-13	11-Dec-13	Successful
636	male	10-Mar-12	SDSP	11-Apr-13	20-Nov-13	Successful

637	male	15-Mar-12	SDSP	11-Apr-13	23-Oct-13	Successful
642	female	30-Mar-12	ORZ	21-Aug-13	11-Dec-13	Successful
643	male	2-Apr-12	SDSP	11-Apr-13	23-Oct-13	Successful

Prior to release into the wild the condors are moved to flight pen for 30 days so that they familiarize themselves with the new surroundings. The condors must be physically and behaviorally healthy. They must socialize with other condors waiting to be released. Condors to be released have also been isolated from humans in effort to prevent taming. Aversion training is an important objective to condition condors to avoid humans and human made structures.

A FWS field team employs aversion training, hazing, and trapping of habituated condors as a means to manage their behavior. Unfortunately, these techniques may lead to condor injuries, and subsequently death. The field team documented some of the newly released condors died as a result of collisions with power lines. The field team used mock power poles within the pre-release flight pens to deliver a nonlethal shock when a condor landed on the structure. This aversion training became a critical part of the condor releases into the wild. The field team has documented the benefits of this approach for condors released in the wild. The protocol continues by recapturing condors that exhibit behavior presenting an immediate risk of physical harm or death to the condor.

The field team takes other specific actions to ensure a condor's protection post-release. Condors are released in pairs to encourage socialization. Supplemental carrion is provided near the release pen to lure other free flying condors in to feed and interact with newly released condors. The team monitors condor roost' to be certain newly released and other free flying condors have become familiar with the location of water and supplemental feeding sites. Supplemental feeding sites act as a substitute for the parental care that the released condors would have received had they reproduced in the wild.

The objective of the recovery program is to establish three additional and separate populations of 150 condors. If the objective is accomplished by 2020, FWS would be pressed to delist the condor.The geographically separate populations would be in Arizona, the other in California. Each would have a minimum of 15 breeding pairs. The number of release sites would grow as additional habitat is identified. However, there is controversy among experts at the San Diego Wild Animal Park and Los Angeles Zoo associated whether the objective is achievable from captive breeding programs.

Utilizing the bird's ability to double clutch, biologists seek to improve the unique captive breeding technique by removing the first egg from the nest. The result is often a second and sometimes even a third egg. The objective is to incubate the extra eggs in captivity and rely on caretakers, using a hand puppet shaped like a condor head, to care for the condor chicks during the early stages.

Environmentalists cite studies on the negative impacts of captive breeding programs to rally the media and the public to support their opposition of captive breeding. They point out that the stress induced by the process of capturing and housing the condor can be detrimental to their reproduction process. Disruption in the natural order of the condor's lifecycle is vigorously opposed. Some conservationists agree with environmentalist but most do not concur. FWS has evaluated and is in the process of promulgating quality standards so that the health and well being of the condor is ensured through their capture and housing processes. However, this set of standards will not be realized unless a budget increase for condor captive breeding program is approved coinciding with a shift in program for condor recovery.

Other studies suggest condors have had difficulty breeding in captivity due to the stress associated with human induced pressure to do so. Breeding rates for captive birds are higher than that of naturally occurring pairs when negative conditions associated with the trauma and stress of the new habitat is eliminated. The budget and new regulatory requirements are controversial among political activists and stakeholders

Condors in the Wild

Many conservation advocates believe that the condor has more successful opportunity to breed in the wild due its familiarity with the natural surroundings than if the condor were to be in captivity. Further, there are a number of federal budget analysts that support condor breeding in the wild due to the high costs associated with breeding in captivity. The cost/benefit analysis concluded that a program focused on maintaining conditions favorable to condors breeding in the wild would cost only roughly $1 million per year versus $3 million per year estimated to fund captive breeding.

One aspect of the Condor Conservation Program is that federal wildlife specialists work with the private sector wildlife professionals to conduct proactive conservation activities focused on removing or reducing ecological threats to condor breeding. This begins with a rigorous assessment using the best scientific information available to determine what barriers can be removed from condor habitat. Close co-operation between state conservation officials and other appropriate stakeholders is critical. This information, such as, successful approaches in the past, availability of land to acquire, and associated funding is the basis for the analysis required to mitigate specific known threats.

As part of the Conservation Program nesting attempts and outcomes for the 2013 breeding season are outlined below. Foster Eggs are captive laid eggs used to replace the wild laid egg when it was not viable. Fledging is the act of the chick successfully leaving the nest and nesting at a different location.

Nest #	Date Located	Egg #	Lay Date	Foster Egg Used	Date Hatch	Nest Fate
AB13	27-Feb	FW113	12-Feb	no	10-Apr	Fledged 29-Aug
HC13	22-Feb	FW213	14-Feb	yes	25-Apr	Fledged 28-Sep
HC13	20-Feb	FW313	19-Feb	no	NA	NA
SP13	2-Mar	FW413	27-Feb	yes	17-Apr	Failed 04-Nov
KR13	2-Mar	FW513	18-Feb	no	16-Apr	Failed 30-Nov
SC13	14-Mar	FW613	12-Mar	no	NA	Failed 18-Apr
OD13	27-Mar	FW713	23-Mar	no	19-May	Fledged 06-Nov
PC13	3-Apr	FW913	3-Apr	no	30-May	Fledged 17-Nov

The 2013 nesting season spanned over 10 months, with nests active from February until November. There were seven active nests during the season, four of which fledged chicks and three of which failed.

Nest guarding has proven effective at increasing the number of wild-fledged chicks in the Southern California population. The field team monitors and records nesting activity within the nest of the condor. Nesting success is defined by the number of chicks to fledge out of the number of nests. This technique has increased the population in the wild since nest guarding was implemented across all nests in 2007. In 2013, each nest was monitored utilizing nest cameras for three of the nests. One nest camera was installed the previous year and two additional cameras were installed in 2013.

The field team attempted five interventions on four nests in 2013. Four of these attempts were successful. Three interventions took place during the egg stage. Two eggs were found to be nonviable during routine nest entries. Both of these eggs were replaced first with dummy eggs and later with two viable eggs from captivity.

Advocates for this approach are also seeking increased funding to support the planning and associated costs of completing studies detailing the effects of environmental threats such as wind farms on the nesting and flight patterns of the California condor. The actual construction of conservation sites in California, Nevada and Arizona led to the deaths of 3 and injuries to 7 California condors as well as numerous reports of injuries and deaths to other indigenous species. The other species include the short-winged New Mexico fruit bat and the long-eared mid-western parakeet due to the carelessness and lack of training of the staff for the condor's habitat. The studies and development of training materials, in conjunction with the Department of Energy, will require 14 new full time employees (FTEs) to complete in accordance with the National Environmental Protection Act (NEPA). There are fixed costs associated with equipment rental and renewal of GSA building leases integral to providing the infrastructure necessary to facilitate safety and optimal conditions to promote breeding in the wild.

The Consultation and Habitat Conservation Plan Program (CHCPP) continues to operate a successful collaborative process between the Fish and Wildlife Service and other state and federal agencies to identify opportunities to initiate effective conservation activities that increase breeding among condors in the wild. Other federal agencies such as the Forest Service are required to consult with the FWS to balance any adverse impacts associated with their development actions.

The FWS' 5-year status review on the 'California Condor Recovery Program' identified another human factor associated with the decline in condor populations. They found that condors in the wild sometimes unknowingly ingest and then feed their offspring pieces of garbage such as, nuts, bolts, washers, wires, shards of glass, bottle caps, and plastic that is disposed of by humans. These items together are referred to as "microtrash." Condor chicks are able to tolerate small quantities of microtrash. However, large amounts often result in a variety of negative effects, including digestive tract impaction, internal cuts and bleeding, and even death. Future recovery programs will seek to address this issue.

Condor Protection Command and Control

The human factor in southern California focused on hunting, predatory egg encroachment, poisoning by cyanide traps set for coyotes, collisions with power lines, wind farm blades, and lead poisoning that occurs from ingesting carrion hunters do not remove from the wild all negatively impact the condor population. In 1986, only 22 California condors were known to be in the wild. The CPA developed strict policies outlawing hunting condors or any game in condor habitat using lead shot. The Act also banned the use of cyanide pills to kill other scavenging animals. This act and state/ federal consideration of promulgating a regulatory regime to protect condors in the wild as well as acquiring additional condor habitat is an approach which has been promoted by some in the advocacy community. However, the costs of promulgating new rules and dedicating staff used to enforce the rules requiring budgetary increases.The process to evaluate this approach commenced when government officials announced that the FWS was analyzing regulatory approaches to protect the condor. Further, stakeholders such as, Friends of California Condors Wild & Free were active both directly and indirectly having engaged professional advocates to raise public awareness on the plight of the condor and supporting the command and control methodology. The public voiced concern that the government was dangerously slow implementing policies to facilitate increased condor breeding and population recovery. The public was polled, and it was clear they believed disreputable lobbyists were culpable in the government's failures. Certain conservation groups such as the Defenders of Wildlife and Conservation and Research for Endangered Species concluded that the condors were better off left in the wild if a full regulatory regime was promulgated to protect the condor. FWS studies reinforced the premise that human activities were responsible for fatalities and a change from status quo was indicated. The congress initiated oversight and appropriation committee hearings to evaluate FWS' performance and the cost/benefits associated with both the regulatory regime and the budget allocated to condor related activities.

The Friends of the California condor testified that the California condor should be managed by a traditional command and control methodology for several reasons:

- Condor's are vulnerable to the encroachment of windmill farms into their habitat;
- Condor's fatalities are documented as having resulted from lead poisoning from bullets and from eating poisoned coyotes that have died from eating cyanide traps;
- The encroachment of condor habitat given housing and commercial development is detrimental. Furthering the impact of climate change;
- There must also be stringent regulations which prohibit use of lead based ammunition and poison traps; and,
- Finally, strict criteria for specific conditions limiting construction and use of wind energy facilities and operations in condor habitat must be imposed.

The preservation of condor foraging habitat is a priority for condor conservation according to the Recovery Plan and the Complex's Comprehensive Conservation Plan. When possible, land managers within the species' range are encouraged to use lead-free ammunition when dispatching animals and allow dead livestock to remain on their properties.

The field team also continues to provide outreach and information to government agencies to ensure they integrate information on condor biology and habitat use into land planning documents. The field team performs a number of additional types of outreach activities with the intention of creating awareness and educating the public about condor conservation issues. The FWS authorizes refuge tours, co-hosts events with program partners such as the Friends Group, and make presentations to local schools. When possible, the FWS accommodates media requests and contributes to several social media outlets and scientific publications.

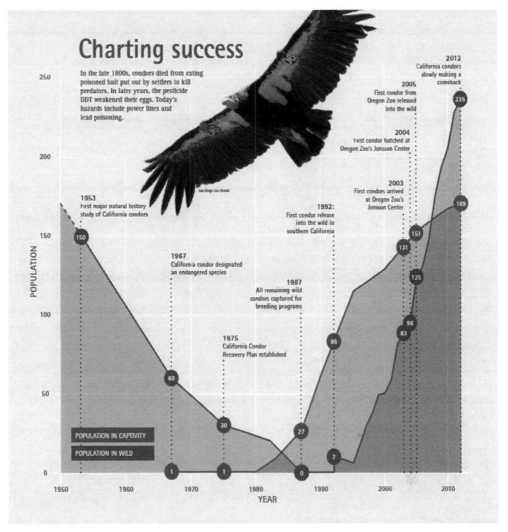

Charting success

In the late 1800s, condors died from eating poisoned bait put out by settlers to kill predators. In later years, the pesticide DDT weakened their eggs. Today's hazards include power lines and lead poisoning.

2012 California condors slowly making a comeback — 235

2005 First condor from Oregon Zoo released into the wild

2004 First condor hatched at Oregon Zoo's Jonsson Center

2003 First condors arrived at Oregon Zoo's Jonsson Center — 169

1953 First major natural history study of California condors — 150

1992: First condor release into the wild in southern California — 151, 131

1967 California condor designated an endangered species

1987 All remaining wild condors captured for breeding programs — 125

1975 California Condor Recovery Plan established — 96, 83, 86

60, 30, 27, 7, 1, 1, 0

POPULATION IN CAPTIVITY
POPULATION IN WILD

POPULATION

YEAR

1950   1960   1970   1980   1990   2000   2010

0   50   100   150   200   250

Expert Studies

There are a number of studies which are relevant to the government's decision-making process. FWS' biological studies are required by the Endangered Species Act. The objective is to address complex issues and knowledge gaps required to facilitate sound decision-making associated with condor protection. The second objective is to implement effective condor breeding policies. Further, the government is contracting with private sector institutions and organizations to improve and update the government's institutional condor database. Thus, the government's responsibility is to analyze various protection alternatives, cost scenarios, and the benefits associated with those cost scenarios. Government decision-makers are encouraged to evaluate studies promulgated in the private sector whether government funded or not. The focus is having the most recent and credible information available to improve their knowledge base.

Surveys conducted by the FWS have concluded that while the general public prefers and supports natural breeding policies, the public is demanding that the most beneficial actions to facilitate condor breeding be undertaken regardless of the costs.

Advocacy efforts for wild and free breeding practices have been led by the Hopper Mountain National Wildlife Refuge Complex. As is known, Federal employees are permitted to educate the public but not lobby. Many family members of FWS employees have joined Friends of California Condors Wild & Free, a nonprofit 501c3 facility and advocacy group, focused on preserving the California condors.

Scientific studies are documenting unfavorable impacts to condors associated with eating carrion poisoned by lead bullet fragments from hunters and by the U.S. Military who use land adjacent to the condor's prime habitat for target practice. The studies account for impacts associated with local rancher's use of cyanide traps set for coyotes that prey on their cattle. The studies conclude that habitat degradation associated with coyote cattle kills and migration of wildlife from condor habitat has resulted in food chain disruption. As carrion feeders, condors often find lead shot or fragments of lead rifle bullets in gut piles left by hunters and in the remains of sick or injured domestic animals and «varmints» dispatched by ranchers.

Lead rifle bullets tend to leave about 15-30% of their mass behind in the carcass when the bullet passes through-sometimes over 200 fragments from one bullet. Copper, steel, and other forms of non-lead ammunition are less toxic and most importantly, do not fragment.

The Arizona Game & Fish Department (AZGFD) has the responsibility to make it easy for hunters to find the right non-lead alternative for their guns; the list is under the "Non-lead ammunition" link found at www.azgfd.gov/condor. Major players in the condor recovery program in Arizona and Utah are not in favor of a ban on lead ammunition. They point out that when this "non-essential, experimental" population of condors was re-introduced to the area, it was under a law stipulating that "current and future land…uses such as…sport hunting should not be restricted due to the…condors." They point out that the reasons for switching are compelling, that hunters have a proud tradition of stepping up to the plate to conserve wildlife, and that education is likely to be more effective in changing behavior than the passage of a new and hard-to-enforce law. There are also numerous studies documenting changes in condor mating rituals impacting condors both in the wild and in captivity. The studies evaluate breeding patterns and what can be predicted in the wild under various conditions versus captivity under various conditions. There appears to be consensus that one sturdy egg is being produced in a captive environment versus one thin-shelled egg in the wild.

Some condor experts conclude that past use of the pesticide DDT prevented the hatching of 20 to 30 percent of condor eggs in the wild. Conversely, other condor experts conclude that the availability of veterinary services for condors in captivity has resulted in a 20 to 30 percent increase in condor breeding in captivity. Compounding the egg issue is an overall increase in the raven population, the main predatory threat to the condor eggs.

Alternative Budget Scenarios

The annual budget associated with the implementation of a habitat maintenance program focused on enhancing condor breeding in the wild is delineated below:

Breeding in the Wild – Annual Costs

Item	Quantity	Unit Cost	Cost
Full Time Employees	5	40000	200000
Tracking devices	35	5000	175000
Surveillance Cameras	10	1500	15000
Trucks	3	55000	165000
Observation Stations	5	50000	250000
Tracking Software	5	1500	7500
Posted signs	30	100	3000
Public Education Newsletter	1	10000	10000
Cooperative Grants Contracts	1	50000	50000
Total			875,500

The annual budget associated with the implementation of a captive breeding program focused on increasing the probability of condor reproduction is outlined below:

Captive Breeding Program – Annual Costs

The annual budget associated with the implementation of control and command regulations focused on preserving the condor habitat and increasing populations is outlined below:

Item	Quantity	Unit Cost	Cost
Full Time Employees	10	70000	700000
Exhibitory Construction	1	500000	500000
Transportation Cages	6	10000	60000
Food	365	200	73000
Training	4	10000	40000
Incubators	6	40000	240000
Veterinary Care	2	80000	160000
Laboratory Equipment	2	150000	300000
Housing Costs	2	120000	240000

Item	Quantity	Unit Cost	Cost
Zoo Maintenance	2	37500	75000
Total			**$2,388,000**

Control and Command Regulations – Annual Costs

Item	Quantity	Unit Cost	Cost
Land Acquistion	3	100000	3000000
Enforcement FTE	5	50000	250000
Regulatory Development	2.5	75000	187500
Operations FTE	5	50000	250000
Cooperative Research Grants	1	250000	250000
Observation Posts	3	50000	150000
Public Education	1	50000	50000
Tracking devices	6	10000	60000
Expert Studies	5	20000	100000
Statutory Enforcement	1	1000000	1000000
Total Costs			**$5,297,500**

Revenue Services	Quantity	Price	Total Earned
Refuge Entry Pass	1300	50	6500000
Classroom Education Programs	12	3000	36000
Total Revenue			**$686,000**

Stakeholders & Political Positions

1. **Baseline Advocates:** Provide objective, up-to-date data and scientific information to facilitate on-going decision making. The analysis is balanced, objective, and transparent in discussion the viable approaches to protect and increase the condor population.
   - **Industry**
     - ○ *The National Audubon Society* – Audubon California was established in 1996 as a field program of the National Audubon Society. They work in California to conserve and restore natural ecosystems,

focusing on birds, other wildlife, and their habitats for the benefit of humanity. They support condor breeding in the wild as well as land acquisition to expand condor habitat; and,

o *Hopper Mountain National Wildlife Refuge Complex* – Advocates from this group wishes for the condor to remain in the wild and are adamantly against and captive breeding program.

- **Government**
  o *White House Office of Management and Budget* – Current position is that the appropriate approach to condor protection and to facilitate increased breeding should be the most cost effective;
  o *Department of the Budget Office* – Current position is that status quo is not working and therefore a change in policy and operations is required; and,
  o *Secretary of Interior's Office* – Current position is that the strongest approach to protecting and increasing successful condor breeding should be implemented regardless of cost.
- **Community Involvement**
  o None Active.

2. **Lobbying Advocates**: Provide an accurate analysis of information/data which emphasizes one alternative.
   - **Industry**
     o *Conservation and Research for Endangered Species* – Most advocate for command and control mechanism;
     o *Captive Breeding Zoo Representatives* – The captive breeding zoo representatives is an advocacy group comprised of zoo officials that prefer the captive breeding alternative; and,
     o *National Rifle Association* – The NRA supports captive breeding and rejects command and control mechanisms.
   - **Government**
     o *Partisan Politicians in Congress*
       ▪ Republicans – A majority believe the best approach is to continue condor breeding in the wild without intervention;
       ▪ Democrats – A majority believe the best approach is to initiate condor captive breeding programs; and,
       ▪ Independents – A majority believe that there must be a catalyst to mix operations and sensitivity to costs guided by authorizing the least amount of government intervention.
   - **Community Involvement**
     o *Friends of California Condors Wild & Free* – Advocates from this group recommend that government decision-makers require the use of non-lead centerfire ammunition when hunting within the current and historic range of the condor and implement a program for the California Department of Fish & Game to provide big game hunters within this range with non-lead ammunition.

3. **Education Advocates:** Education advocacy conduct and report on peer reviewed scientific studies on condor related issues; also, publish the findings and testify to committees, educate the public, and provide relevant information to and regulatory bodies.

- **Industry**
  o None active.
- **Government**
  o *U.S. Fish and Wildlife Service* (**FWS**) – Current position is that the strongest approach to protecting and increasing successful condor breeding should be implemented regardless of cost and regulatory action needs to be implemented for protection enforcement; and,
  o *U.S. Forest Service (USFS)* – Holds the same position as the FWS.
- **Community Involvement**
  o *Golden Ram Sportsman's Club* – The Golden Ram Sportsman's Club has been California's premier club for the avid outdoorsman. Founded by hunters, for hunters, they balance traditional conservation and environmental methodology;
  o *Community Partnerships* – Examples include; Partners for Fish & Wildlife, Costal Program, Central Valley Joint Venture, Sport Fish & Wildlife Restoration, Tribal Partnerships and Grants, San Francisco Bay Joint Venture are all active in supporting habitat revitalization and environmental protection; and,
  o *Local newspapers or publications* – Education advocates seeking to protect the condor population through investigative journalism stories, documentaries, and interviews and cover stories.

CALIFORNIA CONDOR SIMULATION

Section I

The California condor simulation includes Executive Branch, Congressional Branch, and stakeholder roles. There are up to 17 roles which can be part of the simulation. Simulation participants develop materials to successfully achieve their Role's objectives. All advocacy materials must be developed using the information articulated in the case study ONLY.

The ten key roles include: (1) OMB, (2) DOI, (3) FWS, (4) Office of Secretary, (5) USFS, (6) Congress, (7) conservationists, (8) environmentalists, (9) Hunting Community Advocate, and (10) Public Advocates. A summary of the roles follow:

1 White House Office of Management and Budget Executive (OMB)
2 Department of Interior (DOI)
3 U.S. Fish and Wildlife Service Director
4 Secretary of the Interior
5 U.S. Forest Service (USFS) Director

6   Congressman
    6-1 Republican
    6-2 Democrat
    6-3 Independent
7   Conservationists
    7-1 Conservation and Research for Endangered Species
    7-2 Friends of California Condors Wild & Free
8   Environmentalist
    8-1 Hopper Mountain National Wildlife Refuge Complex
    8-2 National Audubon Society Member
    8-3 Captive Breeding Zoo Representative
9   Hunting Community
    9-1 National Rifle Association
    9-2 Golden Ram Sportsman's Club
10 Public Advocate/Media
    10-1 Local newspapers or publication author Community Partnership Representative

The simulation requires interface, coordination, and ultimately negotiation between the roles to achieve the following objectives:

- Understand how to interface with career and political executives as an advocate for your agency/organization;
- Understand the differences between the three categories of advocacy;
- Understand the nuances of effective advocacy to the federal government; and,
- Understand the basis for government decision-making.

Section II

Participants must draft their own advocacy documents outlining the decision criteria associated with their position. The methodologies governing development of credible issue analysis and delivery mechanism are articulated in chapters 6-10 of this publication. Each participant must articulate a comprehensive recommendation and justification for the recommendation. The staff acting as the President will make the final executive branch decision following interface and negotiations between participants.

A representative of each position will advocate for their recommendation to the other position stakeholders. Following the presentations, the Secretary and President will decide the issue. It should be the most reasonable, objective, and cost efficient for preserving and protecting the condor population.

Section III

Upon completion of the advocacy campaign and Executive Branch decision-making process, the simulation continues to the Congressional phase. The advocate whose position was chosen to be the recommendation will then present their argument to a congressional committee of three appointed congressman (seminar participants) to evaluate the Executive Branch's decision-making process associated with the Executive Branch decision. The congressional members must develop their own written advocacy campaign to base the questions on and build the record they support. Along with the presenting advocate there should be a representative from the two other most supported positions. The congressmen appointed to the committee will be from stakeholder states and be those familiar with the condor issue. Following the decision-maker's testimony at the hearing and the statements and questioning by the congressmen, all participants will vote to finalize the changes in policy and the approach the FWS will implement.

Shintech Environmental Justice Case Study and Simulation

The Issue

Should the Louisiana Department of Environmental Quality (LDEQ) issue construction permits pursuant to its delegation of authority from EPA to Shintech for a PVC manufacturing plant in the St. James Parish?

The state of Louisiana acts on permit requests as required by applicable federal statute and associated regulations pursuant to a federal delegation of authority from EPA to act on permit requests. The state of Louisiana conducted a public participation process in which environmental justice activists, industry stakeholders, local elected officials, and residents had an opportunity to advocate their policy positions to state and federal regulatory officials. The state's regulatory officials' public participation process included public hearings in which analysis of Shintech's application, and responses to inquiries by any public hearing attendees were addressed. Most of the public's questions focused on potential positive or negative economic, environmental, health or safety impacts on St. James Parish. The Shintech permit application drew national attention due to the ground breaking environmental justice issues that were raised during the public participation process. The issue was so controversial that the EPA's regional office elevated the situation to the President's democratic appointee heading the EPA. Many requested that the Administrator rescind the delegation of authority to the State and evaluate the EJ related permit requests at EPA. This result would have been EPA deciding whether to issue permits. The Administrator indicated she would work in tandem with the State by evaluating the EJ related issues during the State's process.

The political and business sectors supported Shintech's proposed new facility. However, it was clear that Shintech would have to commit to comply with more stringent environmental permit requirements. Further, Shintech would have to commit to a significant economic enrichment plan to stimulate the St. James Parish's economy. This commitment would be expressed by increasing the number of permanent jobs associated with the new plant, increasing tax revenues, and proposing tangible methods and solutions in order to mitigate potential health and other adverse environmental impacts associated with the construction and operation of the new facility.

The community activists, environmental justice and civil rights advocates, as well as some residents took the position that the new plant should not be constructed in St. James Parish. Their position was that Shintech could not mitigate adverse health and safety impacts to the local residents of Convent. Opponents also stated that local residents were compromised by the cumulative effect of industry's existing emissions in the so called "Cancer Alley" environment.

Overall, there were many that believed that environmental justice related concerns would best be served by expanding the community's economic base with new industry but requiring compliance with more stringent emissions standards.

It is important to note that environmental justice is a relatively new movement. The basis is that all community residents are guaranteed equal protection associated with their access to economic opportunity and individual health that is not **unduly impaired** by toxic emissions. Supporters of the movement believe that minorities and low-income communities are more likely to live in close proximity to facilities which produce toxic and hazardous emissions. Further, residents are less involved with public and government decision-making, therefore, not as protected from the adverse impacts, as upper or middle class communities. Finally, the reality of a community with EJ related issues is less enforcement of environmental standards. The cumulative impact of these emissions results in inequity and injustice. Therefore, disparately impacted communities and the residents should require that industry mitigate adverse impacts to bring more equality and fairness if there are proposals to site near or expand facilities.

Introduction

In 1994, President Clinton signed an Executive Order that directed all federal agencies to examine and to avoid disproportionately high and adverse health and economic impacts on minority and low-income populations associated with construction and operation of facilities with significant new emissions.

The policy prompted renewed interest in Title VI of the Civil Rights Act of 1964. Title VI prohibits discrimination in any federal program or federally-funded program, and applies to any agency that receives federal funds, including state and local agencies.

The federal government has integrated environmental justice criteria into many of its agencies' missions and established grants and cooperative agreements for non-profits, community organizations, and other entities participating and impacted by industry expansion. Environmental justice task forces and collaboratives are also present at the state and municipal levels, to assist community organizations examining issues to minimize local problems associated with industrial expansion.

EPA uses its grants and cooperative agreement authority to support national environmental justice priorities. The EPA is directed to use the funding to enforce Title VI complaints and to fund federal and state-wide grant opportunities addressing requirements delineated in EPA's Request for Proposals (RFP).

EPA federal assistance was available to any stakeholder involved in the Shintech permitting issue. However, any stakeholder seeking the federal financial assistance was required to submit a grant application addressing the disparate impact, environment, and health or safety impacts associated with the permits sought.

There are several financial assistance programs. The first is the Environmental Justice Small Grants Program. The grant program assists recipients develop collaborative partnerships that address environmental and public health impacts associated with development in their communities.[1]

The second is The Environmental Justice Collaborative Problem-Solving (CPS) Cooperative Agreement Program. The CPS Program is designed to help communities understand and address exposure to multiple environmental harms and risks.[2]

The congress will decide whether either federal assistance program is cost-beneficial based on the resolution of the permit issue and acceptability of Shintech's plan for mitigating the environmental and public health issues.

This case study and simulation focuses on the manner in which corporate responsibility and interaction with the communities' environmental justice objectives must be addressed.

Background

In 1996, Shintech Incorporated, a U.S. subsidiary of Shin-Etsu Chemical of Tokyo, Japan, proposed to construct an integrated $700 million polyvinyl chloride (PVC) facility in Convent, Louisiana (St. James Parish) consisting of three (3) chemical plants and an incinerator. Shintech indicated that this location was attractive because the neighboring Dow Chemical Company was able to easily provide raw materials such as ethylene and salt, access to deep waterways, ports and rail transportation, and the existing chemical industry infrastructure.

St. James Parish is located along the Mississippi River between Baton Rouge and New Orleans. This area has many names. Environmentalists coined it "Cancer Alley" due to the cumulative impact of 132 million pounds of toxic emissions each year. State Officials have termed it the "Industrial Corridor" due to the amount of manufacturing and production facilities in the area, and industry leaders from the region refer to it as the "Chemical Corridor."

For decades, Louisiana's industrial corridor has been the backbone of the State's economic growth and due to the jobs and tax revenue provided by industry, it is integral to the State's financial solvency. In terms of environmental and social justice, there is an ongoing debate which revolves around whether compliance with federal and state toxic emission standards balanced with economic expansion and quality of life improvements are sufficient to permit industrial expansion in communities populated by poor and at-risk minorities.

---

[1] Availabe at: http://www3.epa.gov/environmentaljustice/grants/ej-smgrants.html
[2] Availabe at: http://www3.epa.gov/environmentaljustice/grants/ej-cps-grants.html

The U.S. Census reports St. James Parish had a total population of 21,216 in 2000. 10,606 or 50% of residents were categorized as White, and 10,476 or 49.4% categorized as African-American. The area was considered low-income, at-risk community with a per capita income of $14,381. The population within a 4-mile radius of the proposed plant site was 84% African-American.[3] Within the proposed plant construction plans Shintech indicated the plant would provide local residents with full time employment opportunities. At that time St. James Parish already had a 60 percent unemployment rate while being the home of seven oil refineries and somewhere between 175 and 350 heavy industrial plants. These industries emitted 132 million pounds of toxic substances into the environment annually,[4] and waste-processing companies' additional toxic waste from other states into the area – 52 million pounds worth in 1995. Many civil rights groups have presented studies that indicate that the presence of industrial facilities does not reflect positively on the employment rate of that area. People living near the factories and waste dumps were plagued with disease, which many attributed to the industrial chemicals and waste. The incidence of asthma, stillbirths, miscarriages, neurological disease and cancers had ballooned, and residents believed that the waste has also poisoned the pets, fish and other wildlife.[5]

2000 St. James Parish Census Report				
Census Populations, Population Estimates and Percent of Total Population for St. James Parish and the State of Louisiana				
	St. James Parish		State of Louisiana	
Race/Ethnic Group	Number	Percent	Number	Percent
White	10,606	50.0%	2,856,161	63.9%
Black	10,476	49.4%	1,451,944	32.5%
Native American	19	0.1%	25,477	0.6%
Other	36	0.2%	87,129	1.9%
Two or more Races	79	0.4%	48,265	1.1%
Hispanic Origin	130	0.6%	107,738	2.4%

* Source: US Census Bureau, 1990 & 2000 Census Data

---

[3] http://www.scpdc.org/wp-content/uploads/St_James_Comp_Plan_Briefing_Booklet.pdf

[4] United Church of Christ Commission for Racial Justice, From Plantations to Plants: Report of the Emergency National Commission on Environmental and Economic Justice in St. James Parish, Louisiana, September 15, 1998, accessed from the Environmental Justice Resource Center internet site http://www.ejrc.edi/convent_report.html on 29 August 2006.

[5] Barbara Koeppel, "Cancer Alley, Louisiana," The Nation, Vol. 269, No. 15 (8 November 1999): 16.

Per Capita Income for St. James Parish and the State of Louisiana		
Year	Per Capita Income (Current $)	
	St. James Parish	State of Louisiana
1998	$ 18,611	$ 21,772
1999	$ 18,183	$ 22,014
2000	**$ 18,468**	**$ 23,082**
2001	$ 19,359	$ 24,719
2002	$ 20,602	$ 25,249

* Source: US Department of Commerce, Bureau of Economic Analysis

Labor Force Data for St. James Parish and the State of Louisiana						
St. James Parish			St. James Parish	State of Louisiana	United States	
Year	Labor Force	Employment	Unemployment	Unemployment Rate		
1999	8950	8140	810	9.1%	4.70%	4.20%
2000	8819	8109	710	8.1%	5.00%	4.00%
2001	8768	8010	758	8.6%	5.40%	4.70%

*Source: US Department of Labor, Bureau of Labor Statistics

Efforts to recruit more manufacturing facilities to the state and improve the business climate for major industry were a priority in Louisiana. The Louisiana Department of Economic Development (LDED) was tasked with identifying non-adversarial environmental permitting procedures and promoted "toxic tort reform." Republican Governor Mike Foster played a central role in the process. In fact, Governor Foster supported Shintech's proposal to build the PVC facility in the state.

The LDED and the Department of Environmental Quality (LDEQ) were the two government agencies most directly associated with balancing industry's economic considerations and environmental compliance as well as health related issues. LDED acted as a liaison between potentially incoming manufacturers and other state agencies. The LDEQ is the primary environmental permitting agency for the state of Louisiana. There were also two influential trade groups which advocated business interests, the Louisiana Chemical Association (LCA) and the Louisiana Association of Business and Industry (LABI). The LABI represented the general interests of the business community through active involvement in the political, legislative, judicial and regulatory process.

The economic impact (new jobs/small businesses) of Shintech's operation on the community was a major factor associated with gaining resident and community support. St. James Parish had the highest unemployment rate of all six parishes in the six-parish South Central Planning and Development Commission (SCPDC) district.[6] The Parish incentivized Shintech by providing tax breaks in return for giving 35% of its jobs to local residents. The Shintech pro forma projected an increase in local tax revenue of $12 million.

The environmental risk and costs were similarly significant. There were new technologies associated with achieving environmental compliance which were the addition of equipment monitors, scrubbers, pollution control devices, and the utilization of a closed loop system based on stricter multimedia regulations.

The plant's construction costs were estimated at $700 million inclusive of two thousand (2,000) temporary workers to be employed. However, the new plant would employ 165 new full time employees and 90 contract positions when operating. The $120 million in property tax relief and credits worked out as a cost to the state of about $75,000 for each of the proposed jobs.

Shintech's pro forma was reinforced by the College of Business at the University of New Orleans (CBUNO) who conducted a report that concluded construction of the plant would support 13,133 temporary jobs, represented $288 million in income, and would generate $25 million in local and state taxes. The finished plant would create and support 5,988 new jobs representing an annual income of $107 million, and would generate $10.5 million in annual taxes in St. James Parish.[7] For a state where the per capita income was just $16,912, many local residents showed support for the project due to the economic opportunities it provided to the citizens. [8] A state economic development official estimated that the local school district would benefit from a 2% construction tax, equating to $5.6 million during the plant's construction phase. Officials predicted that the schools would continue to benefit by almost $1.3 million yearly after the completion of the plant construction.

CBUNO Report Findings	
Estimated Item	*Amount*
Temporary Construction Phase Jobs	13,133
Estimated Income from Temp Jobs	$288 million
Estimated Local Tax Revenue	$25 million
Estimated Full Time Jobs	5,988
Estimated income from Full Time Jobs	$107 million
Estimated Annual Tax Revenue	$10.5 million
2% Construction Phase Tax Revenue	$5.6 million
Estimated Annual Tax Revenue for Schools	$1.3 million

---

[6] Available at: http://www.scpdc.org/wp-content/uploads/St_James_Comp_Plan_Briefing_Booklet.pdf
[7] Available at: http://scholarworks.uno.edu/cgi/viewcontent.cgi?article=1583&context=td
[8] Available at: http://www.leanweb.org/pub/shincase.pdf

Stakeholder Groups

There were numerous primary and secondary stakeholder groups that were involved in the case including coalitions of residents, local and outside activists, attorneys and scientists, and their views were segmented. Proponents saw the Shintech project as an opportunity to increase economic development in the form of new jobs and tax revenue in a severely impoverished community for small and new businesses. While there was a concern about possible pollution, the proponents of the project supported Shintech officials' assertions that the plant would utilize technology enabling it to operate in a clean and safe manner. However, opponents of the project cited that the pollution issues associated with cumulative impacts stemming from the emissions from other plants could not be mitigated. The Shintech plant would add over 600,000 pounds of air pollutants annually and would have dumped nearly 8 million gallons of toxic waste water into the Mississippi River every day.[9] Further, historical evidence made it clear that these industries tend to locate in minority communities so that it is easier to explain health issues away even though risks are elevated in lower income and poor communities at a much higher rate than in non-minority communities. Finally, activists pointed to data demonstrating that local residents were rarely hired in management or higher pay jobs. Thus, permitting the Shintech facility in the St. James Parish would add to the toxic burden already endured by residents without mitigating benefits. St. James Parish was already the home to eight major chemical plants and a sugar refinery,[10] and in 1996 the chemical plants released more than 17 million pounds of toxics into the environment.[11]

The communities' most effective opponents were Emeralda West and Erik Poche who partnered with Greenpeace, who developed and supplied residents with materials detailing why the facility should not be constructed. However, Poche's self-interest had little to do with environmental health and safety risks but was rather centered on whether the land would be available for sugarcane farming. He might have a hard time locating land to farm since the land he was leasing was being sold to Shintech. So, he organized an informal meeting of parish residents and potential activists at Dale Hymel's restaurant, the President of the Council for St. James Parish to oppose the plant without discussing his personal agenda.

Due to the strength of the parish political network and the economic development model that was being promoted, grassroots supporters formed the pro-development group, The St. James Citizen Coalition (SJCC) in attempt to create a link between their group and the economic rhetoric that was being disseminated. SJCC supported the proposed PVC plant due to the proposed $500,000 job training program, monetized benefits to local schools and businesses, the commitment to hire local, and other

[9] Peter Montague, "PVC & Dioxin: Enough is Enough," Rachel's Environment & Health News, No. 616 (16 September 1998), accessed from the internet site http:www.rachel.org on 28 July 2006.

[10] Mark Schleifstein, "Foster, Clinics Face Off on Rules; Legal Debate Goes Beyond Shintech," The Times-Picayune, 2 August 1998, National section, p. A1

[11] "TRI Data Summary, Environmental Releases, Transfers, and Production-Related Waste," accessed on 27 September 2006 from the Scorecard internet site at http://www.scorecard.org/env-releases/county.tcl?fips_county_code=22093#data_summary

community oriented commitments that Shintech was making to its citizens and community leaders. Shintech signed an agreement with the St. James chapter of the NAACP and the pro-Shintech citizen's group to fund a nonprofit corporation called the St. James Environmental Economic Development Program, Inc. thus confirming the chapter's backing of the plant. The NAACP made the announcement of the agreement in a "friend of the court" brief on the appeal of the DEQ water permit brought by plant opposition. However, the Congressional Black Caucus had asked the E.P.A. to keep Shintech out of St James Parish.

There were other local opponents to the proposed Shintech facility who came forward after the informal meeting hosted by Dale Hymel. Pat Melancon, a white mother of six children organized two public hearings with representation from Parish, State officials, the community and Shintech. There was a surprising early commitment expressed by the parish officials which was the catalyst for formulating a grassroots environmental organization called St. James Citizens for Jobs and the Environment (SJCJE) which Pat became the first president. Although the earliest members of the group were all women, Pat was effective in quickly expanding and diversifying the group to represent a board cross section of residents. There were diverse in age groups, gender, and professions that had lived in the parish for a long time.

The major tension between SJCJE and the parish government was the extent to which parish officials were "in bed with industry" and not protecting the environment and public health of its citizens. SJCJE recruited LEAN, a state-wide environmental organization who supported grassroots environmental groups in Louisiana, as well as a community assistance group called Labor Neighbor Project. The Tulane Environmental Law Clinic (TELC) was also made aware of the issue and became involved. Together they developed an advocacy campaign focused on public awareness techniques which focused on the potential adverse impacts dioxins had on the human body. The campaign also provided data on nearby plants' pollutant releases and the associated fines that had been levied by the EPA. Finally, because of the proximity of a number of industrial plants in their parish located close in proximity to poor, black communities, environmental racism and injustice to the community's residents took on a strong political profile.

Governor Foster reacted harshly to the TELC's intervention and appeared before the New Orleans Business Council in May 1997. The Council was composed of 58 of Louisiana's most influential corporate executives who were also some of Tulane's biggest donors. Foster claimed that the clinic were "a bunch of modern day vigilantes who are just making up reasons to run businesses out of the state." He also told the executives that unless the "bunch at the Tulane law clinic is gotten under control," the executives should reconsider their financial support for Tulane University. Foster threatened to revoke Tulane's tax exempt status which would have impacted over 7,000 employees and was the largest workforce in the state. The governor believed that when the clinic ceased to be constructive and became subjective for the sole purpose of being obstructionist to the new facility, they went too far.

The reception from then Secretary for Economic Development echoed the governor's views. In fact a letter to Tulane's President suggested that the clinic was engaged in barratry. The Secretary also identified that the law school's low success rate on the Bar exam was due to many of the students flunking during the time that they spent at the clinic interfering with their studies. Finally, he felt an internal investigation and an associated investigation by the state Supreme Court was warranted. The investigation resulted in a change in the Louisiana Supreme Court regulation which governs the activities of student lawyers. In brief, the change made the financial eligibility criteria for potential clients more stringent, ultimately limiting the range of individuals/groups that can receive free legal services from law students.

The Politics of Siting and EJ

Four years before Shintech announced its plans for the plant, the Louisiana State Advisory Committee to the U.S. Commission on Civil Rights issued a report on environmental racism in Louisiana. The Committee concluded that many black communities located along the industrial corridor between Baton Rouge and New Orleans were disproportionately impacted because the permitting process did not require consideration of cumulative risks associated with increased emissions from hazardous waste and chemical facilities. Despite their articulation of disproportionate risks, regulating authorities failed to establish regulations or safeguards that environmental activists' believed protected local residents from the hazardous waste and toxic emissions generated by chemical facilities.

From the onset of the process, state and local officials were not neutral about the possibility of having the facility in their state. In an attempt to woo Shintech, Governor Mike Foster wrote Shintech CEO Chihiro Kanagawa a letter of support stating that he was fully prepared to work closely with Shintech to "bring their project to a speedy, profitable, and mutually beneficial fruition."

The St. James Parish Planning Commission president took the unusual step of preparing a personality profile of all of its members, to include their views towards the industry and presented it to Shintech. The commission was comprised on eighteen males, five were black and thirteen were white. Included in the profiles were descriptions of whether the individual was pro-industry or "quiet and noncontroversial." The parish council is the local elected body charged with making local permit decisions on behalf of their electorate.

Shintech submitted three applications to LDEQ for state operating permits issued pursuant to Title V of the Act. The following timeline outlines the construction permit request process Shintech participated in:

July 23rd, 1996 – Shintech submitted three applications to LDEQ for state operating permits issued pursuant to Title V of the Act. These applications requested that Shintech be allowed to operate a chlor-alkali production facility, a PVC production facility, and a VCM production facility in Convent, Louisiana, located in St. James Parish.

July 23rd, 1996 – Shintech submitted an application for a PSD preconstruction permit for the same three facilities.

November 7th, 1996 – LDEQ noticed a single draft permit for the Shintech plants, addressing the PSD and operating permit applications, and opened a public comment period on the draft permit.

December 9, 1996 – A public hearing is held on the draft proposal for Shintech's permits. The LDEQ submitted the draft permit to EPA's Region VI at this time. The EPA submitted written comments on the draft permit on November 20, 1996, and again on November 27, 1996.

February 18th, 1997 – The LDEQ issues proposed PSD and operating permits for the three Shintech Plants. The Agency's Region VI provided oral comments to the LDEQ on the proposed permits but did not provide written technical comments. The EPA's 45-day review period under CAA section 505(b)(1) of the proposed Shintech Permits submitted on February 18 ended on April 3.

May 23rd, 1997 – The LDEQ issued a final PSD permit and three final Title V operating permits to Shintech for its chlor-alkali, PVC, and VCM plants.

On April 2, 1997, the Tulane Environmental Law Clinic (TELC), on behalf of the community group St. James Citizens for Jobs and the Environment (SJCJE), filed an Environmental Justice Petition with the United States Environmental Protection Agency (the "EPA" or "Agency") requesting that the Agency revoke previously issued air permits for Shintech, Inc.'s proposed polyvinyl-chloride ("PVC") plant in St. James Parish, Louisiana.[12] In addition, an Administrative Complaint was filed with EPA under Title VI of the 1964 Civil Rights Act and EPA's Title VI regulations, which charged that Convent residents' civil rights were violated by the Louisiana Department of Environmental Quality (LDEQ) in its decision to issue the two air permits. The environmental justice issue centers on whether the siting of the plant in St. James Parish violates President Clinton's Executive Order. The controversy was widely viewed as the EPA's test case for implementing the Executive Order. In September of 1997, EPA surprisingly responded to the opponents, agreeing with one of the technical objections that were raised and required a reopening of the Shintech permitting process. Opponents had claimed that a vinyl-chloride monomer cracking furnace was not classified correctly and as a result, did not meet the emission requirements for such furnaces. In the course of EPA's review, the EPA agreed to this complaint and also found forty-nine other technical deficiencies in the permit. The EPA Office of Civil Rights agreed to investigate the complaint on August 8, 1998 (U.S. EPA 1998).

---

[12] See Environmental Justice Petition for the Denial of Shintech, Inc. Title V Air Permit (Apr. 2, 1997) [hereinafter Environmental Justice Petition] (on file with the American University Law Review).

The pressure on EPA was immense and is the reason that the National Environmental Justice Advisory Council (NEJAC) and the EPA's Science Advisory Board (SAB) played such a prominent role in this process.

The EPA conducted its investigation to determine if the Department of Environmental Quality (DEQ) was administering *their environmental programs in a manner that does not have a discriminatory effect based on race, color or national origin. (U.S. EPA 1998:2)* Ironically, while the EPA study investigated the DEQ permitting process statewide, it was also the recipient of a complaint for Shintech's proposed St. James Parish facility.

Selected TELC Actions on Behalf of SJCJE	
Date	**Issue**
January 2, 1997	Filed a lawsuit against the Louisiana Department of Environmental Quality (LDEQ) for initiating a five-cent per page fee for photocopying public documents which had previously been free.
May-97	Filed a motion to recuse LDEQ Secretary Dale Givens from proceedings involving Shintech on the grounds that he was biased in favor of the company.
May 22, 1997	Filed a petition (incorporating petitions of 3 April and 16 April 1997) with EPA objecting to operating permits LDEQ issues to Shintech under the Clean Air Act.
June 13, 1997	Filed a lawsuit asserting that St. James Parish authorities were biased and improperly issues a Coastal Zone Land Use permit to Shintech, and requesting that the federal government revoke the permit.
June-1997	Filed a complaint with the EPA claiming that the Shintech plant would violate the 1964 Civil Rights Act and requesting that construction of the plant be stopped on civil rights grounds.
June 30, 1997	Petitioned the EPA Environmental Appeals Board to review a Prevention of Significant Deterioration (PSD) air quality permit issued by LDEQ.
July 16, 1998	Filed a civil rights complaint with the EPA alleging that the LDEQ's issuing of air and water permits to Shintech discriminated against minorities, and requesting that EPA halt federal funding to the LDEQ.
December 7, 1997	Filed a motion with the LDEQ demonstrating pro-industry bias on the part of the Department's top three officials and asking that they recuse themselves.

April 7, 1998	Filed a lawsuit to force the LDEQ to release internal documents relating to the Shintech proposal, and to a prior lawsuit involving air permits.
April 13, 1998	Filed a lawsuit calling for court hearings into allegations of bias by three LDEQ officials.

Without all three permits, the project could not be constructed and benefits of the project would not be realized. Local citizens in opposition of the facility put pressure on the U.S. EPA through public hearings to insure that the LDEQ addressed EPA's EJ criteria before making their final decision on the air permit.

The LDEQ, timely issued two permits required to begin construction; land use and water; but the decision on the air permit was delayed. EPA was part of the reason for the delay because their Science Advisory Board (SAB) was not able to objectively certify a methodology for determining disproportionate "burden." They concluded more time was required to establish a methodology for evaluating cumulative risk and assessing environmental burden before determining whether the project posed unreasonable risks to the community.

EPA took the lead in providing guidance to environmental stakeholders by issuing *Interim Guidance, Draft Revised Investigation Guidance,* and *Draft Recipient Guidance.* Following the issuance stakeholders were still concerned. Industry leaders, scientists, and policy experts still sought clarity on disparate impact, how complaints can be filed, how a community's participation in the decision-making process is determined, and how industry and community interests are best optimized.

EPA's guidance document became the vehicle to address the backlog of 58 citizens' complaints. These complaints allege discrimination resulting from the potential issuance of Shintech's environmental permits.

EPA's Office of Civil Rights (OCR), is responsible for reviewing and investigating Title VI complaints and enforcement issues as well as allegations of discrimination. However, OCR either did not promptly investigate the Title VI complaints, or the complaints were dismissed for jurisdictional or technical reasons. Between September 1993 and July 1998, EPA did not uphold any of the 58 Title VI complaints filed with EPA, including 50 that challenged state or local permitting decisions.[13]

Shintech's St. James case was integral to developing EPA's Title VI discrimination policy in environmental proceedings because of the clear mishandling of the complaints. Delays in promulgating an equitable methodology on determining unreasonable burden along with the national activists' success in painting Shintech as anti-environmental capitalists were the reasons Shintech withdrew its plans to build a PVC plant in Convent.

[13] Mank, Bradford, "Environmental Justice and Title VI: Making Recipient Agencies Justify Their Siting Decisions" (1999). *Faculty Articles and Other Publications.* Paper 138. http://scholarship.law.uc.edu/fac_pubs/138

Policy Precedents

Federal officials noted several policy precedents which resulted from the aforementioned case:

1. The politics of activist's external to the community adversely prejudiced local interests employed to determine whether environmental risks versus community benefits could be mitigated by a project.
2. Local governments and its residents should negotiate indisputable benefits to the community, effectively communicate them and balance the opposition activists' no-growth agenda against those dedicated to improving a community's health and economic circumstances.
3. Both opponents and proponents of the project should prioritize public participation and transparency with the company, regulators, and community activists.

Environmental Justice issues focus on two ideological arguments relevant to the community. First, local community residents and leaders can advocate for industrial expansion projects based on the reality of improved economic conditions in their community. In Shintech's case, supporters argued that the plant would provide for the community a new place of employment and training offered by the company, they would hire plant managers living in the community, the purchase of goods and services from that community, the investment in the local community by providing "seed" money to establish new local businesses and finally improvements to the community's quality of life. Examples of quality of life improvements include: constructing new health clinics, (better jobs, better income and better trained and educated workforce) utilizing technologies such as pollution control devices, equipment monitors, scrubbers, etc., to reduce emissions and health related risks.

Secondly, residents and leaders who oppose industrial expansion base their opposition on industry's inability to mitigate the cumulative toxic emissions from a new plant, and the social injustice of siting new plants in poor communities with disproportionate minority populations. These opponents do not accept industry's commitment to comply with or accept and exceed increased environmental permit related requirements and standards and further believe the "burden" on the community cannot be traded off notwithstanding the community's new economic condition.

The regulatory process was vigorously used by the opposition to demonize the project on an emotional versus substantive basis. Thus, not giving Shintech a chance to prove that they would follow through on their commitments to the community. The LDEQ did not explicitly force Shintech to comply or face sanctions that would mean plant closure. Contrary to public opinion, EPA did not make a precedent setting decision in the Shintech case, and Shintech's decision to shift its site was based on business realities.

Residents of Convent opposing the plant had high profile public support from a variety of celebrities, national political leaders such as members of the Congressional Black Caucus, and religious leaders such as the Reverend Jesse Jackson and the Southern Christian Leadership Conference. The proposed PVC plant was supported by the governor, local government officials, and the state chapter of the National Association for the Advancement of Colored People (NAACP). Opponents of industrial expansion mustered a public outcry confounding elected officials who believed the Shintech project would invigorate the economy and diversify the local workforce.

Conclusion in St. James Parish

This dispute pitted two ideological arguments against each other. First, supporters argued that EJ would best be served by bringing in new industry with stipulations that they support the local economy in ways that the local citizen's best saw fit. This group included influential political and business leaders who argued that the citizens of St. James would be served best by the increased jobs, revenues, and resources that Shintech would provide.

Second, opponents to the Shintech plant argued that environmental and social justice could only be served by eliminating potential environmental and health threats to local residents. The argument was framed to argue that the citizens of Convent already had too great a burden imposed on them by industry. Opponents always defaulted to discrimination arguments. "Environmental racism" was the key phrase employed by those unsupportive of industrial expansion, thus inflaming political tensions across the spectrum.

On September 18, 1997, Shintech announced that it would suspend efforts to obtain permits for the Convent plant and instead proposed building a smaller facility in the nearby community of Plaquemine. Shintech used lessons from the Convent experience regarding environment justice related concerns. Prior to the announcement about the new facility's location, a Shintech manager held three public meetings to explain the details of the project. David Wise, the plant manager for Shintech's facility stated that the new plant would be subject to the most rigorous regulations in the country, as newly constructed plants were required to have low emission levels. In addition, the plant would be located within the Greater Baton Rouge area, which had been designated an "ozone non-attainment" area by the federal governmens. Ozone non-attainments means that any plant within the area has to keep emissions that contribute to smog below regulated limits.

Stakeholders and Positions

I. ***Baseline Advocates***: Provide objective, up-to-date data and scientific information to facilitate on-going decision making. The analysis is balanced, objective, and transparent in discussinn the viable approaches to protecting the environment while encouraging business development.

- **Industry**
  - *Shintech's Project Advocacy Expert Consultant* – Provided technical data available to proponents and those that oppose constructing the PVC plant near the city of Addis; and,
  - *New Orleans Business Council* – Conducts analysis and on business development opportunities in the New Orleans region.
- **Government**
  - *Environmental Protection Agency (EPA)* – Conducted their own EJ review to calculate disparate impact analysis and ordered their SAB to conduct a separate review to determine if there were any requirements on criteria articulated in President Clinton's EO that either Dow or Shintech were not addressing;
  - *Louisiana State Government* – Governors' Office and cabinet agencies demonstrate support for business development in their "industrial corridor";
  - *White House Council on Environmental Quality (CEQ)* – Participating in the plant siting process and requested LDEQ submit progress reports to the CEQ; and,
  - *White House Department of Environmental Quality (DEQ)* – Same position as the CEQ.
- **Community Involvement**
  - *Louisiana Environmental Action Network (LEAN)* – A state wide environmental organization that supports by providing analysis for various grassroots environmental groups.

II. ***Lobbying Advocates:*** Provide an accurate analysis of information/data which emphasizes one alternative.

- **Industry**
  - *Shintech* – Refers to construction area as "Chemical Corridor" and is seeking permits for the construction of a new PVC manufacturing plant in Addis, Louisiana;
  - *Shintech's Technical Institute Expert Consultant* – Held operating training programs for the residents of the parishes who filled out application to enroll and learn the necessary skills to work at a chemical facility;
  - *Dow Chemical Company* – Dow sold Shintech the land for the plant and partnered with Shintech to assist them with managing the regulatory and political aspects of siting and constructing a new PVC plant;

- o *Louisiana Chemical Association* – Supports Shintech's PVC construction plants; and,
- o *Louisiana Association of Business and Industry* – Advocacy group for business and associated industry partners supports construction of PVC plants.

- **Government**
  - o *Republican Governor Mike Foster* – Supported plans to construct the new PVC plant in St. James and later near Addis;
  - o *Louisiana Department of Economic Development (LDED)* – Conducted economic impact studies highlighting the impacts related to job creation and positive impacts on the unemployment rates of the region;
  - o *Louisiana Department of Environmental Quality Control (LDEQ)* – Staff reviews and decides whether permits will be issued to companies that apply for them. LDEQ issued the first two permits in St. James and also issued the permits pre-construction near Addis;
  - o *State Economic Development Secretary Kevin Reily* – Supported the Governor and the studies conducted by the LDED demonstrating positive impacts on employment;
  - o *St. James Council Member Erik Poche* – Outspoken city council member opposing the construction of PVC plants in the region; and,
  - o *Dale Hymel President of the Council for St. James Parish* – Activist and president of local opposition group.

- **Community Involvement**
  - o *Dean of the College of Business at the University of New Orleans* – Supports the Governor and Shintech's plan for PVC plant construction;
  - o *Tulane University Environmental Law Clinic (TELC)* – Provided community activists with free legal assistance and submitted Title VI administrative complaints regarding disparate impact of environmental burdens based on race;
  - o *Greenpeace* – Presented studies to support their opposition the manufacturing and use of PVC because of its potential to release dioxin during its manufacturing process and when PVC is incinerated.
  - o *Emeralda West* – Community activist in opposition of the PVC plant construction plans;
  - o *Congressional Black Caucus* – supported the construction of the Shintech plant and found no civil rights violations;
  - o *Pat Melancon* – Community activist and civil rights leader on EJ issues and is opposed to constructing Shintech's PVC plants;
  - o *St. James Citizens or Jobs and the Environment (SJCJE)* – Grassroots organization in opposition to the construction of Shintech's PVC plants;
  - o *St. James Citizen Coalition* – grassroots organization in support of the proposed PVC plant and the proposed $500,000 job training program.

    o Southern Christian Leadership Conference (SCLC) – Objected to and opposed both the proposed Addis plant and the St. James plant without compromise;

    o *Jesse Jackson's* – Sent a letter to EPA Administrator urging EPA to "use its moral and legal authority to stop Shintech from locating in Convent, Louisiana." However, Jesse Jackson, after hearing objective technical data on the issue dropped his opposition to the plant near Addis; and

    o *Louisiana Communities United (LCU)* – Supports the construction of the Addis plant as a result of working with Shintech in conducting a cost/benefit analysis.

III.   **Education Advocates**: Conduct and report on peer reviewed environmental impact studies PVC and other chemical manufacturing projects; also, publish their findings and testify to committees, educate the public, and provide relevant information to and regulatory bodies.

- **Industry**
  - o *Shintech's Public Participation Expert Consultant* – Responsible for designed, educating and facilitating proceeding for public participation for controversial EJ projects. Host public meetings to hear citizens' concerns and ideas regarding plant construction; and,
  - o *Louisiana State Advisory Committee* – Opposed to constructing the PVC plants but failed to establish regulations that pleased environmentalist.

- **Government**
  - o *EPA Office of Civil Rights (OCR)* – Provides leadership, direction, and guidance in carrying out EPA's equal employment programs;
  - o *EPA Science Advisory Board (SAB)* – Advises the EPA by: reviewing the quality, credibility, and predictability for using scientifically technical information as the basis for EPA regulations and evaluating the utility of EJ research programs;
  - o *National Environmental Justice Advisory Council (NEJAC)* – Established by charter in 1993 to provide independent advice, consultation, and recommendations to the Administrator of EPA on all matters related to EJ; and,
  - o *Iberville Parish and West Baton Rouge Parish Executives* – The local elected officials pointed out that the environmental activists opposed to the Shintech plant had not provided any evidence that the risk of cancer or other health impairments were any greater due to the Shintech's project, based on the science.

- **Community Involvement**
  - o *NAACP* – Conducted analysis associated with the economic benefits the plant would provide to the community as well as projecting new hires at all levels of plant operations; and,

> o *National Black Chamber of Commerce* – Provided analysis regarding future jobs and economic growth provided the construction of Addis plant.

SHINTECH FACILITY SIMULATION

Section I

The Shintech environmental justice simulation includes Executive Branch, Congressional Branch, and stakeholder roles. As is the case in the first simulation, simulation participants develop materials to successfully achieve their Role's objectives. All advocacy materials must be developed using the information articulated in the case study ONLY.

The seven key roles include: (1) Executive Branch Officials, (2) State Government Officials, (3) Local Government Officials, (4) Shintech Consultants, (5) Trade Association Directors, (6) Grassroots Organizing Directors, and (7) Community Activists. A summary of the roles follow:

1   Executive Branch Official
    1-1 White House CEQ
    1-2 EPA OCR
    1-3 EPA SAB
    1-4 National Environmental Justice Advisory Council person (NEJAC)
2   State Government Official
    2-1 Republican Governor Mike Foster
    2-2 Louisiana DEQ staff member
    2-3 Louisiana DED staff member
    2-4 Louisiana State Advisory Committee
3   Local Government Official
    3-1 Dale Hymel, President of St. James Council
    3-2 Erik Poche, St. James Council Member
    3-3 Congressional Black Caucus
    3-4 Iberville Parish and West Baton Rouge Parish Executives
4   Shintech Consultant
    4-1 Project Advocacy Expert
    4-2 Technical Institute Expert
    4-3 Public Participation Expert
5   Director of Trade Association
    5-1 Louisiana Chemical Association
    5-2 Louisiana Association of Business Industry
6   Grassroots/Community Organization Director
    6-1 St. James Citizens or Jobs and the Environment (SJCJE)
    6-2 St. James Citizen Coalition
    6-3 Louisiana Communities United (LCU)

6-4 Louisiana Environmental Action Network (LEAN)

6-5 NAACP

6-6 National Black Chamber of commerce

7   Community Member/Group

7-1 Dean of the College of Business at the University of New Orleans

7-2 Tulane University Environmental Law Clinic (TELC)

7-3 Emeralda West

7-4 Pat Melancon

7-5 Jesse Jackson

The simulation requires interface, coordination, and ultimately negotiation between the roles to achieve the following objectives:

- Understand how to interface with career and political executives as an advocate for your agency/organization.
- Understand the differences between the three categories of advocacy.
- Understand the nuances of effective advocacy to the federal government.
- Understand the basis for government decision-making.

Section II

Participants must draft their own advocacy documents outlining the decision criteria associated with achieving each role's objective. The methodologies governing the development of credible issue analysis and delivery mechanisms are articulated in chapters 6-10 of this publication. Each participant must articulate a comprehensive analysis of the issue from their role's perspective, and if applicable, a recommendation and justification for the change to the status quo.

A representative of each position will make a verbal presentation utilizing the written materials unique to their advocacy category: baseline, lobbying, or education to the other position stakeholders. Following the presentations, participants acting as members of the Office Louisiana's Department of Environmental Quality will decide the issue. It should be the most reasonable, objective, and cost efficient course for the people of St. James Parish, the state of Louisiana, and Shintech.

Section III

Upon completion of the advocacy campaign and issuance or non-issuance of the permits required to construct the new plant, the simulation continues to the Congressional phase.

The advocate, whose position was chosen as the most effective, will present their argument to a congressional committee of three appointed congressman (seminar participants). The committee will evaluate the decision-making process and decide whether the environment justice financial assistance will be appropriated or not. The congressional members must develop their own written advocacy materials to base their questions on and build the record they support.

Along with the presenting advocate there should be a representative from the two other most supported positions. The congressmen appointed to the committee will be from stakeholder states and be those familiar with environmental justice issues. Following the decision-maker's testimony at the hearing and the statements and questioning by the congressmen, all participants will vote on whether congress should appropriate funds to EPA to provide funding for the two federal grants: The Environmental Justice Small Grants Program, and The Environmental Justice Collaborative Problem-Solving (CPS) Cooperative Agreement Program.

31044728R00166